Is Inflation Ending? Are You Ready?

A. Gary Shilling

Kiril Sokoloff

Is Inflation Ending? Are You Ready?

McGraw-Hill Book Company
New York St. Louis San Francisco Auckland
Bogotá Hamburg Johannesburg London
Madrid Mexico Montreal New Delhi
Panama Paris São Paulo Singapore
Sydney Tokyo Toronto

Library of Congress Cataloging in Publication Data

Shilling, A. Gary.
  Is inflation ending? :Are you ready?

  Includes index.
    1. Inflation (Finance)—United States.   2. Industrial
management—Effect of inflation on.   3. Investments—
Effect of inflation on.   I. Sokoff, Kiril.   II. Title.
HG540.S49   1983   332.4′1′0973   82-23962
ISBN 0-07-056879-0

1 2 3 4 5 6 7 8 9 0   BKP/BKP   8 9 8 7 6 5 4 3

ISBN 0-07-056879-0

The editors for this book were William R. Newton and Eric Lowenkron,
the designer was Naomi Auerbach, and the production
supervisor was Teresa F. Leaden. It was set in Melior
by University Graphics, Inc.

About the Authors

DR. A. GARY SHILLING is President of A. Gary Shilling & Company, Inc., economic consultants to a number of leading financial institutions and industrial corporations.

He received his A.B. degree, magna cum laude, from Amherst College where he was also elected to Phi Beta Kappa. Dr. Shilling earned his M.A. and Ph.D. in economics at Stanford University. While on the West Coast he served on the staffs of the Federal Reserve Bank of San Francisco and the Bank of America.

Before establishing his own firm, Dr. Shilling was Senior Vice President and Chief Economist of White, Weld & Co., Inc. Earlier, his experience included setting up the Economics Department at Merrill Lynch, Pierce, Fenner & Smith at age 29, and serving as the firm's chief economist. Before going to Merrill Lynch, he was with Standard Oil Co. (New Jersey), where he was in charge of United States and Canadian economic analysis and forecasting.

Dr. Shilling has published numerous articles on the business outlook and techniques of economic analysis and forecasting, and he currently serves as Associate Editor of Business Economics, the journal of the National Association of Business Economists.

Dr. Shilling is well known for his forecasting record. In the spring of 1969 he was among the few who correctly forecast that a recession would start late in the year. In mid-1971 he stood almost alone in forecasting a strong expansion in 1972 and 1973. In 1973 he forecast that the world was entering a massive inventory building spree to be followed by the first major worldwide recession since the 1930s. During the ensuing recovery, despite alarmist forecasts of recession "any moment now" which were common throughout 1978 and 1979, Dr. Shilling persisted in projecting that the expansion would be sustained through the remainder of the decade. At the same time, and while many thought that raging inflation would last forever, he predicted that the changing political mood of the country would lead to an end of severe inflation as well as to potentially serious financial and economic readjustment problems.

KIRIL SOKOLOFF is a registered investment advisor and editor of *Money Makers: A Report on the Activities of Wall Street Bargain Hunters, Smart Mutual Funds, Professional Traders, Corporate Insiders, Smart Corporate Purchasers and Successful Businessmen,* which is published from Katonah, New York. Sokoloff is author of five investment books, including *Investing in the Future, Street Smart Investing, The Thinking Investor's Guide to the Stock Market,* and *The Paine Webber Handbook of Stock Bond Analysis.*

For six years, Sokoloff was with the *Business Week Letter,* most recently as managing editor, where he wrote a biweekly commentary on investment strategy, personal finance, and stock market selection. He was also senior editor, finance and investments, at McGraw-Hill, where he edited nearly 50 books on investment and financial subjects.

Sokoloff was formerly a commercial loan officer at Citibank with responsibility for lending money to forest products companies, and an investment banker at G. H. Walker & Co., specializing in private placements and the underwriting of stock issues for small companies.

Contents

Foreword

Gary Shilling and Kiril Sokoloff have written a book on one of my favorite topics: inflation. In fact, the intensity of my feelings on the subject has resulted in some critics labeling me as obsessed. I can only suggest to them that they should be too. I am convinced that unless we better control inflation, not only our economic stability, but the ultimate survival of all our basic institutions is at stake. For when inflation distorts the economic system and destroys the incentives for real improvement, people will no longer support that system and society will disintegrate. We can see this process happening today.

Shilling and Sokoloff correctly identify the number one cause of inflation in my view: government spending. Consider that in 1929, federal spending as a percentage of the gross national product was 3%. In 1982, the federal government absorbs nearly a quarter of the GNP. When we add in state and local government spending, the figure rises to 36% of the GNP. Add in off-budget expenditures, and it climbs again to almost 40% of the GNP. To pay for this uncontrollable growth, the government has inflated and borrowed. Shilling and Sokoloff cite the 1979 Congressional Joint Committee on Taxation's finding that inflation has increased the government's income significantly faster than its expenses. If prices rise 10%, the federal government's revenues go up 16%. Higher interest rates that result from federal borrowing puts pressure on the Fed to increase the money supply, and inflation is pushed up to even higher levels.

Since the mid-1960s we have witnessed a series of booms and recessions in which serious overheating of the economy created severe price pressures; accelerating inflation caused recessions by restricting housing construction, personal spending, and business investment; the recessions created unwanted unemployment, setting off another round of excessive stimulus leading again to overheating—inflation—recession—unemployment—and more government intervention.

Inflation should be identified for what it is. The most vicious hoax ever perpetrated for the expedient purposes of a few at the cost of many. And there should be no uncertainty about its devastating impact, particularly for low-income families, the elderly, and working people who do not have the means to keep their incomes rising even more rapidly than inflation.

Shilling and Sokoloff forcefully argue that the American people have gone from an attitude of trust in big government's ability to solve our problems to the attitude that big government is our problem: the causal connection between big government deficits and our economic woes is too hard to miss. They see this new consensus among the American electorate and the subsequent change in the country's political leadership bringing about a gradual decrease in government spending relative to the GNP, and a leveling off of inflation to 2 or 3%.

If inflation is ending, they warn, the transition is likely to be rocky. Shilling and Sokoloff offer a provocative set of strategies for the difficult transition to the postinflation environment they believe is lying ahead. I recommend this book to those who want to know how we got where we are today and who just might want some clues about planning for what is certain to be an uncertain future.

William E. Simon

Preface

History is sometimes kind and sometimes not to people who are ahead of their times. The Vikings were the first Europeans to reach North America but got no credit until very recently. Only after the Crusades gave Europeans a taste for spices and other products from the far east was Europe ready for Columbus's discovery, although he didn't end up where he thought he would.

On the other hand, Winston Churchill's constant harping about the German threat in the 1930s probably was responsible for his becoming prime minister when World War II broke out. Closer to home, Roger Babson warned his investment clients about an impending stock market crash for years before it finally occurred in late 1929. People made fortunes in stocks between the time when he first forecast disaster and its actual occurrence, but he still gets credit for having been right.

In 1975, we first started forecasting the end of inflation, and we expected its demise to follow the 1973–1975 recession. It seemed to us then that the mood of the country had changed, confirming a trend that began in the late 1960s— that a significant watershed in national sentiment had been reached. Earlier, unemployment had been people's number 1 economic concern, but we believed that the nation's top fear had become inflation. Previously, most Americans trusted government and saw it as the solution to almost any problem. This attitude, we felt, had been replaced by distrust and the belief that government spending and deficits were responsible for inflation, especially in view of the Vietnam war and Great Society programs and the inflation that resulted from the coincidence of those two large spurs to government activity.

Furthermore, our analysis demonstrated that the public was indeed correct. The historical link between government's share of the economic pie and inflation has been too clear to miss. Consequently, this shift in sentiment in a country whose government is freely elected seemed to be tantamount to a change in political direction and hence to indicate an end of inflation. After all, we reasoned, if politicians don't follow the voters' wishes, they will be retired early and replaced by those who will.

As of this writing, in the summer of 1982, it still appears that our assessment of the change in the mood of the country, and hence the rationale for an end of inflation, was correct, although the timing was premature. When a watershed is crossed, it's not always obvious at the time. Anyone who has driven across the Continental Divide in the American west knows that no great mountain peak looms up to mark the point where water flows to the Pacific Ocean instead of the Mississippi River. If it weren't for the signposts, the exact point might look like just one more hill.

Politicians had a similar difficulty identifying the watershed in national sentiment, especially since they had been proceeding so successfully and for so long up the path of instituting more and more government programs in response to almost any social or economic problem. We simply missed the fact that it would take a great deal of persuasion from the voters to break this momentum and reorient the political process.

Also, in 1975, we probably underestimated the effects of Watergate. Normally, after a war as unpopular as Vietnam, the nation elects extremely conservative leaders. In reaction to Watergate, however, voters wanted fresh faces that were unsoiled by Washington and voted in Jimmy Carter, who failed to limit government activity as he had promised, backed up by a new crop of advocates of big government spending in Congress as well.

Perhaps the burst of government activity that followed and the resulting surge in inflation were necessary to convince the electorate that enough was enough. In any event, we believe that the 1980 election finally ushered in the political shift that matched the nation's shift in sentiment of a decade earlier. Furthermore, we believe that this shift will be with the country for some time, despite the current concern over the recessionary problems that began in 1980. Earlier, many people thought that they gained on balance from government programs or that those programs aided others, with no net cost to themselves. Many of the same people now firmly believe that the inflation resulting from these government activities has cost them dearly.

With the voters and now, finally, political leaders oriented toward reducing the size and scope of government in relation to the economy, the case for an end of high inflation rates seems clear. There is further and more immediate evidence for this conclusion in the weakness in 1981 and early 1982 in the prices of gold, antiques, real estate, commodities, and all the other traditional inflation hedges.

It appears, then, that the end of inflation is finally coming. We only hope that our first forecasts of its demise, starting in 1975, are remembered more like Roger Babson's early prognostications of the 1929 stock market collapse and less like the Vikings' initial voyages to North America.

A. Gary Shilling and Kiril Sokoloff

Acknowledgments

This book is the result of a long study. It began in 1975 with my hypothesis that the mood of the country had shifted and would lead to political changes which would remove the underpinnings of a highly inflationary environment. Many people contributed to this study, which led to the rather hectic but suprisingly efficient final assembly of the book in the summer of 1982.

Special thanks to my coauthor, Kiril Sokoloff, who had enough confidence in the end-of-inflation hypothesis to suggest in early 1977 that the book be written. Without his continuing encouragement, the book might never have gotten to the writing stage.

I also want to thank my friends and colleagues who read the book in final draft form and offered numerous constructive suggestions. Included here are Alfred L. Malabre, Jr.; Frank A. Riess; J. Anthony Boeckh; George F. Port; Peter F. Weir; and especially Charles T. Maxwell and Peter L. Bernstein.

I am also extremely grateful for the help of my colleagues at Shilling & Company in developing and testing the end-of-inflation hypothesis and in preparing material for the book. Anne D. Willard, Dr. Walter C. Dolde, Dr. Glenn C. Picou,

Dr. Vincent J. Malanga, Dorothy E. Beardsley, and Barbara J. Muller all contributed immensely. Finally, when it came time to put the book together, it was Josephine Galizia, Elizabeth M. Harmison, and especially Anne D. Willard, Dorothy E. Beardsley, and Karen G. Mishler who stepped to the fore. Without their tireless efforts under conditions of considerable strain, this book would surely not have been completed.

A.G.S.

To suggest that inflation is ending has required a contrarian approach to the business and investment outlook. Indeed, at the end of the 1970s, such a suggestion would have been considered ludicrous. However, as the din of arguments for continued inflation grew louder, a select group of far-seeing investment thinkers came to the view that disinflation was the more likely alternative. Foremost among these are William K. Joseph, Charles L. Grimes, Richard Russell, Peter H. de Haas, Martin Pring, Robert S. Salomon Jr., Marion Evans, William Goldman, Anthony Lane Adams, John Boland, Robert Farrell, the late James R. Hunt, Brian Fitzgerald, Jed Laird, and Sidney Homer. My heartfelt thanks to each one—for the enjoyable discussions we had on the likelihood of disinflation and for sharing with me their incisive analysis.

Special thanks also to the McGraw-Hill Book Company, and our editor William R. Newton, for the willingness to undertake this project at a time when its major thesis appeared so unlikely.

The greatest debt of all is owed to the entire staff of A. Gary Shilling & Co., whose help in the preparation of the manuscript was incalculable. Their enormous contribution, both in the preparation of material for the book as well as the many ideas that are contained in it, is deeply appreciated. It was only through their efforts and assistance that a nearly impossible deadline was met.

K.S.

Is Inflation Ending?
Are You Ready?

The Death of Inflation

1

About every 50 years, an event takes place in a nation that alters the whole course of its future. We believe that we are now at such a watershed period in U.S. history.

Since the mid-1960s, the United States has experienced a gradually escalating inflation, culminating in the late 1970s at the double-digit level—an experience that seriously distorted the economy. Now it appears increasingly likely that inflation is ending; indeed, it probably peaked in the 1978–1980 period. By the end of inflation, we don't necessarily mean declining prices or even flat prices, though long-term price performance of that nature is certainly possible. Perhaps more likely is a return to a 2% to 3% level of annual price increase. While still above the recent historical norm, this range would probably be low enough to prevent the rekindling of expectations of soaring inflation and the distortions that such expectations soon lead to.

More important, whether prices end up increasing slowly, holding constant, or decreasing modestly, the difference between that atmosphere and the climate of high inflation of recent years is so dramatic that the ramifications for almost everyone in our society are enormous. The effects will also be felt on a worldwide basis because U.S. inflation has been heavily responsible for inflation in other countries. This book will discuss the implications of the death of inflation to businesspeople, individuals, and investors.

Whether one accepts the possibility that inflation may be ending or not, it is clear that the country is in unprecedented times. Something is happening that is very clearly different from the experience since World War II. The economy does not seem to be responding (or recovering) in a normal cyclical pattern. Interest rates remain historically high, with real interest still at the highest level in decades. More business failures are occurring than at any time since the great depression. Commodity prices have slumped badly, and the real estate boom appears to have ended. Moreover, one can't help but worry about the growing list of financial problems.

We believe the case for inflation's demise is very strong and mounting almost daily. First, voter resistance and budgetary restraints should ultimately reduce the federal government's share of the economic pie. Since we have found a close correlation between government spending as a percentage of GNP and inflation, any decline in that percentage would relieve inflationary pressures. A number of other factors are also working to end inflation: high real rates of interest which discourage speculation and encourage saving, a more disciplined monetary policy, deregulation (competition is one of the greatest spurs to lower prices), improving productivity growth, the puncturing of the shortage mentality as surpluses grow and demand is sluggish worldwide, the possibility of declining rather than rising oil prices as OPEC loses control over pricing, and a continuing strong dollar, which makes imports less costly and keeps pressure on domestic producers that must compete with foreign-manufactured goods.

These economic trends are confirmed by the presence of the classic signs of an inflationary peak. Speculation in inflation hedges staged a classic blowoff in 1979–1980, with prices getting sufficiently overextended to suggest a major peak.

Indeed, the level of speculation in tangible assets was such that people often camped out overnight to get in on the next day's housing auction in southern California, and foreigners were buying and selling cooperative apartments in New York City without even visiting them.

The numerous hyperinflation survival books were also a classic sign of a peak in inflation. In 1979–1981 there were three best-selling books predicting hyperinflation and literally scores of others telling people that inflation would continue forever.

If inflation is ending, the transition is apt to be a rocky one. For one thing, the nation has become conditioned to rising inflation and rising expectations of inflation. People have grown accustomed to oil and tangible asset prices that keep going up. They now take wage increases for granted, whether they are merited or not. Borrowing, too, has become a way of life for many people. And the nation has learned that holding cash—or liquidity—is unwise in a highly inflationary environment. Inflation has been highly disruptive, and it took a long time for people to adapt to it, but the nation finally has learned how to play the inflation game successfully—just as the rules are being changed. An end to inflation would come as an enormous shock to the people with expectations of a continuing environment of inflation, and it poses risks that are numerous and grave.

The money markets appear to be especially vulnerable to financial disturbance. Short-term business borrowing has ballooned, and any crisis of confidence in this market might make it difficult for certain companies to roll over their borrowings. Another source of potential trouble is the money market funds, which invest the bulk of their assets in bank certificates of deposit (CDs) and commercial paper. Problems in these two areas could quickly spill over into the money funds, causing a redemption stampede.

Other potential disasters could result from the growing surplus of commercial real estate; a large drop in oil prices and the financial vulnerability of high-cost energy investments; a crack in housing prices, where speculation with borrowed money has been significant; problems in the farm sector caused by weak agricultural prices, dropping farmland values, and heavy debt burdens; bankruptcies of less-developed nations which have huge external debts and whose economies are largely dependent on weakening commodity prices; a growing number of problem banks and thrift institutions; declining corporate liquidity; and deteriorating finances of municipalities. Furthermore, it is worrisome that the Kondratieff wave, the 50-odd-year cycle of boom and bust, appears to be right on schedule, as evidenced by the growing litany of financial woes.

If inflation ends, there will be a totally different set of winners and losers in the economy from that prevailing in the last 15 years. Chapter 10 lists nearly 100 new winners and losers.

Borrowers will be losers, and savers will be winners. Continued high real interest rates and a dearth of inflation-fueled price increases will encourage people to save rather than go into debt. Financial assets, such as stocks and bonds, should prosper, while tangible assets, such as housing, real estate, diamonds, and commodities, should continue to suffer. Of course, given the financial risks, the timing of purchases of stocks and bonds is critical. In any event, quality should be the cornerstone of investment in stocks and bonds because financial strength will be the key to survival in the period ahead.

By the same token, preservation of capital probably will become a key investment strategy in the 1980s. The unwinding of the kind of speculative excesses the nation has seen in recent years usually leaves a long-lasting impression on investors' memories. Speculation may fall into disrepute in the 1980s as long-term investing regains favor.

Indeed, a whole new business strategy will be needed. Elements of this strategy would include ruthless and permanent cost control, an orientation toward volume expansion, an adaptation to continuing high real interest rates, maximization of long-term performance instead of short-run profits, avoidance of tangible-asset plays, and a realization that deregulation of many industries will continue.

Before we discuss the arguments for an end to inflation, it may be worthwhile to explore the causes and effects of inflation. Not only will such a recounting help in understanding our end-of-inflation arguments better, it also will lay the groundwork for determining the new winners and losers.

Inflation's Roots: Government Spending but Other Causes As Well

2

While there are a wide variety of forces that can be cited as contributing to inflation, we believe that government activity is the primary and central cause. Historical data back to 1749—which is as far back as we can trace them—provide strong evidence for the correlation between high levels of government spending and high inflation. We would not want to vouch for the accuracy of the data in 1749, and we're not completely sure about 1750, but the 5-year moving average of annual changes in wholesale prices shown in Exhibit 2-1 provides a useful overview of the nation's most recent 2¼ centuries. You will note that times of inflation tend to coincide with times of war and other periods of high government spending.

Starting at the beginning of the graph, the French and Indian War resulted in an inflationary bulge, and perhaps fittingly, America's greatest period of inflation occurred during the "glorious" Revolutionary War. Here we're measuring inflation in terms of British currency. If we used those "not worth a continental" dollars, the inflation bulge would easily run off the page. Even the Barbary pirates did their bit, and the inflation associated with that "police action" was even

EXHIBIT 2-1

Inflation and Government Spending. *(U.S. Bureau of the Census,*
Historical Statistics of the U.S., Colonial Times to 1970, *pt. I, 1975; U.S. Department*
of Labor, Bureau of Labor Statistics.)

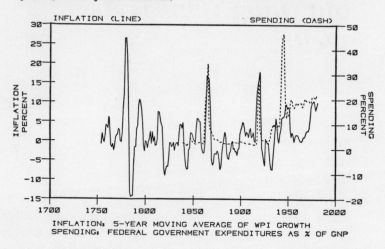

INFLATION: 5-YEAR MOVING AVERAGE OF WPI GROWTH
SPENDING: FEDERAL GOVERNMENT EXPENDITURES AS % OF GNP

greater than the inflation created by Vietnam and its aftermath of worldwide inventory boom, food shortages, oil crisis,
etc.

Later wars also led to inflation bulges, and more recently
we've made the list of shooting wars less monotonous by
adding the cold war and the war on poverty. The latter had
its origin in the depression and the impact that major disaster
had on national attitudes. At that time, fully a quarter of
those who wanted to work didn't have jobs. Supplies of men,
machines, and materials were plentiful, and demand, with
all those people unemployed, was weak. The free enterprise
system didn't seem to be working anymore, and the solution
of the New Deal was to have the government step in and
provide the needed demand.

And step in it did. Federal spending as a percentage of
gross national product (GNP) was about 3% in 1929, roughly
the same peacetime level it had run over the previous century; by 1982 it amounted to almost one-quarter of GNP.

But even this figure does not tell the whole story. State and local government spending, which was equal to about 5% of GNP immediately after World War II, had risen to almost 10% of GNP by 1960 and to almost 14% by the mid-1970s. Hence, by the late 1970s, federal, state, and local government spending together accounted for roughly 36% of GNP, or more than a third of total economic activity.

But there are also the so-called off-budget items, which, while relatively small in magnitude, have been growing at enormous rates. Expenditures of government-sponsored entities and enterprises, including the postal service, the Federal Financing Bank, and direct loans to synfuels, rural electrification, and other programs, grew eightfold between 1965 and 1980, from 0.2% to 1.6% of GNP. Of even greater concern, government-guaranteed loans, which channel money to borrowers who are deemed poor risks by the private credit market, have doubled to 1.3% of GNP over the same period.

If one adds up all these areas, government's total share of the pie comes uncomfortably close to 40% of GNP.

Whether the New Deal, which started this stratospheric climb in government involvement in the economy, can be fully credited with getting us out of the depression is debatable. The eventual return to full employment may have been more closely related to the rise of military spending in Europe, the rebuilding of the military structure in this country, and finally, World War II. Nevertheless, the inclination then was to give credit to the New Deal for the economic revival.

Then the U.S. entered World War II, a popular war from which it clearly emerged as the leader of the free world. The nation was the only major country that had been untouched in the direct sense by war, and was the last bastion against communism in the cold war period. After the war, the U.S. didn't experience the postwar depression that had been widely anticipated—by economists in particular, we might add. (One of the authors can only thank his parents for his not being old enough at the time to join in that chorus.) Rather, the nation entered two decades of substantial economic growth.

It was also a period of growing government involvement. This favorable economic performance and government spending programs continued to be associated with each other in the eyes of many. During that period of ever-growing confidence in government, the nation saw that confidence lead to perhaps the most insidious of economic fallacies: the free lunch doctrine. There was, many came to believe, a bottomless economic cookie jar. Resources were limitless, and all that was needed to solve any economic or social problem was another government spending program that produced benefits but had no real costs. Thus, government involvement in the economy—although it ultimately developed some self-reinforcing aspects that were very far from what the electorate wanted, as discussed in Chapter 4— did initially receive its impetus from the desires of the electorate.

The correlation of inflation with these changes in the government's share in economic activity is striking, as shown in Exhibit 2-1. From 1749 to the present, wholesale prices rose 1.5% per year on average, while in "war" years, shooting and nonshooting, the average increase was 12%. In peacetime, on the other hand, prices actually declined 1.3% per year.

The reason for the persistent connection between rising prices and expanding government share is quite simple. The federal government transferred purchasing power from the private sector to itself by putting excess demand in the economy, which was manifested by inflation. Then Washington paid for this rising spending by squeezing out of the private sector the expanded tax revenues that resulted from inflation. Inflation increased incomes and nominal profits, pushed individuals into higher tax brackets, and created taxable but artificial profits through increases in the value of inventories and underdepreciation of corporate assets.

Thus, inflation obviously worked very much to the government's advantage at the same time that it worked to the detriment of the household and business sectors of the economy. In fact, in 1979, the Congressional Joint Committee on Taxation reported that inflation had increased the government's income significantly faster than its expenses. According to the committee, if prices rise 10%, the federal government's revenues go up 16%. Accordingly, even if all government costs grow at the same rate as inflation, Washington still realizes a net gain that it can use to fund new spending.

Nonetheless, inflation has not been raising revenues nearly fast enough to keep pace with the expansion in government programs. Not only has the price of delivering the programs risen, the total volume of goods and services purchased and the number of beneficiaries receiving payments have skyrocketed. This means that government has had to borrow, and in eye-opening amounts. By the end of fiscal year 1982, deficits were running well over $100 billion per year and the federal debt was over $1 trillion. The relationship between big deficits and inflation is also clear, as illustrated in Exhibit 2-2.

There is, however, an important difference between deficits incurred during recessions and those occurring during expansions. Note the early 1930s, for instance. At that time, there was an increase in the deficit accompanied by an actual *decline* in prices, which seems inconsistent.

Private sector loan demand dried up because of slack economic activity. Consumers retrenched, and businesspeople's need for credit dwindled along with their inventories and capital spending plans. Hence, although falling tax revenues, rising unemployment benefits, and increases in other recession-related outlays expand federal deficits in recessions, there is plenty of room for government to borrow the money it needs to finance them without straining credit supplies or expanding the money supply unduly.

When deficit spending continues into periods of expansion—as happened in the late 1970s—the real trouble develops. Even then, explosive inflation can be mitigated if the def-

---

EXHIBIT 2-2
Inflation and the Federal Deficit. *(U.S. Bureau of the Census,* Historical Statistics of the U.S., Colonial Times to 1970; *U.S. Department of Commerce, Bureau of Economic Analysis; U.S. Department of Labor, Bureau of Labor Statistics.)*

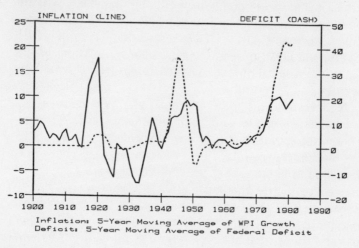

icits created by prodigal fiscal policies are funded by selling government securities to the private sector. The increase in saving that would result from private purchases of government securities would then offset the increased government spending, with cuts in private spending making room for expanding government outlays.

But private investors demand higher returns as the federal financing burden rises, and thus, higher interest rates are needed to induce consumers and businesses to save the required additional amounts. Consequently, it's not surprising that in reality, the desire to limit increases in interest rates puts tremendous political pressures on the Federal Reserve to inject additional credit into the system. At the same time, by boosting the price of everything, inflation increases the amount of money the Fed has to provide to facilitate everyday transactions.

Of course, as a politically independent institution, the Fed has never been required to accommodate credit demands or hold down interest rates in order to promote government expansion. But the Fed does pay close attention to the political orientation of the President and Congress.

Senior Federal Reserve officers have put it to us this way: The Supreme Court exists because the Constitution says there shall be a Supreme Court. On the other hand, the Fed exists because in 1913 Congress passed, and the President signed, the Federal Reserve Act. Fed officials point out that what Congress and President giveth, Congress and President can taketh away. For example, a bill could be passed tomorrow that would transfer all the monetary policymaking functions to the Treasury, leaving the Fed to simply count coins and bills.

Until recently, the nation's orientation has been toward accommodating government expansion and promoting low unemployment with little concern about inflation. Small wonder, then, that the Fed has not only supplied ample credit to finance federal deficits without large increases in interest rates and increased transaction demands but has also expanded the money supply rapidly at other times in order to keep the economy expanding.

This notion that the Fed is de facto subordinate to the prevailing political sentiments, despite its de jure independence, is just the point that we feel is missed by the monetarist school of thought, and it pinpoints our major disagreement with that school. Such theorists see growth in money supply as the primary and perhaps only cause of inflation. Growth in government spending is not very important, they believe, because if credit isn't available, somebody else's spending will simply be curtailed while government's share of the pie expands. The net result should be no increase in money demand.

The connection between growth in money supply and inflation is technically valid, as is evident prima facie in Exhibit 2-3. But in a practical sense, concentration on exces-

---

EXHIBIT 2-3

Inflation and Growth of Money Supply. *(U.S. Department of Labor, Bureau of Labor Statistics; Board of Governors of the Federal Reserve System; U.S. Department of Commerce,* Long Term Economic Growth 1860–1970, *June 1973.)*

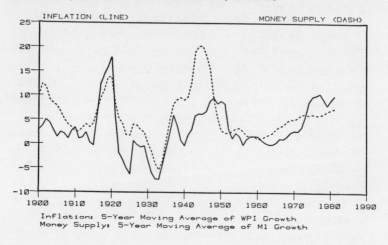

sive money growth as the cause of inflation isn't terribly fruitful.

If the nation is engaged in a shooting war and government does not want to increase taxes enough to pay for it, is it likely that the Fed will keep the money supply growing at a sedate 3% annual rate and watch interest rates move to banana-republic levels as the credit markets are destroyed? Concentration on the money supply rather than government's share of the pie as the prime mover suggests the ridiculous conclusion that the inflation bulge commencing in about 1915 occurred solely because the Fed didn't know enough to keep credit expansion under control.

While we are convinced that government spending is the number 1 cause of inflation, there are other factors—mostly government-related—that also are involved. We see six principal factors that have aggravated inflation: "inflation by fiat" (price increases created in the private sector by government action but not by direct government spending), income indexation, sluggish productivity growth, OPEC increases in the price of oil, a shortage mentality, and a weak U.S. dollar.

Inflation by Fiat

"Inflation by fiat," a term we coined in 1977, refers to all those little ways in which, with the stroke of a pen, Congress, the administration, and the regulatory agencies can have a tremendous impact on prices in key sectors of the economy. Such actions include dairy and other farm price supports, sugar tariffs and import quotas, steel trigger prices, the minimum wage, and increases in Social Security taxes. These factors are shown, along with their inflationary impact, in Table 2-1. Just this partial listing of programs added $22 billion to $27 billion per year to consumer costs in the late 1970s, equivalent to a 1% to 2% increase in the consumer price index (CPI).

If it were possible to quantify all "inflation by fiat" items—including government subsidization of housing, economic and environmental regulations, wage and price controls, and so on—the number would be significantly larger. In fact, it is doubtful whether the government would have been able to enact inflationary measures of this magnitude by voting them directly into the budget. But the insidious thing about fiat inflation is that it is a difficult issue on which to keep a congressional scorecard.

The first item in Table 2-1, farm price supports and acreage set-asides, lumps together a variety of different programs for various crops that guarantee minimum prices to farmers or pay them to set aside acreage if it is thought that the crop will be so large as to keep prices low. The cost of the programs varies somewhat with the weather and hence with the expected crop size, but the bill can run as high as $4 billion to $5 billion.

The second item, the dairy price support program, actually was instituted immediately after World War II, but its impact was not significant until 1977. This program guar-

Table 2-1   *Inflationary Impact of Government Actions*
(Billions of Dollars)

	Increase in Consumer Costs				
	1978	1979	1980	1981	1982
Farm price supports	4.5	4.5	4.5	0.0	4.0
Dairy price supports	3.5	3.5	3.5	1.8	1.8
Sugar tariff quota	2.3	2.2	2.0	2.0	3.0
Steel trigger prices	2.6	5.4	4.0	4.5	4.5
Minimum wage	6.7	6.7	5.4	6.7	0.0
Social Security taxes	2.9	4.8	2.7	8.0	8.5
Total cost	22.5	27.1	22.1	23.0	21.8
Consumer price index effect, %	1.6	2.0	1.5	1.0	1.0

SOURCE: A. Gary Shilling & Co. Inc.

antees that the government will buy any excess dairy supplies at a certain set price. Prior to 1977, the price at which
the government purchased dairy products and the market
price were close enough that there was no strong impact on
consumer prices. But in 1977, the Carter administration set a
minimum support level of 80% of parity, with semiannual
adjustments, that tacked on roughly $3.5 billion to consumer
costs in 1978–1980.

Programs supporting sugar producers are another fiat
item. A tariff was in effect until 2 years ago, and it raised
sugar prices to the extent of allowing domestic producers to
charge prices equal to the cost of cheaper imported sugar
plus the tariff and yet still remain competitive. More recently
quotas were introduced to limit the supplies of imported
sugar, and those have had essentially the same effect. This
piece of favoritism is good for another $2 billion added to
consumer costs.

The steel trigger price mechanism was introduced during
the Carter administration at the behest of domestic manufacturers who argued that Japanese steel was being subsidized
by the Japanese government and was therefore being sold in

this country below cost. In response, the administration devised a formula to equalize the cost differential by pushing up imported steel prices. This had the effect of slowing the rise of steel imports and guaranteeing the market for domestic manufacturers. Regardless of the merits of the case, the effect of the trigger price mechanism was to substantially increase prices for the American consumers of steel. Only recently, in January 1982, was the trigger price mechanism suspended.

The minimum wage was one of the biggest contributors to fiat inflation in the late 1970s, with a price tag approaching $7 billion in some years. This was partly due to the direct impact of minimum wages in pushing up labor costs, but it also resulted from the fact that increases in the minimum wage work to push up the entire wage structure. It is not surprising that increases in the minimum wage are strongly backed by organized labor.

Rising Social Security taxes, the last item on the list, increase labor costs in two ways: directly by boosting the tax that the employer has to pay for each employee, and indirectly by tending to push up wages to help offset the increases in employee taxes. These factors together combined to make Social Security the biggest fiat inflation item in 1981, at a cost of $8 billion.

This number measures the effect of Social Security *taxes* but does not take into account the way in which Social Security *benefits* tend to be inflationary by reducing the incentive to work both for the marginally disabled and for those reaching early retirement age. In this way these benefits reduce the labor pool and hence put upward pressure on wages in general.

Our discussion gives only a few of the many examples of fiat inflation. It goes without saying that the costs of complying with government regulations in such diverse areas as accident and safety, pollution control, grain inspection, and interstate commerce, although difficult to quantify, have increased rapidly in recent years. They may have significant benefits, but like any costs, they must ultimately be passed through to consumers in the form of higher prices. In some cases, the added cost of government regulation actually forced some facilities to shut down, creating shortages of certain goods and hence higher prices. An example was the closing of gray iron foundries over much of the last decade because of pollution-control regulations, leading to a shortage of castings.

This bring us to the most ironic example of inflation by fiat: wage and price controls. To some, the combination of these two ideas—legislated inflation and control of prices and wages—may seem something of an oxymoron. The idea of such controls is always, of course, to curb rather than excite inflation. The result, however, tends to be the reverse.

The wage and price controls of 1971 provide an example of this. For a while the controls seemed to be working. During Phase I—a 90-day mandatory, comprehensive wage-price freeze—the rate of inflation was brought down significantly. The percentage change in overall prices in August, when the controls were put in place, from 3 months earlier, was 4.0% at an annual rate as measured by the CPI; in November, growth in the CPI from 3 months earlier was down to 1.7% at an annual rate.

The only problem was that once controls were lifted, inflation burst out even more violently than before. The reasons for the resumption of inflation were simple. In a free market, changing prices regulate demand relative to supply. If prices are held constant by regulation, however, inventories of items in relatively low supply will be run down because there is no increase in prices to hold down demand and encourage supply. Consequently, when controls are lifted, prices on items that have become scarce will tend to jump up wildly, producing soaring inflation.

Furthermore, wage and price controls essentially put management and labor in a starting gate stance, ready to raise prices and wages as soon as the controls come off. Once they are removed, constant fear of reimposition of controls tends to make business and labor try to boost prices and wages even faster so that if controls are put back on they will be affected less.

Indexation

As government spending, loose monetary policy, and fiat inflation steadily pushed up inflation rates, labor became more and more concerned about the erosion of workers' purchasing power, and cost-of-living adjustments (COLAs) became an important part of economic life. COLAs, which provide for periodic automatic adjustments in wages on the basis of movements in a specific price index, are, of course, unabashedly inflationary. They assure that whenever general prices rise a certain amount, wages—the largest component of production costs—will also rise, pushing up prices, tripping the automatic COLA mechanism, thereby pushing up wages, and so on.

COLAs cover about 10 million civilian employees, or about 10% of all civilian workers, as well as almost 40 million recipients of Social Security, veterans, and other benefits—a very significant chunk of the population. But their ultimate impact is much more widespread, since the whole wage structure tends to move up along with COLAs in order to maintain compensation differentials.

Even if COLAs accurately reflected increases in the cost of living for those receiving them, they would obviously be inflationary. To make matters worse, however, COLA clauses are typically geared to the national CPI, which has a tendency to overstate price increases for many consumers, especially Social Security recipients.

There are two major reasons for this. First, the CPI attaches fixed weights to the items that constitute the standard market basket of goods and services. It assumes that consumers over time purchase exactly the same relative amounts of goods and services from year to year. Currently, those weights are based on a survey conducted over the 1972–1974 period—just a bit out of date.

In fact, of course, the relative quantities of goods purchased by the typical consumer change constantly, and one of the principal ways they change is in response to price movements.

Changes in relative quantities of goods purchased occur when consumers substitute similar goods for one another when one type of good becomes particularly expensive. For instance, when prices of red meat rise sharply, consumers may buy more chicken and pasta. If trains become more expensive than air travel, people take planes instead. This type of substitution becomes particularly prevalent in a highly inflationary environment and has a substantial effect on stabilizing consumer budgets, but the CPI does not take this factor into account.

The CPI also tends to exaggerate the cost of housing by assuming that house purchasers "consume" the total value of the house in the year of purchase. Thus it doesn't account for the fact that many households are bearing costs for shelter on the basis of purchase prices and mortgate rates that were established years ago at much lower levels.

To the extent that retirees—who comprise the bulk of recipients of Social Security and other pension programs tied to COLAs—are almost all people who bought their houses long ago, it is particularly inappropriate that payments to them should be affected by an exaggeration of housing costs in the CPI. If anything, since retirees frequently sell the houses they lived in while working—and under current tax law are not taxed on the proceeds even if they don't buy new houses—their incomes actually tend to be *higher* when the housing component of the CPI is rising sharply.

There is also a more insidious way in which COLAS tend to promote inflation. By insulating large proportions of the population against the ravages of inflation, they make inflation increasingly palatable politically.

This type of situation is perhaps best illustrated in countries with a pronounced socialist bent, such as Italy, which in 1976 established the *scala mobile,* a system of automatic wage indexation implemented on a quarterly basis. During the time this system was in effect, wage rates in Italy rose consistently above consumer inflation rates, in some years by as much as 10 percentage points. The protected members of the electorate were thereby kept happy enough to live peaceably with double-digit inflation rates. By mid-1982, however, the unfortunate repercussions of this system on the unprotected workers, especially the 11% of the work force unemployed at that time, forced the government to end the *scala mobile* agreement.

It might be argued that if *all* Italian workers had been covered, the *scale mobile* would have worked. But the ultimate and ironic reality of COLAs and inflation indexing in general is that if the system really worked, it would not be needed. The theory of indexing is that it keeps everyone even with inflation. But as was explained earlier, rapid inflation is the result of one sector in the economy—the government—spending more than it can afford without resorting to inflation. Consequently, if inflation exists, it is impossible for the private sector in total to keep even. Indexing would work only if every sector's spending retained a normal relationship with its income. But in that case inflation would not be significant, and indexing would be redundant.

We can see this point more clearly in many Latin American countries because of their extreme excesses in government spending and inflation. Inflation is used there to increase the government's share of the economic pie and also to benefit the dictator's personal friends and associates—the winners. The losers are the peasants, many of whom are attracted to the cities from wretched agricultural existences in the hope of an improved life but who in reality suffer a decline in living standards in the process.

In this country we don't have a large and politically weak peasant class that can be constantly pushed to lower relative living standards. Instead, we have a vast middle class composed of blue- and white-collar workers who have a lot of effective votes and can blow the whistle on losses in real income caused by inflationary government policies.

Productivity

Productivity growth—or rather the lack of it—is another force that has exacerbated the inflation problem over the past decade. Productivity growth is important because it expands the total economic pie and allows everyone to get a bigger slice without reducing someone else's. In terms of output per worker-hour, it is an offset to increases in labor compensation that otherwise would be purely inflationary. If compensation in a given year rises 5% but output per work-hour goes up 3%, the net inflationary effect is 2%. If there is no productivity growth, the full 5% flows through to inflation because there are no more goods and services produced to absorb the additional compensation payments. Labor thinks it's getting 5% more, but either someone else's share is reduced or the compensation is simply dissipated by the resulting inflation. In effect, productivity growth has the wonderful property of enlarging the total pie while offsetting inflationary tendencies.

Despite wars and other disruptions, productivity growth, averaged over 10-year periods to iron out cyclical fluctuations, has maintained a steady rate of 2% to 2½% per year since 1900. Even in the 1930s, output per worker-hour as measured by either the National Bureau of Economic Research or the Bureau of Labor Statistics averaged a 2.39% annual advance, as shown in Table 2-2. The exception, of course, is the 1970s, with only a 1.14% rise per year on average.

The sources of poor productivity over the past decade are complex, but some can be identified. The first is the reversal of the relative attractiveness of investing in labor as opposed to capital goods. After having been burned badly by the

Table 2-2 Productivity in the Nonfarm Business Sector
(Average Annual Growth by Decade)

	NBER*	BLS†
1901–1910	2.34	—
1911–1920	2.64	—
1921–1930	2.07	2.43
1931–1940	2.39	2.39
1941–1950	2.46	2.31
1951–1960	2.28	2.07
1961–1970	2.49	2.44
1971–1980	—	1.14

*NBER = National Bureau of Economic Research.
†BLS = U.S. Department of Labor, Bureau of Labor Statistics.

1973–1975 recession, businesspeople generally adopted a very cautious approach toward all aspects of their operations. This was evident in the conservatism with which they accumulated inventories and their reluctance to move ahead with capital investment projects.

Indeed, rather than incurring the risks of having to finance newly acquired plants and equipment, businesspeople in the late 1970s adopted a policy geared toward hiring additional labor to meet increases in demand. The fact that business was constantly being warned of an early economic downturn all through this period also made a policy of adding labor as opposed to capital seem rational. After all, in a recession unneeded labor can be laid off, but unutilized capital equipment just sits there deteriorating while the payments to finance it continue.

Another incentive to adding labor faster than capital was the fact that labor was relatively cheaper than investment in new equipment during most of the 1970s. Exhibit 2-4 shows the ratio of the price of capital—reflecting purchase price, depreciation, and financing costs—to the price of labor. After falling steadily for over two decades, capital became more expensive in the mid-1970s, especially as interest rates soared. Even by 1981 the ratio was still flat and far above its

EXHIBIT 2-4

***Price of Capital Services Relative to
Price of Labor.*** *(U.S. Department of Labor,
Bureau of Labor Statistics; U.S. Department of
Commerce, Bureau of Economic Analysis; Moody's
Interest Rate Series and S&P 500 Dividend Yield and
Price/Earnings Series, both reported in Board of
Governors of the Federal Reserve System*, Federal
Reserve Bulletin; *George M. Von Furstenberg,
"Corporate Investment: Does Market Valuation
Matter in the Aggregate?"* Brookings Papers on
Economic Activity, *2:1977.)*

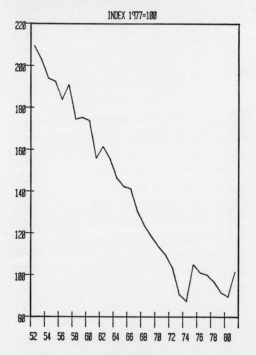

INDEX 1977=100

normal trend level. In sum, there was a general substitution of labor for capital in the late 1970s, and as a result, many productivity-enhancing investments simply didn't get made. Finally, the uncertainty over the business outlook that was created by inconsistent government regulations and rapid changes in federal policy clearly inhibited capital investment.

A shift in income to labor and away from profits, as

shown in Exhibit 2-5, was a third inhibitor of productivity growth. Labor's share of national income ran about 70% until the mid-1960s but then rose rapidly to 75% by 1970 and has held there ever since. Meanwhile, corporate profits' share of national income was almost the mirror image, falling from about 14% to 10% between 1955 and 1981. No wonder capital investment and the resulting productivity gains have been below par.

Demographics is another major factor that slowed productivity growth in the 1970s after influencing the 1960s as well. The postwar babies entered the labor market in huge numbers as raw and inexperienced first-time job holders. Many older women joined the labor force for the first time as well; while they were more mature than the younger people, they also lacked experience.

Another major source of productivity drag for the overall economy has resulted from the growth in the share of activity

---

EXHIBIT 2-5
Compensation of Employees (Line) and Corporate Profits (with Inventory Valuation Adjustment and Capital Consumption Allowance) (Dash) As a Percentage of National Income. (U.S. Department of Commerce, Bureau of Economic Analysis.)

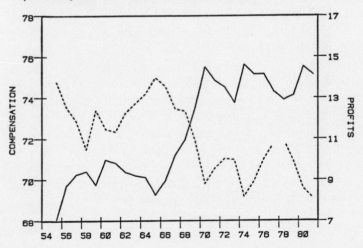

accounted for by government, which is inherently ineffient. If you don't believe this, take a trip to your local post office— essentially an excursion into the nineteenth century.

If one needs evidence on the inefficiency of government in general and the Postal Service in particular, simply note that the government's monopoly on first-class mail, granted by the Constitution, must constantly be defended in court against challenges by private courier services. Such challenges are indicative of the post office's extreme inefficiency in view of the tremendous economies of scale built into its nationwide system—a system that if properly managed should make it almost impossible for any newcomer to gain even a toehold.

The sharp rise in energy prices over the last decade also made its mark on productivity gains by making prematurely obsolete portions of the capital stock which were so energy-dependent as to be uneconomical. Official Commerce Department estimates of the capital stock do not take account of such relative price effects and thus the effective capital stock. Independent private estimates, however, place this overstatement caused by the explosion of energy prices and other factors in the range of 15% to 25%. Since the average worker has less capital to work with, his productivity is thereby lower.

A final factor depressing productivity was the attitudes that developed in a high-inflation environment. Anyone involved in productive rather than speculative activity began to look like a fool. Imagine yourself in a cocktail party conversation with a new acquaintance several years ago. You told him that by very hard work and lots of new and expensive equipment, financed at high interest costs, you enhanced productivity at your plant by 4% over the past year. He countered by explaining how he bought a building a month before and sold it a few days later for a personal profit of $1 million. Who came out ahead in that conversation?

There has also been a decline in the work ethic in the last several decades, reflected in laborers who have come to see extraordinary gains in wages and benefits as their right, regardless of what they actually did to earn them and regardless of the economic and financial well-being of their employers. Work rules in particular, often dictating that two or three people do what half a person could do easily, reduced productivity.

The extremes of this attitude are illustrated by the words of Joseph Jarzabkowski, maintenance worker at U.S. Steel's South Works, quoted in *The Wall Street Journal* of July 30, 1982. When he was hired in 1974, "a manager told me I wouldn't have to work more than four hours a day," even though he was being paid for 8 hours. But more recently, the company has been reducing staffing levels and requiring workers to do more than one job. Mr. Jarzabkowski says that he "used to wait around until I was called to fix something, but now the company is finding other fill-in jobs for me to do" when maintenance work isn't needed. He says he often works "nonstop for eight hours."

Oil Price Increases

Beyond the domestic scene, international events also seemed to conspire to exacerbate inflation. Foremost among these were the tremendous increases in oil prices administered by the OPEC cartel in the mid-1970s and again at the end of the decade.

Many regard these increases as totally exogenous, entirely outside the control of the U.S. government or any other body within this country. We disagree; even the oil embargo that precipitated the first round of oil price increases wasn't totally unrelated to U.S. government actions. It wasn't that the Saudis, recognizing the peak of inventory building, the frenzied feeling of running out of everything, and the bad weather conditions of the early

1970s, said, "Hey, here's a great opportunity to slap on an embargo and run up oil prices." Quite the contrary. They instituted the embargo to bring pressure on the United States and other countries to change their middle east policies, and they were amazed at how effective their actions were.

In any event, after the first oil shock, U.S. government policy clearly had a lot to do with the further increases in oil prices of the late 1970s. The basic attitude in Washington was to try to avoid the increased cost of oil, which, in reality, was a highly deflationary factor.

If the oil price increase had been accepted as such by our government, it would have required a substantial reduction in production, as consumers and businesspeople retrenched on nonenergy outlays in order to offset the sharply higher costs of energy-related products. In effect, recognizing the OPEC price increase as a giant tax increase imposed from outside our borders would have required a slowdown in the economy, which would have entailed a painful adjustment with distinctly slower activity.

Rather than bite the bullet, however, Washington's attitude was, "We'll get it back." By late 1973, the Fed had eased money substantially and had begun to push interest rates lower in order to help everyone obtain enough credit to offset the higher petroleum prices. The administration and Congress were in there pitching as well. They made it clear that they wanted to help those consumers and businesses that could least afford the higher cost of energy. Of course, it was those very consumers and businesses that would be the most affected by price increases and thus most likely to respond by reducing their energy consumption. Consequently, Washington's policy amounted to an effort to isolate the economy from higher energy costs.

Finally, the energy price controls added the capstone to this policy of denying that the price structure had changed. By holding down energy prices, controls greatly muted the normal market signals which otherwise would have strongly urged energy suppliers to increase their production while at the same time encouraging energy users to conserve wherever possible.

Both monetary and fiscal policy, then, were aimed at offsetting the effects of higher petroleum prices, and in a way that was highly inflationary despite the energy price controls. Higher petroleum prices were passed through to final product prices and then worked their way through to higher wage and salary demands as consumers sought to keep their standards of living intact.

The inflation set off by this mechanism meant that the dollars received by OPEC from the United States were worth less and less in terms of American goods and services. But the effect was magnified since virtually all of OPEC's oil payments were in the form of dollars, and foreign currency traders did not fail to notice the deliberately inflationary policy of the United States. The weakness in the dollar that resulted was substantial and further reduced the value of the dollars that OPEC received. We were, in effect, outinflating OPEC, throwing the ball back into their court.

What's intriguing about this U.S. government policy is the way it contrasted with that of Germany during the same period. There the Bundesbank administered very tight credit, which pushed real interest rates 3 or 4 percentage points above real rates in the United States in 1973 and 1974, as shown in Exhibit 2-6. Ironically, the Germans were reacting to their experience in the 1920s, when they had quite successfully used the printing press and the resulting declining value of the mark to pay World War I reparations. The result, however, was a wrecked economy that paved the way for Nazi takeover in the 1930s. In effect, then, we in the 1970s tried the same thing that the Germans had accomplished in the 1920s. But they knew from experience that it wouldn't work; we thought we might get away with it.

The game came to a grinding halt, however, in 1979, when the political situation in Iran blew up, shortly to be fol-

EXHIBIT 2-6
Real Interest Rate Spread between West Germany and the United States. (Board of Governors of the Federal Reserve System, Federal Reserve Bulletin, Banking Statistics; *U.S. Department of Commerce, Bureau of Economic Analysis; U.S. Department of Labor, Bureau of Labor Statistics.*)

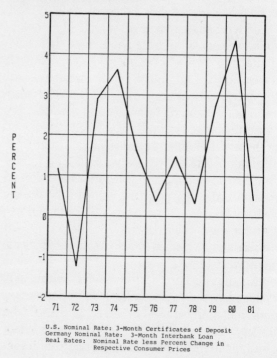

U.S. Nominal Rate: 3-Month Certificates of Deposit
Germany Nominal Rate: 3-Month Interbank Loan
Real Rates: Nominal Rate less Percent Change in
Respective Consumer Prices

lowed by the Iran–Iraq war. The resulting disruption in oil flow and tightening of petroleum supplies led to a very rapid and decisive response by OPEC. In effect, OPEC told us loudly and clearly that our attempt to hit them with a double whammy of high U.S. inflation and a declining value of the dollar would not be accepted. Oil prices were promptly pushed up from an average of $14 in 1978 to an average of $21 in 1980 and peaked at over $34 per barrel in early 1981.

In effect, then, this second increase in oil prices was largely the result of U.S. policies that tried to deny the first price increase and failed to recognize it for what it was—a once and for all transfer of purchasing power from this country to OPEC.

The Shortage Mentality

Energy was not the only staple that suddenly seemed in short supply in the 1970s. Food also seemed to be a major problem, especially in the early part of the decade. The Russian grain purchases of 1972 combined with a major crop shortfall in the United States and a shift in the Humboldt current off South America that caused the anchovies to disappear from their normal fishing grounds. This produced a massive worldwide shortfall of animal feed. The energy and food problems coincided with a third: the real but temporary shortages created by the most frantic worldwide inventory-building spree in 50 years, which led many to believe that we were running out of everything, that supply bottlenecks had become the normal way of life.

The reaction to several years of bad weather, particularly in Russia, and the resulting surge in grain prices was dramatic. People were convinced that bad weather would be with us indefinitely. You may remember that the sunspot theorists were hitting the front pages of newspapers with regularity. One of the authors recalls making a speech at that time to an agricultural convention. Afterward, one fellow came up and explained that he was a meteorologist and had carefully studied weather records going back to Babylonian tablets. As a result of his studies, he had determined that there was a 3000-year weather cycle. The world had just crossed the peak and had to look forward to 1500 years of bad luck. We suggested that he keep tabs on things and let us know when it was time for a turnaround.

The Weak Dollar

As the United States proceeded from an already inflationary base into the price spiral of 1978–1980, further complications set in from developments in the foreign exchange markets. Set afloat during the Nixon administration in a market where communications technology permitted information and funds to flow across international boundaries almost instantaneously, the dollar began instantly to register foreign assessments of U.S. policy toward controlling inflation. Investors began shifting out of dollar assets and into other currencies, and the dollar virtually collapsed.

From 1976 to 1980, the trade-weighted value of the dollar fell 18%, as shown in Exhibit 2-7, and a declining dollar meant higher import prices. Of course, importers no doubt slowed price growth and squeezed profit margins to maintain their competitive positions in the U.S. markets. But the bot-

---

EXHIBIT 2-7
Weighted-Average Exchange Value of U.S. Dollar. (*Board of Governors of the Federal Reserve System,* Federal Reserve Bulletin.)

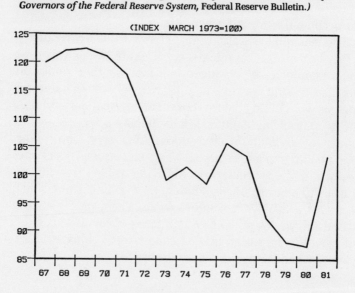

tom line was an acceleration in import prices as the dollar fell. This gave U.S. competitors against imports the opportunity to raise their own prices, and most did so promptly. Since 24% of the goods sold in this country are imported and since that percentage probably should be at least doubled to account for U.S. goods that compete with imports, the overall effect of a weak dollar on domestic inflation was substantial.

How did these inflationary pressures affect our economy and social fabric? In Chapter 3 we shall attempt to explore the answer.

Bitter Fruits: How Inflation Has Devastated Our Economy and Social Fabric

3

The effects of inflation, especially in the past several decades, have been almost too numerous to list and too profound to contemplate. However, we believe that there are seven important effects that exceed all others in importance: the undermining of our financial institutions and financial assets; the deterioration in corporate balance sheets and profits; a weakening of the household financial position; an enormous flight into tangible assets; the burgeoning of the underground, or "off-the-books," economy; the fact that government benefits from inflation and thus has an incentive to perpetuate it; and the impact on society and its values. Let us see how truly dramatic the effects of our inflation have been.

Financial Institutions and Financial Assets

In the late 1970s, investors demanded ever higher returns to offset the effect of inflation on capital. Interest rates skyrocketed while fixed-income assets collapsed. At the same time, thrift institutions were in the middle of a shift in their deposit mix away from demand balances and passbook savings and toward negotiable order of withdrawal (NOW) accounts, large CDs, and other rate-sensitive sources of funds. This reliance on other sources of funds was necessary simply to prevent disintermediation; i.e., massive flows of funds out of savings accounts that occur when money rates soar far above government-mandated ceilings on rates paid to depositors at thrift institutions.

However, the result of this ploy to retain and attract funds was, as shown in Exhibit 3-1, that an increasing proportion of liabilities at savings and loan associations were interest rate–sensitive. If thrift assets had been equally interest-sensitive, this wouldn't have been so bad, but unfortunately, the bulk of their assets were locked in at low interest rates. Despite the increasing use of alternative mortgage instruments that were more sensitive to changes in market rates,

EXHIBIT 3-1
Savings and Loan Rate-Sensitive Liabilities (Percent of Total Savings and Loan Capital). (Federal Home Loan Bank Board, Office of Economic Research; Board of Governors of the Federal Reserve System, Federal Reserve Bulletin.)

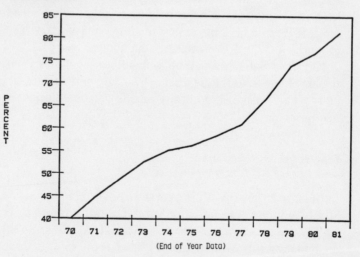

(End of Year Data)

the bulk of the industry's mortgage portfolio consisted of traditional fixed-rate, long-term loans. Thus, when short-term rates hit stratospheric heights in 1979 and stayed there, thrifts' interest margins turned negative and the return on assets went into free fall, as shown in Exhibit 3-2. It was no surprise that many institutions plunged into the red.

Other financial institutions also discovered their own peculiar vulnerability to inflation and the resulting high rates. For instance, life insurance companies took the long-term nature of their product too literally, finding that policyholders had a very short-term orientation when returns on insurance reserves lagged behind other market rates. Since interest rates on policy loans are in the 4% to 8% range, these loans in 1980 stood at $41.4 billion, an eightfold increase from their level in 1960.

Some insurers have had to allocate as much as 40% of investable cash flow to fund policyholders' loans in recent

---

EXHIBIT 3-2
Return on Savings and Loan Assets for All Federal Home Loan Bank Board Districts. (Federal Home Loan Bank Board, Office of Economic Research.)

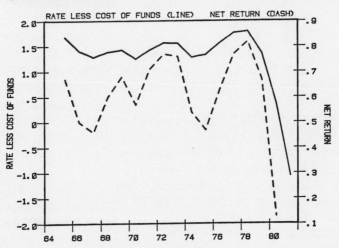

years. To make matters worse, policyholders increased the rate at which they surrendered their policies, which represented not only an additional drain on cash but also a reduction in premium inflow.

Pension fund sponsors were also victims of inflation. Wages and salaries that are the basis of pension benefits exploded as employees sought increases commensurate with inflation. Even worse was the fact that benefit formulas were heavily weighted toward final years' salaries, which meant pension liabilities increased much faster than salaries. This in turn set off a clamor on behalf of those who were already retired, seeking equity with recent pensioners and compensation for the ravages of inflation. The Employee Retirement Income Security Act of 1974 (ERISA) reinforced these problems, since it required not only funding of pension liabilities newly incurred but also amortization of the unfunded existing liabilities.

Stocks and bonds were also major casualties, many of which were held by pension funds. Little needs to be said about bonds, as the 40-year bear market finally became obvious to everyone in the late 1970s. Stocks are another story, and many people do not appreciate just how severe the damage has been. As illustrated in Exhibit 3-3, when deflated for inflation, stock prices were recently selling at levels that had not been seen since the mid-1950s and that were actually below the 1929 peak.

The poor performance of stocks and bonds has a carryover effect to those who own them, whether individuals or institutions. Many financial institutions, for example, hold a large amount of fixed-income securities, and if they were required to mark these assets down to current market rates, their capital base would be eroded significantly. In many cases, the institutions would become insolvent.

Clearly, the thrift institutions, which are the primary mortgage lenders, have been hit the hardest, and a number of failures have already occurred. Life insurance companies are the next most vulnerable. As of 1980, bonds and mort-

EXHIBIT 3-3
Real Stock Prices (S&P 500 Index Deflated by Consumer Prices). *(Standard & Poor's Corporation; U.S. Department of Labor, Bureau of Labor Statistics.)*

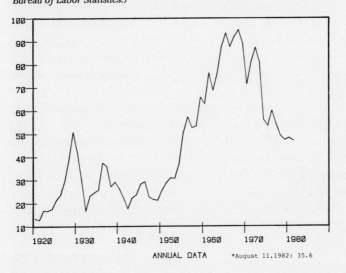

ANNUAL DATA   *August 11,1982: 35.6

gages constituted almost 70% of their assets. At this writing, the difference between assets valued at cost and the true market price for the typical company portfolio is 25% to 40%.

Corporate Balance Sheets and Profits

Corporate balance sheets were also victims of the financial excesses of steadily accelerating inflation. The deliquification of the corporate sector that picked up momentum in the late 1960s reached new extremes in the early 1980s. Investors stayed out of the bond markets in droves, and corporate treasurers weren't eager to lock in historically high interest rates for 10 to 20 years. As a result, corporate borrowing was pushed increasingly into the short end of the credit markets.

Another example of the deterioration in corporate balance sheets is the persistent downtrend in the current ratio of liquid assets to short-term debt, as shown in Exhibit 3-4. The ratio sank to nearly 40% by the early 1980s after being double to triple that level during the prior two decades.

The combined influence of declining liquid assets and rising short-term debt in a rapidly rising interest rate environment began to place severe strains on corporate cash flow. Prior to the mid-1960s, net interest paid (interest paid minus interest received) fluctuated between 5% and 15% of before-tax corporate profits, as shown in Exhibit 3-5.

By the 1970s net interest payments had increased sharply, and jumped to as high as 45% of before-tax profits in 1981, representing $161 billion in gross interest. After netting out interest received, net interest payments amounted to $82 billion, compared with pretax corporate profits of $184 billion in 1981.

Another effect of inflation was a negative impact on corporate profits. In fact, the overall effect of inflation on cor-

---

EXHIBIT 3-4
Ratio of Liquid Assets to Short-Term Debt (Nonfinancial Corporate Business). (Board of Governors of the Federal Reserve System, Flow of Funds Accounts.)

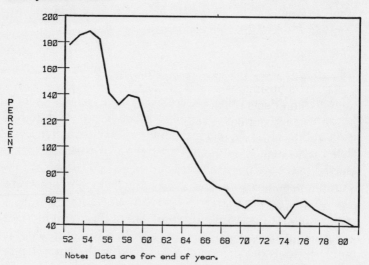

EXHIBIT 3-5
Ratio of Net Interest Paid to Before-Tax Profits (Nonfinancial Corporate Business). (U.S. Department of Commerce, Bureau of Economic Analysis.)

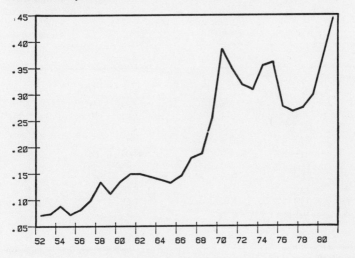

porate profits was much more negative than many observers perceived. By some measures, corporate profits looked great during the high-inflation period of the 1970s. After-tax profits as a percentage of stockholder equity for the Standard & Poor's 400 group of companies rose to 16.5% in 1979 after averaging 11.5% in the robust 1960s, as shown in Table 3-1.

But most businesspeople confused nominal results, which include the effects of inflation, with inflation-adjusted reality. How many annual reports have you seen in recent years in which the chief executive officer (CEO) in his opening letter proudly states that his firm has once again met the sales and earnings projections of the 5-year plan? The obvious question to those CEOs is, "What inflation rate did you build into those plans?" In other words, "Did you really meet your plan or were you confusing the veil of inflation with reality?"

The truth was that returns on stockholder equity (earnings as a percentage of book value) were artificially inflated

Table 3-1   The True Picture of After-Tax Corporate Profitability for the S&P 400

	(1) ROE* (%)	(2) ROE* Adj. for Phantom Profits (%)	(3) Wholesale Price Index (% Change)	(4) ROE* Adj. for Phantom Profits and Inflation (%)
1960	10.1	9.3	0.1	9.2
1965	12.6	13.4	2.0	11.4
1970	10.3	9.3	3.6	5.7
1971	10.8	10.1	3.3	6.7
1972	11.7	10.9	4.4	6.5
1973	14.1	11.0	13.1	−2.2
1974	14.2	7.2	18.8	−11.6
1975	12.1	8.9	9.2	−0.4
1976	14.0	10.2	4.6	5.5
1977	14.0	10.8	6.1	4.6
1978	14.6	10.7	7.8	2.9
1979	16.5	10.7	12.5	−1.8
1980	14.9	9.1	14.1	−5.0
1981	14.0	10.3	9.1	1.2

*ROE = return on shareholders' equity.

DATA SOURCE: Standard & Poor's Corporation; U.S. Department of Labor, Bureau of Labor Statistics; A. Gary Shilling & Co., Inc.

because the numerator of the ratio, earnings, was blown up by inflation-created accounting profits. This occurred as inventories swelled in value because of price increases. Another factor was that depreciation of plant and equipment was inadequate, given the sharp rises in replacement cost.

To the extent that any ongoing operation, just to maintain the current level of production, has to replace inventories and equipment at current prices, the accounting profits created by price increases are essentially phony. Column 2 of Table 3-1 shows what happens if these inflation profits are taken out of earnings and demonstrates that return on equity was really 20% to 30% lower than the nominal numbers would indicate.

But one more adjustment is needed to take full account of the erosion caused by inflation. We still need to include inflation's effects in eroding corporate purchasing power. On this basis, return on equity was actually negative in 1979 and 1980, as shown in column 4.

In effect, government was taxing profits without adjusting for inflation. As a result, in the late 1970s, corporations experienced corporate bracket creep and handed over to the government billions of dollars of taxes on phantom and inflated profits.

Household Financial Position

The household financial situation also suffered from inflation. Individuals had three basic and related responses to inflation. They boosted borrowing, decreased their financial assets, and cut their rate of saving, with the proceeds from all three going into tangible assets. The situation became acute in the late 1970s, when interest rates lagged behind inflation and households were borrowing at what amounted to negative real after-tax rates.

In fact, for a time in the late 1970s, real or inflation-adjusted interest rates were negative even before tax. In effect, banks and other lenders were literally paying borrowers to cart the filthy lucre away. After ranging mostly between 3% and 7% and never exceeding 8.5% for the prior 20 years, household credit expansion (consumer loans plus mortgages) increased to 10% to 11% of disposable income from 1977 through 1979.

To be sure, when interest rates began their inevitable adjustment to persistently high inflation rates, the borrowing game lost a lot of its appeal. By 1980, as a result of high interest rates, household credit expansion had fallen by half, settling back to 5% of disposable income.

But the legacy of the debt splurge remained. The ratio of total household debt *outstanding* to disposable income, a measure of the household's debt-repayment burden, had risen to around 0.75 of disposable income in the late 1970s, as illustrated in Exhibit 3-6, up from the 0.65 level that characterized the prior decade and a half.

The debt situation was exacerbated by the very serious

EXHIBIT 3-6
Ratio of Household Debt to Disposable Income (End-of-Year Data). Household Debt = Consumer and Mortgage Debt Outstanding. *(Board of Governors of the Federal Reserve System, Flow of Funds Accounts; U.S. Department of Commerce, Bureau of Economic Analysis.)*

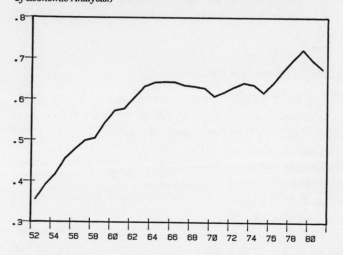

disincentive to save over the past decade. Exhibit 3-7 illustrates the after-tax real return on Treasury bills since 1950 earned by an individual in the top tax bracket. (The top bracket dropped to 70% in the mid-1960s from 92% in the early 1950s and didn't fall to 50% until 1982.) It is remarkable that this return has been negative each and every year over the past three decades, but even more remarkable is how great the disincentive to saving has been. In a year such as 1980, when the return was nearly a negative 7%, the saver couldn't win. Of course, not everybody is in the top bracket, but it's obvious from the exhibit that even those in much lower brackets also didn't get a positive return. One wonders why we all were so willing to get financially fleeced for so long.

Indeed, the top-bracket saver basically had several choices. One was to invest in Treasury bills and watch pur-

EXHIBIT 3-7
After-Tax Real Treasury Bill Return in Top Tax Bracket. *(Board of Governors of the Federal Reserve System, Statistical Release, "Selected Interest Rates and Bond Prices"; U.S. Bureau of the Census, Historical Statistics of the U.S. from Colonial Times to 1970, pt. 2; U.S. Department of the Treasury, Office of Tax Analysis.)*

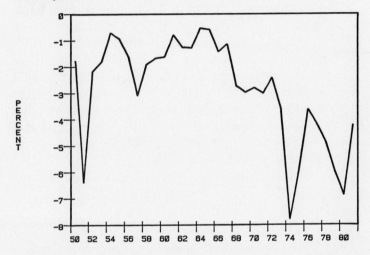

chasing power decline year after year. Another was to buy a sports car which would have left the saver with about the same dollar value at year end but which at least would have afforded the pleasure of use during the year. It is not hard to understand why so many people did the latter; rather, one wonders why more people did not. A third choice was to buy real estate, coins, artwork, or any of the other tangible assets that were advancing so fast in price that a sizable real after-tax return seemed assured. Of course, this was the route taken by many.

The Flight into Tangible Assets

The flow of funds into tangible assets and away from financial assets during the 1970s was dramatic. In 1975, when the recession created a great deal of caution over real estate and other tangibles, 70% of consumer saving went into financial assets and only 30% into tangibles. But by 1979, with rebounding inflation and unbounded confidence in tangibles, consumers put 80% of their saving into tangibles and only 20% into financial assets.

The full impact of this shift from financial to tangible assets in terms of household wealth is illustrated in Exhibit 3-8. The ratio of household financial assets to physical assets declined from a peak of almost 70% in the late 1960s to less than half that amount by the late 1970s. How did this shift manifest itself? Basically, new money flowed into collectibles, including coins, antiques, artwork, gold, silver, and diamonds, and into residential real estate, commercial real estate, farmland, and corporate acquisitions instead of into financial assets such as stocks and bonds.

Let's look at "collectibles" first, a word which was not

EXHIBIT 3-8
Ratio of Financial Assets to Tangible Assets, Household Sector.
(Board of Governors of the Federal Reserve System, "Balance Sheets for the U.S. Economy 1945–1981"; Unpublished data, May 1982.)

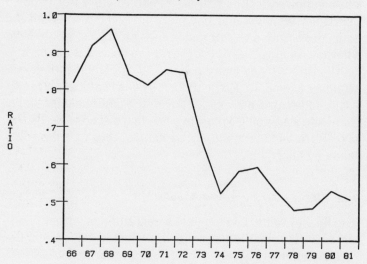

even part of the popular lexicon in the early 1970s. But that changed quickly as inflation accelerated and business surged at auction houses. Indeed, after years of taking their commissions from the seller (10% of the purchase price), Sotheby Parke-Bernet doubled their commissions on every sale by charging an additional "buyers' premium" of 10% of the purchase price. Christie's soon followed suit, making it emphatically clear that in the art world at least, a seller's market prevailed. Later Sotheby's expanded its New York operations by building a $15 million gallery that specialized in rugs, furniture, and other tangibles. It also introduced "arcade auctions" to capture the low end of the market: the less wealthy consumers eager to get a piece of the tangibles boom.

But perhaps the most prominent and widespread mania for tangible assets occurred in the residential real estate market. To begin with, the government made it particularly easy to invest in this market by providing tax and other subsidies to home ownership. Second, once prices began to rise rapidly, more and more young people who had always assumed that home ownership was part of their American birthright began to fear that if they didn't get into the housing market right away, they never would. Others already owning houses felt that if they didn't trade up immediately, they never would.

The rush for housing was so strong that previous financial constraints went by the wayside. Until the mid-1970s, the conventional wisdom was that people were expected to spend about one-quarter of their income on housing. But by 1981 the national average of income going for housing payments was running close to one-third, and in some urban areas the figure approached 40%. Increasingly, people had to rely on a second income to help meet mortgage payments. Sometimes that second income involved not two people working but one person taking a second job.

Of course, housing had a number of powerful forces behind it. First, there was an immense and growing number of 25- to 44-year-olds, who constitute the prime housing market. Second, housing came to be seen as a good investment. Many buyers bought much bigger and more elaborate houses than they really needed, extended themselves to buy a house before they could really afford it, or bought vacation homes which they hardly ever used. Soaring residential real estate prices also tempted a number of speculators into the market: people who had no interest in living in the property they bought but who merely acquired properties to sell them sometimes literally overnight at a tidy profit.

On June 2, 1977, *The Wall Street Journal* quoted one expert as saying that in the San Francisco area, rental houses actually outnumbered houses for sale instead of there being the normal ratio of 1 rental home for every 10 for sale. It turned out that many houses were owned by speculators who rented them out while waiting for the inevitable capital appreciation.

As house prices rose, homeowners began to look at their houses as a source of funds to finance purchases of everything from cars and boats to trips to Las Vegas. It became routine to refinance a house and extract much of the capital gains, especially in areas such as California, where the price explosion was ridiculous. Friends of ours at an institution that services a large portfolio of home mortgages in California told us that 90% of the houses with first mortgages in their portfolios carried second mortgages and that 50% had third mortgages.

The contrast between this attitude toward mortgages and that prevailing a generation ago is worth noting. Several decades ago, the memories of the depression days were still vivid, as many houses had been lost because of nonpayment of mortgages. Not surprisingly, this led to a strong desire to pay off one's indebtedness and have one's own house "free and clear."

You may recall the movie *Adam's Rib*, starring Spencer Tracy and Katherine Hepburn and released in 1949. They happen to be married in the film, but both are lawyers and represent opposite sides in a court case. The arguments in court become so heated that they fight bitterly and decide to get divorced. Toward the end of the movie, they are meeting with their own lawyer to discuss the division of their property, and of course this division reminds both of them how much they have in common, especially their farm, which they both love. Perhaps the turning point that leads to their reunion occurs when Katherine Hepburn muses that they've just made the last payment on the farm. Not today. Anyone who rejoiced over making the last payment would be considered plain crazy, at least until the last year or so.

Like many other people, the parents of both authors were indelibly marked by the depression, and its effects on over-borrowed homeowners. In fact, the parents of one of the authors bought their house in 1936 from a man who lost it because he had speculated in stocks on very thin margins. They didn't think they could afford it, but the owner saw them as a nice young couple he'd met at church, and so he insisted they do so because he wanted a new home for his house.

None of this was lost on the parents. In the mid-1960s, when their son and his wife bought their first house, the son got a letter from his mother congratulating them on the new house. She went on to point out, however, that she knew what a burden a mortgage was but that it would be gradually paid off and finally that glorious day of the final payment would arrive.

That same son has been concerned about housing speculation for some time. In 1979, he stated on public television, "I wouldn't buy my house for what I can now sell it." Nevertheless, he wishes he still had the 5.5% mortgage on that house or more of the still outstanding 6% mortgage on his present residence.

Commercial real estate has been another beneficiary of the craze for tangibles. It was a particular favorite of financial institutions, especially pension funds and life insurance companies, which were eager to replace the faltering financial assets in their portfolios. For a while, commercial real estate did do well, providing total annual returns, including both rent and capital appreciation, of 25% and more.

Compared to the dismal return on both stocks and bonds, this made investors clamor for more real estate deals. As the investors with the deepest pockets, the life insurance companies and pension funds naturally had the most money to throw onto the table.

Metropolitan Life Insurance Company, for example, concluded what was then the largest real estate deal in history, purchasing the Pan Am Building in New York for $400 million. In 1981, Metropolitan Life entered a real estate joint venture with Metropolitan Structures, a Chicago-based development company. Metropolitan Life's commitment in that venture alone could reach $3 billion over the decade.

Prudential Insurance made a well-publicized entry into the real estate area with its $4 billion Prudential property investment separate account (PRISA). PRISA grew very rapidly until 1982, understandably so after total returns of 23.3% in 1980 and 16.2% in 1981. Growth, however, was limited by a lack of suitable investment properties, and many pension funds stood in line to put money into PRISA while others were turned away. Huge as this $4 billion is, it represents only about a quarter of the total real estate investments of private pension funds.

Farmland was another major real estate area that boomed, beginning its first price surge when the Nixon administration encouraged trade with the Soviets. The resulting "sneak" grain purchases in 1972 by the Soviets and the subsequent infamous Soviet grain deal resulted in nearly 30 million tons of corn and wheat being shipped to the Soviets in 1972–1973, causing U.S. grain exports to rise some 75% above the average level of exports in the prior 5 years.

This manifestation of détente with the Soviet Union may have been well timed politically, but it was poorly timed for the economy. As noted in Chapter 2, during 1973 the United States suffered a major crop shortfall, the anchovies disappeared from the coast of Peru because of a change in the Humboldt current, and virtually all countries went on a com-modity-buying spree as a hedge against future price increases.

With a minimum amount of grain left in storage, this tri-ple whammy sent agricultural commodity prices soaring, along with prices for most other commodities. The season's average farm price of corn, for example, went from $1.57 per bushel in 1972 to $3.02 per bushel in 1974, and soybeans climbed from $4.37 per bushel to $6.64, with the price actually rising above $10 per bushel for a brief time. Need-less to say, farm income soared. Moreover, with the prospect of operating in a free market with access to eastern Europe as well as the general belief that food shortages would be permanent, there was every expectation of ongoing strength in demand for U.S.-produced agricultural products.

Thus in a very short period of time the disposition toward agriculture shifted to unbridled optimism. This shift was quickly apparent in the heightening of interest in American farmland by farmers, foreign investors, and nonfarm inves-tors looking for a way to cash in on the boom.

Farm income has historically been an important factor affecting the volume of farmland sales and the pattern of price appreciation of farmland. Thus, the fact that farm income rose to $33 billion in 1973 after averaging about $15 billion in the 1970-1972 period goes a long way toward explaining the 1973-1974 run-up in land values. What was surprising at the time, though, was the fact that when farm income fell back to the $18 billion level in 1976-1977 because of the onset of renewed crop surpluses and a downturn in the livestock industry, land prices continued to soar relative to inflation. Furthermore, even when the recovery in farm income came in 1978-1979, it never equaled the 1973-1974 highs; but farmland prices, nevertheless, continued to rise relative to inflation.

The last time farmers got caught up in this kind of en-vironment was in the ill-fated boom after World War I.

Also, just as in the 1970s, inflation rose rapidly during the shortage-plagued World War I period, and farm prices and income prospects appeared extremely favorable. However, the positive environment faded with the onset of peace, a severe recession in 1920–1921, and a subsequent break in inflation. Farm prices—like all other prices—softened appreciably, and as a result, farm income dropped some 25% from the level achieved in the 1915–1919 period.

During the World War I boom, farmers acquired a huge external debt, which became quite onerous once farm income started to decline. The inability to repay that debt ushered in a wave of foreclosures in the early 1920s and precipitated an 8-year drop in land prices relative to inflation from 1920 through 1928.

While farm income in the middle and late 1970s behaved much as it did in the early 1920s, other factors were at work which forestalled a land price collapse in this latter period. To gauge farmland price movements, we devised an econometric model which relates changes in land prices to factors such as farm enlargement pressures, the expectation of capital appreciation as measured by past appreciation, government payments to farmers, and of course, farm income.

Aside from farm income, all these factors pointed to higher land prices. Farms were getting larger, farmers had realized significant capital gains over the past few years, and the government was still in the picture, providing support prices and deficiency payments to farmers. Interestingly enough, even after taking all these factors into account, the cumulative 66% increase in land values from 1976 through 1980 was about 16 percentage points greater than that estimated by the model.

This unexplained run-up, which is illustrated by the gap between the actual values of the index of farmland values and that estimated by the model, as shown in Exhibit 3-9, may be taken as an approximation of the degree to which speculation affected farm real estate transactions in the late

EXHIBIT 3-9

Farmland Values*. *(U.S. Department of Agriculture, Farm Real Estate Market Developments: A. Gary Shilling & Co., Inc. estimates.)*

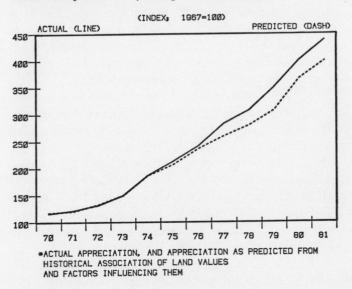

(INDEX: 1967=100)

ACTUAL (LINE)   PREDICTED (DASH)

*ACTUAL APPRECIATION, AND APPRECIATION AS PREDICTED FROM
HISTORICAL ASSOCIATION OF LAND VALUES
AND FACTORS INFLUENCING THEM

1970s. It may well have been caused by the increased involvement in farmland investment by foreigners as well as nonfarm domestic interests.

Another manifestation of the insatiable appetite for tangibles was the rash of acquisitions that occurred toward the end of the 1970s, as the corporate world began to play the inflation game by investing directly in the tangible assets that had proved to be such good inflation hedges. Some notable examples are du Pont's takeover of Conoco, U.S. Steel's acquisition of Marathon Oil, and Standard Oil of Ohio's acquisition of Kennecott.

The advantage of this ploy as long as inflation continues indefinitely is clear. Debts decrease as the dollar falls in value, while assets in the ground keep on rising. Thus, many acquiring companies were willing to go heavily into debt, as illustrated by du Pont, which more than doubled its long-term debt-to-equity ratio from about 15% to about 37% by acquiring Conoco.

Perhaps the most prominent instance of overexuberance for tangibles was seen in the domestic energy industry. As was discussed in Chapter 2, the OPEC embargo in 1973 led to nearly a fourfold price increase from about $3.40 per barrel to about $14.00 per barrel by 1978. Of course, most U.S. oil was subject to controls, and so the response of average domestic prices was restrained to $9.00 per barrel. Nevertheless, the increase that did occur elicited a surge in domestic drilling activity.

However, the surge was modest relative to that which followed the second oil shock in 1979, particularly from a psychological standpoint. Many people believed that the oil price jump in 1973–1974 would not be sustainable and that prices would fall back to somewhere near the preembargo level. But energy prices did not collapse during the latter part of the decade as the experts had expected, although they were flat relative to inflation until 1979.

The Iranian revolution in the winter of that year, however, resulted in the removal of about 5 million barrels of oil per day from the world's supply at a time when inflation was accelerating and the western economies were in the throes of an economic boom. With the world's supply-demand balance tightening dramatically, gasoline shortages reappeared for the second time in the decade, and oil prices started climbing rapidly. By summer the contract price had climbed to about $18 per barrel, and by the end of 1980 it had moved to over $20 per barrel on its way up to $34.

Domestic oil prices lagged behind this run-up because of price controls. But when controls on oil prices finally expired in January 1981, prices in this country quickly climbed to world levels. Despite an accompanying windfall profits tax on decontrolled oil in 1981, the increase which occurred over the 1979–1981 period created tremendous incentives to develop our domestic fossil fuel resources. And the burst of activity was huge. As shown in Exhibit 3-10, oil and gas well completions increased from 50,000 in 1979 to 81,000 in 1981, with the demand for drilling rigs and components rising even more rapidly.

After the second run-up in prices, the country's whole mentality toward the energy problem changed, and most experts became convinced that prices would at best stabilize for a time before moving to higher levels. Even with stable pricing, industry participants clearly expected drilling activity to continue rising.

Indeed, the *Oil and Gas Journal's* initial forecast of drilling activity in 1982 was for about 88,000 wells, or about 10% more than the 1981 record. Moreover, *World Oil* was expecting a continuing surge in drilling to a level of 96,000 wells in 1985.

Needless to say, with this kind of outlook, nearly everyone wanted to join the party. After a 60% increase in funds

EXHIBIT 3-10
Domestic Drilling Activity: Wells Completed, Units. *(American Petroleum Institute,* Basic Petroleum Data Book, Petroleum Industry Statistics, *vol. 1, no. 3, Section III, Table 2.)*

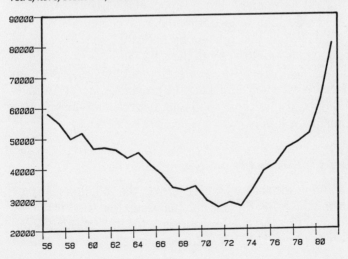

for drilling programs and limited partnerships in 1981, the most conservative forecasts for 1982 were for a similar-sized rise. Figuring that higher oil prices were a sure bet, Dome Petroleum buried itself in $7 billion of debt to acquire, among other things, Hudson's Bay Oil and Gas Co. Of course, major nonenergy companies also went on takeover sprees to acquire energy reserves.

There were also numerous reports that established companies in the service and supply industry had boosted their capacity. For example, Armco Steel's tubular products division is spending nearly $700 million to build two new seamless pipe mills. CF&I Steel Corp., a subsidiary of Crane Co., has under way a second continuous caster and seamless pipe mill in order to be ready for what the company claimed in an advertisement in *The Wall Street Journal* of March 4, 1982, would be 500,000 new wells to be drilled over the 1982–1987 period, or 6 times the exuberant level of 1981.

Meanwhile, hundreds of new rig builders, suppliers, and contractors sprang up in Texas and Oklahoma to cash in on the boom. Furthermore, many nonenergy companies were converting capacity from the production of nonenergy industrial goods, for which demand was weak, to the production of oilfield equipment and components, where the outlook seemed excellent. Indeed, the major oil companies encouraged this conversion process by indicating to these companies that they would need all the nuts and bolts that could be produced over the next 5 years. No doubt the majors multi-ordered equipment and parts to provide some encouragement for capacity conversion and also to ensure themselves an adequate supply.

The Underground Economy

In addition to those who tried to win the inflation game by learning the rules, there is another sector that tried to win by circumventing them entirely. This is the underground economy, or the whole range of transactions that are undertaken in cash, without records, and without the knowledge of the Internal Revenue Service (IRS). Underground economies typically occur when tax burdens become oppressive and people lose their faith in government and become convinced that they are no longer getting value for their tax dollar.

In this country, years of bracket-creep erosion of incomes and growing disenchantment with government solutions to the nation's problems have led to booming growth in this sector. The underground economy probably measured less than 4% of GNP in 1960. Today a very conservative number is 3 times that percentage, with several researchers independently arriving at estimates in the neighborhood of 25%. In absolute terms, what was in 1960 about $15 billion of annual commerce undetected by the national income accountant—and by the tax collector—is now at least $300 billion and by some estimates approaches $1 trillion.

Just how pervasive this kind of activity has become is suggested by a witticism one of the authors heard not too long ago. We were having lunch with the investment department of a major New York bank, and the underground economy came up in conversation. Soon people around the table were recounting their experiences in the cash economy. We pointed out that in suburban New Jersey, it's typical for a mason or electrician to give a 10% discount for cash on residential remodeling work. "There's no discount for cash in New York City," replied one of the senior bank officers who lived in Manhattan. "What's wrong?" we asked. "Aren't you willing to bargain?" "No, no," he retorted. "In New York City, you don't get a discount for cash. You get hit with a premium for paying by check."

Government Benefits from Inflation

The entity that is clearly the biggest winner from inflation is the government. Government spending, including transfers, has been the one major growth sector throughout the recent period. In actuality, government has used inflation as a mechanism to pull revenues from the productive sectors of the economy and transfer them to the less productive or non-productive sectors, as was noted in Chapter 2.

Moreover, government programs have a pronounced tendency to create their own children, i.e., a need to create new programs to solve problems left over by the old programs. A good example is the minimum wage. By pricing the unskilled, the young, and the minority groups out of the labor market, the nation suffers higher unemployment rates as well as chronic welfare cases, all of whom in turn have to be helped out with additional government programs.

There's another aspect as well. In 1979 Walter E. Williams, a prominent black economist, estimated that $34,000 was spent on every recipient of poverty programs. He pointed out that the bulk of this sum went not to the people who needed the money most but to the bureaucracy needed to administer the programs. The result has been the creation of a new industry: the poverty industry.

Why hasn't government been more concerned about inflation? The key reason is that while inflation increases prices for the goods and services the government is purchasing, the impact of inflation on government is not as automatic or immediate as the effects of inflation-created bracket creep on revenues. Much government spending in inflation-sensitive areas, such as indexed transfer and interest payments, responds to price increases only after a lag.

Social Security payments are a case in point. Although these payments are indexed, the amount by which they are adjusted each July is determined by the rate of general price increases over the 12 months that end the previous March. Therefore, so long as prices kept accelerating, the government could keep pushing up its spending without incurring overpowering deficits. (It might be noted that this lagged response of government spending to inflation exerts a drag on the downside. As inflation slows, COLAs for many government programs will still reflect higher previous inflation. Indeed, it is this problem which has aggravated the deficit in recent years.)

In line with this phenomenon, Exhibit 3-11 shows that growth in personal tax revenues and growth in government transfer payments have moved pretty much together over most of the past 20 years. Since 1975, however, tax revenues have increased more rapidly than government spending on transfer payments. Under a progressive individual income tax system, inflation has pushed people into higher tax brackets. What's more, as people at the upper end of the income scale have paid more taxes, this money has been increasingly transferred to those at the bottom end of the scale.

The income redistribution effects of inflation can be seen better by noting a recent study that produced some amazing results, especially since it was prepared by the Brookings

EXHIBIT 3-11
Personal Taxes and Government Transfer Payments. *(U.S. Department of Commerce, Bureau of Economic Analysis.)*

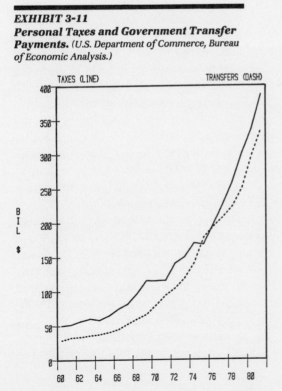

Institution, which is hardly considered a hotbed of conservatism.

Because inflation affects different forms of income and assets in different ways, the Brookings study examined the individual behavior of wages, salaries, interest, dividends, rents, and other forms of earned income during an inflationary period. It also looked at how transfer payments such as Social Security benefits and how taxes and assets such as stocks, bonds, and real estate fared in an inflationary climate. Then the study used an extensive sample of American households to determine the mix of income and asset holdings by income level. Finally, the researchers applied the effects of a 2% increase in overall inflation to this income and asset mix to determine how households at various income levels made out compared with how they would have done otherwise.

The unexpected results were that after 1 year of a 2% increase in overall inflation rates, the income plus asset gains and losses of households with income up to about $11,000 were almost the same as they would have been without the increase in inflation. Their wages tended to rise in step with inflation, and other factors approximately balanced out.

But for middle- and upper-income households, income tax creep, the negative effect of inflation on stock prices, and especially the decline in bond prices were devastating. Families in the income range of $100,000 to $200,000, for example, suffered losses in combined income and assets of about 15% after 1 year of a mere 2% increase in general inflation.

These findings indicate that those who sought to redistribute income and wealth over the last 50 years by means of government programs were more successful than they themselves realized. Many believed that high inflation was particularly detrimental to lower-income people and advocated strongly that additional government aid be authorized to offset the effects. In reality, however, the inflation resulting from ever-growing government activity didn't hurt lower-income people; by being so damaging to middle- and upper-income households, however, it narrowed the income gap significantly.

A major problem with income redistribution is that it is basically self-defeating. Indeed, by shifting income to the lower end, these policies have significantly reduced the saving rate by taking money out of the hands of the big savers in the society and putting it into the hands of big spenders. In fact, as we shall see in Chapter 5, upper-income households (those earning more than $47,800 in 1980 dollars) on average save more than one-third of their after-tax income, while those who have gross incomes lower than $11,500 actually *dissave* an even greater proportion of their after-tax income.

Given these saving propensities, it seems clear that the redistribution of income toward the low end has reduced aggregate saving, constraining the availability of funds for investment and thereby reducing productivity growth and exerting a drag on the economy that ultimately reduces the availability of jobs for the people the programs are supposed to help. The net effect is that rather than gaining job skills and the independence of self-support, many have been pushed into a permanent dependence on welfare that is often passed from one generation to the next.

Government income redistribution policies have another effect. They involve many people besides the ultimate recipients who have a vested interest in seeing the programs continue if not grow. Start with the congressional subcommittee that exists only because of the program in question. Wouldn't the subcommittee chairperson lose status if it were eliminated? Then move on to the department or independent government agency that oversees the program. What would those Department of Agriculture employees do if acreage set-aside programs were knocked out? Consider next those who actually provide the services. How would nursing home operators react if Medicare and Medicaid were threatened? Of course, the actual recipients of the government benefits wouldn't be happy over the programs' demise, but how about those whose incomes depend on the spending of the recipients of government programs? Did you ever notice the reaction of the local merchants when the closing of an obsolete army base is announced? For that matter, did you ever notice the reaction of that district's representative? But now we're back to square one.

The problem is that once the chickens get out of the barnyard, they're hard to get back home. Government benefits that originally looked like fortuitous windfalls for the recipients soon were considered almost natural rights.

Sometimes even diehard conservatives join the parade, looking for government help. A good example of this occurred several years ago in a very conservative beach community we are familiar with. An urgent request was sent to community members, asking them to send letters to their U.S. senators supporting legislation to increase funds for the seashore in that area. A poll asking people in this community whether they favored more government spending would certainly have resulted in a resounding no. But when it came to their own beach . . .

A report we issued in October 1979 and then updated in April 1981 examined just how large the total constituency for government spending had become. We did not, of course, try to include every case similar to the one just mentioned; that would probably have led us to a total of 100%. Instead, we tried to identify the proportion of the population deriving a significant portion of their income from government spending. Such people include recipients of government transfers (e.g., Social Security, government pensions, and welfare), government employees, and people in private jobs created by government spending. Dependents of all these people were also included.

The results of that study are shown in Table 3-2 and indicate that *over half* the population in 1979 could be counted as government beneficiaries, compared with about 37% in 1960, before the large government programs began to blossom.

Table 3-2   *Government Beneficiaries*

	1960 % of Population	1979 % of Population
Government employees		
Federal military	1.4	0.9
Federal civilian	1.3	1.2
State and local governments	3.3	5.7
Dependents of government workers	6.8	5.4
Private employees who are paid by government	3.8	4.1
Their dependents	4.3	2.8
Recipients of government pensions, Social Security, and other transfer payments	14.4	25.6
Their dependents	1.2	0.6
Other recipients of government benefits not counted elsewhere	0.2	2.7
Their dependents	0.2	3.9
Total government beneficiaries	36.7	50.2
Total privately employed and dependents	63.3	49.8
Grand total	100.0*	100.0*

*Totals may not add up because of rounding.
SOURCE: A. Gary Shilling & Co., Inc.

Note that the increase in the roster of government beneficiaries was concentrated not in federal employees but largely in the transfer and pension categories and in the area of state and local government. The last area grew significantly because many of the federal social welfare programs that have been introduced over the last 20 years are administered on the state and local level. Thus both the recipients in government social programs and the bureaucracy that administers them have been the major source of growth in government dependency.

With a constituency for government spending of this size, it is remarkable that the voter rebellion against fiscal irresponsibility has been so strong.

Impact of Inflation on Society

In one sense, inflation has had its greatest impact on national attitude and psychology. One example is the "pass-through" psychology finally adopted by businesspeople who, after years of being badly bruised by inflation, began to conclude that it was a way of life. Why fight suppliers' price increases? most reasoned. After all, suppliers have continuing labor and other cost increases that they can't avoid in an inflationary atmosphere. Indeed, businesspeople shifted their emphasis to educating customers about the legitimacy of their cost increases in the hope that those customers would be similarly understanding.

In many industries, inflation quickly zipped right through the multilayered production system. Do you remember how many people asked in the spring of 1981 why high interest rates hadn't brought U.S. business to its knees? The usual answer typified the inflation pass-through attitude: "Interest costs are just one more inflationary element that is passed through the system, and business has learned to live with it."

Another effect of inflation was growing cynicism about government and a breakdown of any feeling of joint responsibility. The typical attitude can be characterized as a "me first, women and children last" syndrome. After all, my wage increases are earned or my price increases are justified. It's only the other guy's wages and price increases that are inflationary.

Even more important was the loss of individual responsibility. Gone were the days when someone who failed in business or even in family relationships felt the necessity of picking himself up and moving on; instead, there was almost always some government agency or program to pick up the pieces.

A natural offshoot of this was the belief that has flourished in the post-World War II period that when anyone gets into trouble, the fault is society's, not the individual's. The Judeo-Christian concept of free will or free choice was replaced by communitywide—usually meaning government—responsibility. In *The Defenders*, a popular TV series in the 1960s, the criminals defended in each episode were never responsible for their actions. It was always a bad home life or a ghetto environment that forced them into lives of crime.

Not surprisingly, the hero also disappeared from serious literature during this period. The hero—the person who knows where he stands, fights for what he thinks is right, and says, "It's not me that's out of step, it's the world!"—was replaced by the confused individual who asks, "Why don't I fit in with everybody else?"

Of course, the hero did hang on in certain popular forms of literature, especially the movie western. But with the exit of Hopalong Cassidy and the Cisco Kid, even that art form succumbed, and the TV western of the 1960s typically blamed the bad deeds of the desperado on the dreadful experiences forced on him by the Civil War.

Needless to say, with the disappearance of individual responsibility and the hero, any meaningful concept of good and evil and any functional difference between the two faded as well. Thus, characters such as Aaron, the archvillain in Shakespeare's *Titus Adronicus*, became only historical curiosities. What modern playwright would even consider writing anything like the final speech Aaron makes when he has rightly been condemned to be buried alive and starved to death:

> O, why should wrath be mute and fury dumb?
> I am no baby, I, that with base prayers
> I should repent the evils I have done:
> Ten thousand worse than ever yet I did
> Would I perform, if I might have my will:
> If one good deed in all my life I did,
> I do repent it from my very soul.

By the late 1960s, that me-first attitude and cynicism had reached an all-time extreme. With the tremendous number of postwar babies becoming young adults in the 1960s, this attitude also took the form of the pursuit of perennial youth. "Hanging loose"—that is, assuming no responsibilities for anyone but yourself—became chic. Singles clubs abounded. Even young married couples decided to prolong the singles life-style by electing not to have children. Why be tied down with all those unnecessary responsibilities?

Of course, with government launching more and more social programs and with feelings of individual responsibilities waning rapidly, people's concern for helping others by voluntary means also deteriorated. After all, if a social problem really existed, there *must* already be, or soon would be, a government program to solve it.

As it became clear that government would offset virtually any mistake or financial disaster as long as it was big enough, people adjusted their risk levels upward. This is ironic, because many of these government programs designed to reduce risks were instituted in reaction to the financial collapse of the depression.

However, human beings seem to love a certain level of risk. Thus, when the government raised the safety net through regulation of the securities markets, deposit insurance, etc., people merely found new ways to speculate with stock options, commodities, and tangible assets, such as real estate of all types, coins, antiques, gold and silver, diamonds, and artwork.

Until recently the formula has been simple. If you want to take big risks or are prone to dumb mistakes, make sure that you're big enough or that there are enough of you so that the government can't fail to come to your aid.

The inevitability of government bailouts also made people much more convinced that they didn't need to worry about job performance or loyalty. After all, if worse came to worst, you could always get a government job or go on unemployment or welfare. And many people realized a higher spendable income by not working than by engaging in gainful employment.

Finally, job hopping became a respectable activity. The worker who spent time at many firms *had* to be more able than the one who was in the same dull rut for 20 years. Of course, with rapid job changes the rule in the past decade or so, executive search firms flourished. Small wonder that virtually everyone we know who went into head-hunting after dropping out of Wall Street following the end of fixed commission rates and the resulting consolidation of the brokerage industry became an instant success at the new profession.

The Snake Eats Its Tail

What is especially threatening about these effects of inflation, whether economic or psychological, is that they are virtually all self-reinforcing. Despite the fact that government is the prime mover in generating inflation, the effects create a perpetual motion monster that grows larger and larger by feeding on itself. Inflation kicks up mortgage rates, which artificially pushes up the CPI, which boosts COLAs, which exacerbates inflation, which kicks up mortgage rates. COLAs dampen resistance to inflation, which boosts inflation, which kicks up mortgage rates. High inflation weakens the dollar, which raises the price of the imported goods that compete with our products, which heats up inflation and weakens the dollar. Inflation creates uncertainty about the future, which leads to hedge buying, which depresses saving and investment, which reduces productivity and leads to high inflation and uncertainty about the future.

High inflation produces bracket creep, which encourages speculation, discourages productivity, and leads back to high inflation. Consumers and businesspeople are encouraged to borrow to invest in tangible assets, which strains the credit markets, which pushes up interest rates, which are passed through to the consumer in the form of higher inflation that encourages borrowing to invest in tangible assets.

The one common fuel for all these mechanisms, the pernicious psychology that guarantees their perpetuation, is expectations of inflation. If people believe that inflation is here to stay, they will continue to use the strategies that have worked so well in the past: Buy now, pay later; increase debt in order to accumulate tangibles; buy collectibles or real estate at any price, for prices can only go up; accept price increases from suppliers and compensation demands from the work force, for they can easily be passed on in turn; and so on.

Such expectations are the primary factor that makes inflation so hard to beat. They explain why a few months of lower inflation aren't enough to get investors to accept lower interest yields. They explain why people who can't sell their houses at a certain price take them off the market rather than lower the price; if they wait, prices will surely soar again.

Nonetheless, as Chapter 4 discusses, strong forces are at work to end the inflationary spiral as well as the vicious circle of expectation of more inflation.

The Voters Blow the Whistle on Inflation

4

In Chapter 2, we stated that the major cause of inflation is government spending and documented our reasons for holding that belief. Therefore, in order for inflation to end, government spending must be brought under control. At a time when federal deficits are at their highest levels in history and actions to moderate those deficits involve mostly tax increases rather than spending cuts, it may seem that there is little cause for optimism. Indeed, many observers believe that the election of Ronald Reagan was a flash in the pan, merely a reaction to the bungling of Jimmy Carter. Such people believe that the nation's attitudes about government and inflation have not really changed. The nation is hooked on inflation and government spending, they argue.

Those who are intimate with the securities markets often say that a "bull market climbs a wall of worry"—that is, the more skepticism there is about a change in trend, the more the change should be believed. The same probably holds true in the political process as well. Any suggested shift away from a 50-year trend is bound to be met with cries of skepticism or even derision. After all, when you've been right for many decades, it's hard to accept that the end is at hand.

Nevertheless, we think there is compelling evidence to support the view that the nation's attitudes have changed and are not about to shift back.

Confidence in Government Intervention Has Declined

First, the national attitude about government and its ability to solve problems has changed dramatically since the 1960s. It seems hard to believe now, but there was a time when administration economists actually thought they were so adept at controlling the economy by monetary and fiscal means that they could prevent not only major recessions but minor dips as well—the "fine-tuning" philosophy. As Alfred L. Malabre, Jr., of *The Wall Street Journal* points out, those economists were so sure they could eliminate the business cycle that they changed the title of the Commerce Department's monthly *Business Cycle Developments* to *Business Conditions Digest*.

Furthermore, many in and out of the administration in the mid-1960s believed that with just a little more government spending, all the social problems of the nation could be solved—and so were launched the Great Society programs. Finally, there was the conviction that the government was so omnipotent that it could afford to fight a land war in Asia and pursue massive domestic spending programs simultaneously—the "guns *and* butter" concept.

We can easily look back now at how absurd these extreme levels of confidence in government were—levels that had all the earmarks of a peak. And a peak it was, soon to be followed by the aftermath, an era when everything seemed to go wrong: frustration over Vietnam and the disappointment in Great Society programs that failed to live up to expectations, tremendous excess demand created by spending in these two areas that led to strong inflationary pressures here and abroad, and eventually, the massive inventory-building spree that occurred on a worldwide basis and ultimately resulted in the 1973–1975 recession, the most severe in this country since the 1930s and the first one of global significance since World War II.

Even the CIA and Watergate problems were probably part of this reaction phase. They marked, perhaps, the ending of the feeling that Washington was omnipotent and above the law. The net result of this "morning after" was a rapid swing of the pendulum away from the extreme of idealistic trust in government solutions to virtually all problems and toward disillusionment and serious questioning of the government's basic role.

Another side effect of the disillusionment in government was the way Americans viewed themselves. Students in the 1960s believed that the world could be transformed easily into something utopian and were actively involved in trying to change it, but their successors a decade later concentrated on their books and became worried about getting jobs and making money.

We can sum up this shift from rising to declining attitudes by referring to a series of articles in *The Wall Street Journal* in 1966 and again in 1976. Both sets of articles examined what life would be like in the year 2000 in terms of food supplies, communications, medical advances, education, technology, transportation, and so on.

The difference between people's view of the world in 1966 and their view 10 years later is absolutely astonishing. In the mid-1960s the attitude was, "We're on our way to the moon; there's really nothing that cannot be accomplished by the end of this century." Ten years later, there was an almost complete reversal: little conviction that much *can* be accomplished in the remainder of the century and strong belief that even less *will* be accomplished.

This amazing transformation in attitudes is certainly one that has not occurred before in the business careers of most people. However, it's not the first time it's happened in the nation's history. As a matter of fact, it is consistent with a long cycle called the Kondratieff wave, which we discuss in considerable detail in Chapter 9. During this cycle, which lasts about 50 years, there are periods—such as the one we have just left—of tremendous turmoil and disruption, followed by long periods of stability.

For example, World War I and the runaway inflation and huge inventory cycle that followed it led to retrenching in the 1920s and 1930s. After the Civil War, the nation's greatest trauma, there was a long period of stability and 50 years of Republican presidents who were elected to do only one thing—as little as possible. And most of them succeeded. The War of 1812 was followed by the "Era of Good Feeling," in which politics became so dull that political parties virtually disappeared.

Attitudes about Unemployment Have Changed

A second reason for thinking government spending will be controlled is that attitudes about unemployment have changed markedly. Earlier a majority of the population had vivid memories of the depression and its 25% unemployment rate, while few people had seen significant inflation. Consequently, unemployment was consistently ranked as the country's number 1 economic problem in the polls.

By the late 1960s, however, the depression-scarred constituted a much smaller percentage of the population and everyone had begun to witness inflation of frightening proportions. Not surprisingly, the polls began to show inflation as the top-rated national economic concern.

This shift in attitudes about unemployment is nowhere better illustrated than in the current recession, where reactions to the rising number of unemployed are surprising. Even though the unemployment rate exceeded 9% in the first half of 1982, which was even higher than the level reached in the severe 1973–1975 recession and a long way from the 4% figures of the late 1960s, people appeared to be accepting it with an uncharacteristic equanimity. Until the

mid-1970s, the mere suggestion of even an 8% unemployment rate conjured up an image of riots in the streets. Why
don't today's unemployment rates bring forth an uproar in or
out of Congress?

The key reason, in our view, is the much greater national
concern over inflation and hence the reduced interest in
unemployment problems. The Watts riots in Los Angeles in
1965 were credited by some as being the launching pad for
the Great Society programs. In contrast, the Libertyville riots
in Miami in 1980, which were also highly destructive, were
almost forgotten by the general public within a month.

Interestingly, this change in national priorities has even
affected the attitudes of potential rioters. Sociologists tell us
that the zeal for civil disruption has waned because many
feel that nobody is paying attention anymore. Consequently,
there is little to be gained by rioting. It's fascinating to note
that both the French and Russian revolutions occurred not at
the height of repression but after some liberalizing reforms
had been introduced. Apparently, people felt that once those
monarchies had given in to some of their demands, they
could be pushed much further.

Another reason why unemployment is losing its edge is
that the overall rate, although still a politically sensitive
number, does not entail the degree of national suffering it
once did. A great deal of the rise in the total unemployment
rate in recent years has come from the growing percentages
of the labor force accounted for by women and teenagers.
Since these groups tend to have higher unemployment rates,
the overall rate has been pushed up and is not measuring the
same thing it did 15 years ago.

Another distortion is the surging underground economy,
discussed in Chapter 3, which has led to a growing overstatement of unemployment. "Off the books" activities cannot
operate without labor any more than the measured economy
can. Indeed, the underground economy is probably the more
labor-intensive of the two. Furthermore, many of those
counted as officially unemployed are in fact employed in the

underground economy, even while they collect unemployment benefits. Deleting these people from the unemployment statistics would lower the measured unemployment rate, perhaps by several percentage points or more.

A final reason for the lessened concern regarding unemployment today is the substantial level of unemployment and welfare benefits which greatly buffer the blow of being out of work. In fact, as was stated in Chapter 3, these benefits are now so generous that they often appear to discourage gainful employment.

Government Spending Doesn't Appear to Work Anymore

Of even greater importance, however, it has become increasingly obvious that government spending has not accomplished what it set out to do. In contrast to the old conviction that government can solve problems efficiently, there is now an almost universal distrust of politicians at all levels, a feeling that whatever happens, they are bound to foul things up. Furthermore, people now relate inflation to government spending and deficits, in effect having realized that the free lunch was very expensive. The vast American middle class that had been willing to have social programs expand when they were paid for out of economic growth has begun to realize that these programs have become so big that the cost is coming out of their pockets.

The failures of many government programs to satisfactorily solve the problems they addressed and the resulting change in public attitudes did not come as a surprise to several farsighted thinkers. The most famous of these was Ludwig Von Mises, a lifetime proponent of the view that among forms of economic organization, only capitalism is consistent with freedom. Von Mises believed, as had his intellectual predecessors, that the swing to a big government with vast social and economic powers would either degenerate into authoritarianism or be arrested by people concerned with the erosion of their economic freedom.

Despite Von Mises's ideas, the majority opinion among intellectuals over the past half century has supported the liberal program. But as these programs have failed to live up to expectations, a rethinking has begun, with some notable defections from the liberal camp.

Take, for example, Richard Hatcher, who was elected mayor of Gary, Indiana, in 1968 and immediately became successful in the federal grantmanship game. There's no doubt that there was much to rebuild in Gary, then a dying steel mill town being deserted in droves by the middle and upper classes, retailers, and employers. But by 1976, despite more than $100 million in federal grants, Gary hadn't changed much. One of the realizations growing out of the Gary experience is that too many government programs are one-shot events with no longer-term impact. By the mid-1970s, Mayor Hatcher acknowledged both the considerably more modest prospects that should be expected and the necessity for local self-help in achieving lasting progress.

An interesting contrast to Gary's experience is that of Indianapolis. Rather than looking primarily outward to Washington for its civic programs, Indianapolis has mainly looked inward, to itself. As a result, local government has worked *with* rather than *against* local business in revitalizing the community. Indianapolis's leadership has dubbed this strategy the "cookie" concept, and it is the opposite of the "doughnut" concept, in which the central city is permitted to decay and disappear, with economic activity departing for the suburbs. The leadership in Indianapolis became convinced, after the unfortunate experience of Gary and other cities, that business development of the profit-oriented sector can do more to improve living conditions for low-income citizens—and for all citizens—than massive government transfer programs.

One of the most startling challenges to the effectiveness of government programs comes from economists Daniel Benjamin and Lewis Kochin in a study of unemployment compensation in Great Britain during the great depression. Their research shows that these programs actually *raised* the unemployment rate by an average 5 percentage points over the period 1921–1938, and by as much as 10 percentage points at the peaks of unemployment in the 1930s.

The Benjamin-Kochin research is based on careful analysis of unemployment experience in terms of age of labor force participants. The age ranges were critical because unemployment benefits varied enormously by age. Many of the unemployed under age 18 qualified for no benefits, and those who did received relatively low benefits. Benefits for those aged 18 to 20 were twice as high, while the benefits for those over 21 were 50% higher than those for the 18- to 20-year-olds.

How did these different levels of benefits affect unemployment? Conditioned by U.S. experience, we would expect teenagers to have the highest unemployment rates, with the older groups having the lower rates. In fact, just the opposite was true in Great Britain for the period under study. During 1921–1938, the overall unemployment rate in Great Britain averaged 14.6%. Yet it was only about 5% for those under 18 who received no or low benefits. Those in the 18- to 20-year-old group who received higher benefits averaged roughly 10% unemployed, while those above age 21, who got the greatest government help, averaged about 15% unemployment.

The shortcomings of a large government role in the economy are also evident from a review of the experience of the developing countries. Professor Robert M. Dunn, Jr., of George Washington University has pointed out that Korea, Taiwan, Singapore, Mexico, and Brazil have generally led the list of newly developing economies in terms of real growth and other measures of economic performance, while Tanzania, India, and Burma have generally been near the bottom of the list. In terms of economic organization, those countries at the head of the list have employed a much more free-market approach, though admittedly with more central control than in the western industrialized countries. But the emphasis is still basically capitalist, and it provides incentives to individuals to foster economic progress. The countries at the bottom of the growth list, in contrast, have adopted a strongly socialist approach which appears to have stifled individual incentive and economic growth, Professor Dunn believes.

Theoretical Underpinnings for a Reduced Government Role

It should probably be no surprise that after the shift in the general public's attitude about government from positive to negative and after the evidence that so many social programs had disappointing results, economic theories developed that support the case for a reduced government role in the economy. After all, theory often follows fact.

One of these new theories, the rational expectations hypothesis, asserts that people do not persist in errors of expectations and perception but rather adjust them over time until no error remains. "Rational expectations" does not imply that people have perfect foresight or that their expectations will always be fulfilled, but it does imply that people learn and take offsetting actions. Let's consider several examples.

First, let's say the monetary authorities want to stimulate the economy by reducing interest rates. Their traditional approach would be to increase the money supply. As soon as they did so, however, the public would begin to worry that more credit in the system would increase economic activity and also inflation. More inflation would lead to offsetting higher interest rates, people would reason, or to an eventual tightening by the Fed to eliminate the inflation.

Either way, people would assume that interest rates would end up higher. Consequently, the public's immediate response to an expanding money supply would be to cut out the middleman and maintain interest rates at their old level or even push them higher. This, of course, would offset the intended effects of credit ease, and the Fed would have made a round trip to futility.

As another example, assume that Washington plans to cut individual taxes to raise consumer income and thereby induce spending. The public, however, sees increased government spending and deficits as inflationary and consequently saves more and spends less to prepare for the expected higher living costs that people see ahead. The tax cut, then, is offset by more saving, and the effect on spending is nil. Again, the public has foiled economic policy.

In effect, the rational expectations hypothesis says that after years of being misguided by Washington, the public can no longer be fooled. Consequently, the adverse aspects of government actions are now perceived quickly by the public, which immediately takes offsetting actions. And if the public takes offsetting actions, why should the government bother to act at all? This, of course, fits in nicely with the conservative desire to limit government actions.

With the mood of the country shifting toward conservatism, the growing evidence that many government programs weren't successful, and the rising popularity of rational expectations and related economic theories, the political orientations of economics professors around the country have changed. Now conservative professors are no longer an intellectual curiosity and an endangered species, and their influence over current and future students will undoubtedly aid the drive to control government activities over time.

This, of course, represents a distinct change from yesteryear. In the 1950s and 1960s, a conservative faculty member in almost any discipline was generally thought to have no viable intellectual support for his or her ideas. Virtually all the empirical and theoretical evidence with any degree of credibility supported the liberals. One of the authors saw this as an undergraduate at Amherst College in the late 1950s. Every sophomore was required to take an American studies course which examined various problems in American history, such as the controversy between Andrew Jackson and Nicholas Biddle over the Bank of the United States, a sort of central bank in the early nineteenth century. In that particular case, Jackson, the westerner who favored easy credit, was pitted against Biddle, the easterner who stood for monetary responsibility and control. Jackson won by vetoing a bill to renew the bank's charter in 1832, and as a result the nation lacked a central bank until the Federal Reserve System was established in 1913.

Each student in the course was required to do extensive reading on both sides of the issue and then write a paper supporting one side or the other. The strategy soon became clear. One could write an excellent paper supporting the conservative side of the issue and hope for an A minus but probably get a B. Or one could get smart, realize the leanings of the professors who read the papers, and prepare a merely good piece supporting the liberal side for an easy A. Needless to say, Jackson's side of the bank issue became the favorite.

In the early 1960s, while doing graduate work in economics at Stanford University, this same student saw an even clearer example of the dearth of conservative economics professors. A successful businessperson offered to endow an economics chair at Stanford with a considerable gift but specified that it must be occupied by a nationally known economist with a conservative orientation. The economics faculty, eager to get the money, scanned the country but could come up with only one possibility, Milton Friedman, who was happily ensconced at the University of Chicago. (Ironically, Professor Friedman is now on the Stanford campus at the Hoover Institute.) Sadly, Stanford had to decline the endowment.

The Politicians Were Slow to See the Changes in Voter Attitudes

Politicians, as usual, were slow to realize the depth and extent of the change in the mood of the electorate that commenced in the late 1960s. Ever-increasing government spending had worked so well for so long—why should they throw in what still looked like a winning hand?

Furthermore, constituents' grumbling over government deficits and inflation after the late 1960s did not seem nearly as loud or clear to most politicians as the distinct melodic tones of the many well-organized special-interest groups.

Moreover, increasing government spending and proliferating programs and agencies proved to be an excellent way to build power bases in Washington while maintaining a compassionate concern for helping the poor and the unemployed.

Politicians were not the only ones who were slow to realize the shift to a more conservative orientation in the nation. The same was true of leaders in many areas, even as late as 1981. Then, Connecticut Mutual Life Insurance Co. published an opinion survey that compared the attitudes of the general public on a number of moral and social issues with those of leaders in business, the military, news media, government, religion, education, law and justice, and science. Both the general public and the leaders were asked about their stand on the morality of such things as abortion, pornographic movies, premarital sex, homosexuality, adultery, sex before 16, and lesbianism. They also were polled on whether divorce should be more difficult to obtain, whether mothers with young children should work outside the home, and whether married women should work if their husbands could support them.

On almost every issue, the leaders, with the exception of the clergy, were distinctly more liberal than the general public. This suggests that leaders in general, not just in politics, are carryovers from the more liberal days when their opinions were being formed and have yet to catch up with their constituents.

To be fair, it should be noted that there was another reason why politicians took a long time to get the message: Watergate. National aversion to this incident and to the political factions and party associated with it overcame and masked shifting voter sentiment regarding government activity and spending in the 1976 elections. A sizable number of liberals replaced tainted Republicans in Congress, and Jimmy Carter—supposedly the answer to prayers for a politician untainted by Washington—turned out to be another social activist. Consequently, the nation suffered another, and we hope final, round of government stimulation, with federal spending rising $43 billion, or 9.5%, in fiscal 1979 and $86 billion, or 17.4%, in fiscal 1980.

Even so, a few straws in the wind did blow by long before it became widely recognized that a major turning point had been reached in American social and political attitudes. Already in 1976 a new congressional budget process was introduced which was supposed to ensure that the costs of legislation passed by Congress on a piecemeal basis did not add up to a sum greater than government revenues.

This procedure seemed ironclad, and many observers— one of the authors included—were convinced that this was the real thing, that government was finally putting its fiscal house in order. Charls E. Walker, Undersecretary of the Treasury in the early 1970s, was quoted in the *New York Times Magazine* of August 22, 1976, as saying, "Many 'instant historians' rate the forced resignation of Richard Nixon as the 93rd Congress's long-term claim to fame. We disagree. Our nomination is the Budget Reform Act of 1974, which established an orderly and rational Congressional budget procedure."

Alas, changing procedure was not enough. There were no adequate means for enforcement; resolutions were not in fact achieved in the late 1970s, as is well and disappointingly remembered by many. Thus, the politicians needed to have the steel against their ribs before they would actually take steps to pull back on spending.

The Political Swing to the Right Is Not a Flash in the Pan

It was only a question of time before the politicians saw the handwriting on the wall. One concrete manifestation was the Steiger amendment reducing taxes on capital gains in 1978. President Carter had proposed a capital gains tax increase but wound up signing, and taking credit for, a cut.

The first highly visible public affirmation of the revolt against the rapid growth in government size and taxes, however, was probably the victory of Proposition 13 in California in June 1978, which put a ceiling on property taxes at 1% of market value. Similar measures soon followed. In November 1978, voters in 16—or almost one-third—of the states approved more than 80% of the tax reduction measures proposed in those elections. Idaho and Nevada approved proposals very similar to Proposition 13. In Michigan, a Proposal E was passed, limiting the increase in state spending to the increase in the state's personal income. Spending limits were approved by voters in Arizona, Hawaii, and Texas. North Dakota approved a measure cutting individual state income taxes by 37%. In the face of such a massive expression of voter sentiment, even the politicians began to get the point.

The final proof, of course, was the 1980 election. Not only was a conservative president elected, but on the basis of voting records as opposed to party affiliation, so were conservative majorities in both houses of Congress as well. Seen in this light, the conservative sweep in 1980 was not a fluke or a reaction to Carter's ineptness but the culmination of a shift that had begun over a decade before. Moreover, the fact that at this writing 31 states—only 3 short of the 34 that it takes to call a Constitutional Convention—are clamoring for an amendment that requires Congress to balance the budget suggests that the public is bound and determined to keep the heat on politicians to control spending.

For years, we've heard many of our conservative friends ask, "When are those so-and-sos in Washington going to stop the continuing growth in government that is so inflationary and so detrimental to the economy?" Our friends, we believe, are missing the point. Governments in this country are freely elected, and until recently the 50-year trend of rapidly expanding government activity was clearly supported by a majority of the voters.

Some cynics think that this trend can never be arrested, that politicians will continue to be elected by promising more free lunches. We believe, however, that the majority of voters aren't necessarily rejecting outside benefits but now see themselves losing more than they gain from government expansion. Those so-and-sos in Washington are either changing their approaches because the voters are telling them to or are being retired early and replaced by legislators more in line with voter sentiment.

President Reagan's principal economic goal, of course, is to reduce government involvement in the economy—to reverse the 50-year trend during which, with the exception of the World War II bulge, the federal share of the economic pie has grown relentlessly. It seems incredible that the earlier policies, born of the depression, are only being reversed 50 years later, long after they ceased to have any relevance. It does tell us something, however, about the lasting impact of the depression and about the parallel since the early 1930s between economic advances and growing government involvement which many took for a causal relationship.

The Shift in Attitudes Has Come None Too Soon

It appears to us, then, that the long liberal swing that began in 1932 in reaction to the depression has ended. The populace in general came to believe that government involvement in the economy had gone too far and, more important, that they were paying through inflation for all the "free lunch" programs. Even many of the liberals who had initiated and supported these social welfare and income redistribution programs realized they weren't working, and a considerable body of theory recently developed which demonstrates that heavy government involvement is a hell of a way to run either a railroad or an economy.

This shift in attitude toward more reliance on markets and the private sector to allocate the nation's resources and away from government involvement which has been so inflationary will, if history is any guide, last for some time. More important, it comes none too soon. The nation was becoming more and more accepting of ever-increasing inflation rates. Remember when President Nixon imposed price and wage controls in 1971 because inflation was at a 3% annual rate and headed for the horrendous level of 5%? Today 5% is fondly to be wished for. Then, 6% became the accepted "built-in rate" according to most economists, but that soon gave way to 8%. It wasn't long before anything below double digits was the impossible dream.

The problem, however, is not the level of inflation per se. It's the economic distortions and perverse social consequences, discussed in Chapter 3, which developed when inflation became high enough and persistent enough that people assumed it would last forever. More important, it's the risk that the economy will deteriorate into hyperinflation in which the whole system of productive work and investment will disappear and be replaced by all-out speculation in existing assets and a frantic scramble to get rid of money before it becomes worthless. This is the condition toward which we were rapidly moving, avoided perhaps by the eleventh-hour shift in the nation's attitude.

The basic truth is that no democracy can survive long in a hyperinflationary atmosphere and that the damage to the moral and intellectual values in a prolonged and high inflation are incalculable. Inevitably, inflation that is allowed to run out of control will lead to chaos and ultimately to some form of dictatorship because the people will sacrifice freedom in order to bring back stability. It happened in ancient Rome and Greece. Napoleon's rise to power was aided by the money-printing binge in France after the revolution, and hyperinflation in Germany paved the way for the rise of Hitler. The Chinese hyperinflation helped Mao grab power, and almost every Latin American country with hyperinflation is run by the military or by some form of dictatorship.

Most students of financial history would argue that hyperinflation is far worse than depression. It is not necessarily an either-or situation since eventually hyperinflation must end, and with it will come the trauma of stabilization. The longer the inevitable day of reckoning is put off, the greater the adjustment process.

The shift in the nation's attitude appears to have prevented deterioration into hyperinflation and to have set the economy on a course toward much lower inflation. Other forces are working in the same direction, as will be seen in Chapter 5.

Forces that Are Turning the Tide

5

The shift in voter attitudes discussed in Chapter 4 and the unwillingness of the American people to put up with continuing fiscal irresponsibility are at long last having an effect on government actions. To expect absolute declines in the levels of government spending in the immediate future may be overly optimistic, but we can at least look forward to a reduction in the government's share of the economic pie as the private sector grows faster than government spending.

The counterpart of a reduction in the government's share in the economy should be slower growth in the money supply. If we are correct that the nation's sentiment about inflation and the role of government has shifted, then in future years, spending growth will be smaller and federal deficits reduced. This in turn will take pressure off the Fed to print money by monetizing the deficit. What's more, an end of inflation will reduce the growth of money needed for transactions. Without continuing large price increases, there won't be a need to keep more and more money on hand to make everyday purchases. Finally, the Fed is well aware of the change in voter attitudes and the change in these attitudes toward inflation and unemployment, which further insulates it from pressures to artificially hold down interest rates and stimulate the economy. This, too, should reduce the growth in the money supply.

Just as we found government spending and related monetary policies to be the root cause of inflation, we feel that progress in those areas is the central factor that will turn the tide toward lower inflation. But there are a number of supplementary forces at work as well. We have identified five additional factors pointing to the conclusion that inflation is really ending this time: financial shifts discouraging speculation, higher saving rates, improved productivity growth, more competition (because of worldwide commodity and manufacturing surpluses, a strong dollar, and reduced regulation), and a reversal of inflationary expectations and other social attitudes that promote inflation.

The Fun Goes Out of Speculation

We expect several changes in the financial structure to take much of the appeal out of speculative activity. First, we expect real interest rates—both short- and long-term—to remain high by historical standards for some years to come. High real rates help moderate inflation in two key ways. They reduce borrowing to speculate, and they encourage saving. After all, real interest rates measure the extent to which borrowers *cannot* pass on their financing costs. The inflation rate is the average of every business's price increases, or the average of everyone's success in passing on costs. Consequently, the difference between inflation rates and interest rates is the amount that borrowers have to absorb. As was pointed out in Chapter 3, speculation was encouraged when real interest rates were negative and the tangible assets bought with borrowed money were rising in price even faster than inflation. With an ending of inflation and high real interest rates, the reverse is true.

Real interest rates should be kept high by uncertainty on the part of lenders, together with their desire to catch up

Forces that Are Turning the Tide   87

after the combination of negative real rates and capital losses on bonds and other fixed-income investments of the late 1970s. In effect, these factors have induced a structural shift in interest rates to substantially higher risk premiums.

Statistical analysis supports this claim. To determine why real interest rates became so high, we constructed a model explaining yields on 20-year Treasury bonds in terms of inflation, 90-day Treasury bill rates, and the federal deficit. The results obtained from testing this model over the 1956–1974 period and the 1975–1982 period were quite different. They indicate that in the recent period, all things equal, rates are 2.5 percentage points higher than they would have been in the previous period, assuming that all the explanatory factors were held constant.

Similar analysis indicates that interest rates on short-term instruments are also higher under equivalent conditions than they would have been in the past because of volatility itself: The wilder the oscillations in the market, the higher the short-term rates demanded by lenders. This again suggests that rates are higher than they would otherwise be as a result of a feeling of greater uncertainty in the marketplace and a feeling among lenders that they must be compensated for increased risk.

When a structural shift like this takes place, it takes some time to change it. True, a severe financial shock, virtual elimination of the federal deficit, or some other event could convince lenders that the environment has changed. But otherwise, they are likely to remain skeptical, and the nation will probably face high real rates at both the short and long ends of the spectrum for some time, even if inflation is largely eliminated.

There is, however, an additional factor keeping short-term rates high: a flattening in the yield curve, or the relationship between short- and long-term interest rates at any given point in time. Exhibit 5-1 shows the spread between short-term rates (as measured by yields on commercial paper) and long-term rates on corporate bonds from 1835

EXHIBIT 5-1
Interest Rates. *(Board of Governors of the Federal Reserve System, Statistical Release, "Selected Interest Rates and Bond Prices"; Sidney Homer, A History of Interest Rates, 2d ed., Rutgers University Press, New Brunswick, N.J., 1977.)*

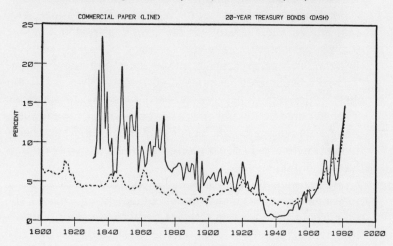

COMMERCIAL PAPER (LINE)   20-YEAR TREASURY BONDS (DASH)

onward. As indicated, short-term rates were almost always above long-term rates—an inverted yield curve—until the depression. Since then, however, the reverse has generally been true, and many believe that this is the way the world was created. In fact, this is suggested by the term used when short-term rates are below long-term rates: a "normal" or "positive" yield curve.

There are probably a number of reasons why the yield curve became distinctly positive about 50 years ago, but we think the key was a monetary policy since the depression that stressed economic expansion and low unemployment. The result, of course, was lower short-term interest rates than would have prevailed otherwise. Indeed, how many times did the Fed restrain the natural rise in short-term interest rates late in a business cycle in order to keep the expansion going and delay the next recession?

With the recent and, we expect, long-term change in monetary policy, this artificial restraint on short-term rates has been removed. Consequently, the strongly positive yield curve may be a thing of the past, although short-term rates probably will not exceed long-term rates again over the course of the business cycle for an extended period of time.

With short-term interest rates closer to long-term rates than in past decades, the short-term rates may experience a double jump compared with past patterns—once in moving closer to long-term rates and again as long-term rates remain higher in relation to inflation. This would greatly reduce the attractiveness of hedge buying, excess inventory holding, and other speculative activities financed by short-term borrowing. In effect, short-term borrowing would make sense only for short-term, self-liquidating purposes or when returns were judged to be extraordinary.

Another factor that should tend to dampen speculative fervor is the dramatic change in financial institutions' attitudes toward the relative maturities of their assets and liabilities. Far too late, many financial intermediaries discovered that borrowing short and lending long in a period of rapidly rising interest rates represents a suicidal strategy. Now the universal aim is to match maturities, and this greatly reduces speculative opportunities.

An excellent example of this can be seen in the housing area. Earlier, a house buyer was able to borrow at a fixed rate for 30 years. As inflation and mortgage rates moved up over the last two decades, those borrowing rates usually became submarket rates, subsidized initially by savers who were confined to low-interest earnings and later by the thrift institutions when they were forced to pay savers more to retain their deposits. The borrower was protected from rising mortgage rates, but if rates ever fell, the loan could simply be refinanced. At the same time the cost of the borrower's liability was fixed and low; the house owner had invested in an asset whose price was rising faster than inflation. He couldn't miss.

Unfortunately, this free lunch had to be paid for eventually, and the price has been the virtual wrecking of the thrift institutions. The net result is the recent introduction of

variable-rate mortgages, which greatly change the game.
With them the home buyer is essentially locked into a relatively fixed spread between mortgage costs and appreciation
of the price of a house. Periods of high inflation and rapid
growth in house prices are also likely to be periods of high
mortgage rates which tend to offset the appreciation in the
house prices. The speculative attractiveness of variable-rate
financing is obviously far less than it was with low fixed
mortgage costs and open-ended appreciation in the price of
the house. The fun is gone.

One last factor that should tend to tarnish the luster of
speculation is the changing tax structure. With the top tax
rate being cut from 70% to 50% and write-offs on interest
being diminished accordingly, the government has become
much less of a partner in the borrow-to-speculate game. The
average tax rate for almost every taxpayer is lower than the
top tax rate, but this rate on the incremental dollar is the rate
that any rational investor or speculator considers before
plunking down his or the bank's money. Moreover, if a flat
tax were implemented, the average and incremental rates
would be the same. With a flat tax, this rate could drop to,
say, 20%, which means that Uncle Sam would not be picking
up the old 70% of borrowing costs and losses or even the
current 50%, but only 20%. Admittedly, the winning speculator would get to keep 80% versus 50% now or 30% earlier,
but the urge to leverage speculations and investments to
today's level would obviously be dampened greatly.

Increased Saving

As was noted earlier in this chapter, high real interest rates
encourage saving which ultimately will finance capital
spending and generate productivity growth. High real rates
mean that for the first time in decades, savers can receive a
positive return after adjustment for inflation and taxes. As
was pointed out in Chapter 3, after-tax real returns of -5%
to -8% were the norm in the 1970s. With the top bracket

now at 50%, interest rates around 12%, and inflation averaging 4.3% in the first half of 1982, the real after-tax return for an upper-income taxpayer works out to a positive 2.1%. Clearly, then, it makes more sense to save now than it has for a long time.

Saving should also increase as people realize that their houses and other tangible assets no longer represent large and automatically growing savings accounts. Declines in prices for tangibles could well boost savings as individuals rebuild their net worth. By the same token, the extended recession which started in 1980 is another reason to expect people to set aside more of their take-home pay. Indeed, until the Commerce Department revised the saving numbers in mid-1982, we were baffled as to why consumers did not show a higher saving rate.

While the new individual retirement account (IRA) program should also encourage saving, it is too early to judge its full impact. Some surveys indicate that about 89% of those eligible for IRAs are aware of their eligibility. By mid-1982, about one in six had already opened an IRA, while another one in six claimed they would open one before the year's end. Thus, about one worker in three planned to have an IRA by January 1983. This ratio is roughly consistent with past participation in IRAs and Keoghs before eligibility increased dramatically in 1982.

If anything, we might expect higher participation now, because a lot of the people who are newly eligible are upper-income salaried employees who are known to be in high tax brackets, disposed toward minimizing taxes, and favorable toward saving. The preliminary data appear to be consistent with this assumption. Apparently, a large proportion of the IRAs recently started have the maximum tax deduction, indicating that participants have strong resources.

One of the most favorable factors for higher saving in the coming decade, however, is an expected increase in the number of households that earn higher real incomes. As shown in Table 5-1, average household saving as a proportion of disposable income increases rather dramatically at higher gross income levels. Households with gross income over $47,800 in 1980 dollars save 33% of their after-tax income, while those with incomes under $11,500 spend $1.37 for each dollar of take-home pay.

Obviously, to the extent that dollars are kept in the hands of the upper-income earners, who are big savers, rather than transferred to households that actively spend, total national saving will increase. Indeed, this is exactly the effect achieved by the changes in the tax structure implemented under the Reagan administration. Since upper-income people pay the most taxes, the proportional cuts in tax rates under the new law give them the largest tax savings and also the greatest increase in after-tax income.

Demographic factors also should contribute to the shift of households toward the upper-income end of the spectrum and hence to saving. As the postwar babies mature and move ahead in their careers, more and more of them should move up into higher income levels. The same is true of the huge number of older women who have entered the labor force in recent years. The upward income shift will also be enhanced by the baby boom generation's higher educational levels and greater tendency toward two-income households.

Table 5-1 Estimates of Consumer Spending and Saving Rates by Gross Income Level

Gross Income, 1980 dollars	% of After-Tax Income Used for:	
	Consumption, %	Saving, %
Under $11,500	136.7	−36.7
$11,500–$22,900	98.6	1.4
$22,900–$47,800	85.6	14.4
$47,800 and over	67.4	32.6

Note: Data derived from 1972–1973 Consumer Expenditure Survey, collected by the Bureau of Labor Statistics. Rates subsequently reconciled with National Income and Product Account data through 1980.

A final factor suggesting less spending and more saving is the likely consumer reaction to a less inflationary climate. Until recently, high and increasing inflation rates coupled with low borrowing costs encouraged consumers to buy ahead and hence build their inventories. How many have bought an extra suit or even accumulated extra canned goods because they believed that the prices of those items would increase soon?

Lower inflation and high real interest rates may well convince people that they don't need to stockpile goods. Even now, with the extremely weak state of business, many are beginning to realize that almost everything they buy that isn't on sale now soon will be. Few autos are being sold currently without some sort of rebate. For the past 3 years, retailers have run almost storewide sales *before* Christmas. In any period during which consumers are reducing their inventories, their consumption will exceed their purchases, and their saving will be augmented by the difference between normal consumption and the lower level of spending.

One of the authors may already be learning about the costs of excess inventories. His basement is full of boxes of unopened tools bought at once-in-a-lifetime bargain prices he was sure he'd never see again. His garage is stacked from floor to ceiling with lawn fertilizer he accumulated over the years at prices he just knew would prove to be cheap as inflation continued. Recently, however, he saw some fertilizer priced below what he paid for it a year ago. Considering the interest rate he could have received on the money tied up in his fertilizer inventory, he's now beginning to believe that fertilizer is for lawns, not for hedge buying.

Productivity

Productivity growth, whose afflictions in the past decade reinforced the inflationary pressures generated by the government, is now due for a turnaround. Many of the negatives for productivity growth that were detailed in Chapter 2 should now turn to positives and should also reinforce the deflationary thrust resulting from the new pressure to contain government activity.

As we shall note later, the recent strength in the dollar, which seems likely to continue, puts tremendous downward price pressure on domestic producers who compete with imports. This heightens the need for them to improve their efficiency and productivity in order to reduce their costs and prices. At the same time, a strong dollar means that U.S. export prices rise in terms of foreign currency, reducing their competitiveness abroad. This too helps contain prices in this country, because U.S. firms that lose sales abroad tend to compete more aggressively in their home markets in order to maintain their overall volume of output. Again, the pressure to reduce costs through increased productivity is intensified.

Productivity should also improve as a result of the investment encouraged by a more stable and hence more predictable economy and by reduced and less erratic government regulation. As was noted in Chapter 2, without a market test or profit motive, government activity is inherently inefficient, and so a shift in economic activity away from government and toward a greater private share should also improve productivity.

A further spur to productivity is the fact that efforts to increase efficiency are more meaningful in an era of little or no inflation compared with a period of double-digit inflation. An end of inflation would shift attention away from speculation, removing what has been a devastatingly strong alternative to productivity-enhancing activities. But it goes much further than that.

By perseverance and the commitment of resources to research and development (R&D), a firm might lower its manufacturing costs by 3% per year. In a time of 3% general inflation, the effects of such cost-saving innovations make a big difference, offsetting the price rise that would otherwise occur. During double-digit inflation, in contrast, the fruits of such efforts get lost in the shuffle, waylaying only a fraction of general price increases.

Demographics provides another area in which the forces for higher productivity and lower inflation will operate. Although none of our industrial clients has bragged about the work ethic of the postwar babies who poured into the labor force in recent years, their productivity as well as that of the many older women who also entered in large numbers almost has to rise as they gain experience and training.

Capital formation will help sustain productivity growth, and new incentives are already in place, thanks to the Economic Recovery and Tax Act of 1981. These include faster depreciation, more liberal leasing rules, increases in the investment tax credit for some categories of equipment, and some special provisions for small business. Capital investment would benefit also from declining interest rates. On a present-value basis, a $100 return in 10 years is worth only $16 today with a 20% discount rate, but $39, or about 2.5 times as much, with a 10% rate.

Soaring energy costs presented a major stumbling block to productivity in the past, but these price signals have encouraged conservation, which is another way of saying that energy productivity has increased. As was stated in Chapter 2, the earlier explosion in energy costs, among other factors, also took its toll on the economy by making about 20% of the capital stock obsolete. This in turn required a considerable amount of catch-up investment. With this catch-up almost completed, however, investment now can be applied to making progress rather than recovering lost ground.

A decreased drain on capital formation is also expected as a result of a more rational and balanced approach to environmental protection. Furthermore, American industry has largely caught up in many areas with the air and water pollution control-related expenditures that were mandated earlier.

Increased Competition

A greater element of competition in world economies is also a major factor in the argument for the end of inflation. We now appear to be in a world of surpluses rather than short-ages, as was feared several years ago. For one thing, an inventory-building panic even remotely like that of the early 1970s seems unlikely for years to come. Businesspeople were so badly hurt in 1974–1975 that they simply don't want to risk building another house of cards. Furthermore, as was noted earlier in this chapter, higher short-term interest rates should take the fun out of inventory building for some time.

Even apart from inventory building, however, the econ-omy is facing almost universal surpluses, with not only con-tinuing unemployment of men and machines in this country but also—for the first time since the 1930s—significant unemployment in Europe and Japan. Previously, those coun-tries were rebuilding from the effects of World War II and catching up with the United States. They had, if anything, chronic shortages of labor and capital equipment.

That process of rebuilding was largely completed by the late 1960s, but the full effects of the shift to a lower under-lying growth rate were not fully felt even in the recession of the mid-1970s, the first one of significance outside North America since World War II. Turks, Yugoslavs, Greeks, and other "guest" workers in northern Europe were simply sent home so that native Germans and Swiss wouldn't be laid off. But the foreign workers were never recalled after that reces-sion, and so in the current recessionary period the native Germans and Swiss are without work.

After such a long period of virtually uninterrupted growth, these countries have developed political and social systems that assume unemployment will remain low. Con-sequently, with today's unemployment problems there is a great deal of frustration, and the best position for a European politician is being out of office—he'll soon get back in. In Norway, the United Kingdom, and most recently Germany, the voters threw out the liberals and put in the conservatives; in France they threw out the conservatives and put in the liberals.

European and other industrial countries are eager to put their unemployed men and women back to work but cautious about reducing their interest rates unilaterally for fear of depressing their currencies. This in turn would increase the cost of imports, and as shown in Table 5-2, most of these countries have considerable foreign exposure. However, these countries have no qualms about increasing their exports as a way of employing more people and machines at home. And the United States has become the happy dumping ground for the world, adding further to already ample domestic supplies of almost everything.

Underdeveloped countries face an even more serious situation because of their huge balance-of-trade deficits resulting from more imports of manufactured goods and oil than exports of raw materials and other items. Many of these countries virtually depend on one export commodity for foreign exchange earnings to offset the deficits. In the case of Peru, Zambia, and Zaire, dependence on copper is so heavy that if the price declines, as it has over the last several years, their inclination is to meet that *falling* price by *increasing* production to maintain foreign exchange earnings. This dis-

Table 5-2 Imports and Exports as a Percentage of Gross Domestic Product, 1980

	Imports, %	Exports, %
United States	12.1	13.1
Japan	13.6	12.5
France	20.7	17.8
Germany	22.9	23.5
United Kingdom	22.0	21.0

SOURCE: International Monetary Fund, *International Financial Statistics*, July 1982.

equilibrium situation is quite in contrast to the usual economic inclination to cut production when prices fall.

Despite these attempts, export earnings of the developing nations are likely to slow significantly from their pace over the past 15 years. During this period, export earnings of the nonoil developing world grew at a 17% annual rate as world trade expanded. This enabled foreign exchange reserves to grow, which in turn provided developing countries with the wherewithal to pay for imported products. With trade slowing and commodity prices under pressure, exactly the opposite should occur.

To further aggravate this situation, budgetary constraints in the developed world may impose a limit on the amount of foreign aid flowing to the developing world. The recycling of petrodollars to developing nations may also moderate as surplus oil revenues dwindle in the face of rapid internal development in OPEC nations amid slowing demand for oil and weakness in its price. As a result of all these factors, the developing nations are likely to be providing a lot less demand than supply over the coming years.

The Soviet Union is likely to be another abundant source of commodities. It will be under considerable pressure to export in order to meet its commitments to communist bloc nations, to import grain to offset continued bad harvests, and to meet interest payments on foreign debt of $20 billion. Consequently, Soviet exports of oil, gas, metals, and minerals, including gold, diamonds, platinum, aluminum, vanadium, zinc, and chromite (note that there are strategic metals in this list), are likely to keep worldwide supplies plentiful and prices down.

We believe that this condition of sluggish demand and worldwide surpluses is likely to be quite broad-based, including not only raw commodities (notably energy and food, the two principal inflation bugbears of the 1970s) but also intermediate products such as steel and petrochemicals and even manufactured goods such as automobiles. A brief look at each of these areas will bear out our assumption that intense competition and downward pressure on prices are likely.

Energy

In the late 1970s, many were convinced that shortages of oil would last forever. On December 19, 1979, *The Wall Street Journal* ran a front-page column headed "Decade of Scarcity: Main Problems of 1980s Will Involve Energy, Many Experts Think." Robert Baldwin, president of Gulf Oil Corp.'s refining and marketing area, was quoted as saying, "The decade of the '80s is the decade of scarcity." The Department of Energy was predicting a steady growth in U.S. energy consumption over the decade, with a 10-year increase of about 27%.

President Carter hoped to slash oil imports by 1990 to half the then current 8.5 million barrels a day. John Lichtblau, executive director of the Petroleum Industry Research Foundation, said, "After 1980 and 1981, it would be a very great achievement if we stay below the 8.5 million-barrels-a-day ceiling." At this writing, in the summer of 1982, oil imports are running at 4.8 barrels per day, not much more than half that figure.

What happened—and what we expect to continue happening—is that the price increases that exacerbated inflation so badly in the 1970s did their job of depressing demand and increasing supplies. Energy conservation over the last decade has been quite dramatic: Energy consumption per dollar of GNP fell from about 60,000 Btu in 1973 to only about 51,000 in 1980, or almost 20%.

Even gasoline consumption, which many thought was demand-inelastic, is under considerable downward pressure from several long-term factors. The average miles per gallon of the new car fleet is increasing. As these cars replace the gas guzzlers whose poor mileage has been dragging down efficiency numbers for the whole fleet, the fuel efficiency for the entire car stock will improve, with positive implications for gasoline conservation. In fact, gasoline consumption by 1986 could fall to about 5.5 million barrels per day, as shown in Exhibit 5-2, from a peak of almost 7.5 million barrels a day in 1978.

Energy conservation has been impressive abroad as well. For example, oil consumption among the Organization for Economic Cooperation and Development (OECD) nations, including Canada, France, Italy, Japan, the United Kingdom, the United States, and West Germany, was about 34 million barrels per day in 1973 and on an upward trend. But since 1973 the group's oil consumption has been below that level in every year but two, namely, 1978 and 1979. And even in those years consumption was only about 1 million barrels per day higher than the 1973 level. Overall demand for oil in the

EXHIBIT 5-2
Gasoline Consumption. *(U.S. Department of Energy, Energy Information Department; A. Gary Shilling & Co., Inc. estimates.)*

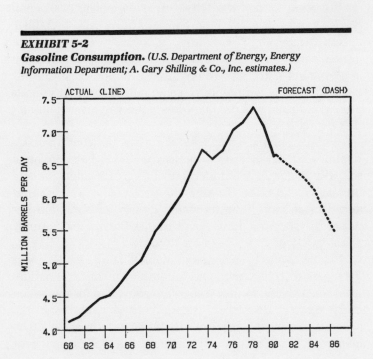

noncommunist world may drop 5% in 1982 from 1981, according to some experts.

The price increases of the 1970s were a major spur to increased exploration and production worldwide. Major discoveries were made in Nigeria, Mexico, the North Sea, and the Beaufort Sea, and production in the United States increased in 1981 after full decontrol of domestic oil prices was accomplished. Indeed, it took just 5 months after full decontrol for domestic production to increase on a year-to-year basis. At this writing, it has increased on a year-to-year basis in virtually every month since then. Furthermore, soon after the Federal Energy Regulatory Commission decontrolled various classifications of natural gas by fiat, the domestic market was glutted, and prices have been falling rather than rising.

The result of this confluence of forces is that OPEC's power over the world oil market may be on the wane, as we shall discuss further in Chapter 8. With non-OPEC production increasing and demand stagnating, OPEC's share of total world production has fallen from 55.4% in 1973 to 49.5% in 1978. That share may be only about 37% in 1982, given the data available at this writing. OPEC's production has fallen absolutely as well, particularly over the past 2 years of global recession, when production cuts of about 45%, from 31 million barrels a day to about 17 million, have been necessary to prevent oversupply from driving down prices.

The loss of production from a major OPEC producer such as Saudi Arabia or Kuwait would undoubtedly tighten the market if it were not offset by the restoration of production by Iran and Iraq to pre-1979 levels. But barring this, there is every indication that the current excess of production capacity will continue. Thus, when demand finally recovers as part of a worldwide economic recovery, petroleum prices need not increase abruptly or sharply.

In fact, a slack oil market could linger for a protracted period, since oil is likely to lose its share of total energy con-

sumption. According to American Petroleum Institute estimates, oil represented 55% of the free world's energy consumption in 1978, but by 1985 it may represent only 47%, and
in 1990 only 45%.

Meanwhile, the share of coal, natural gas, and new fuels
will increase steadily. The United States is still moving in the
direction of fully exploiting its extensive coal reserves, with
the development of a coal slurry pipeline system under
intense discussion in Congress.

Food

As far as bad weather and food shortages go, maybe the
meteorologist mentioned in Chapter 2 was right and we are
on the down leg of a 3000-year weather cycle. So far, however, even 4 consecutive years of disastrous harvests in Russia have not prevented U.S. grain surpluses and low prices
from becoming major economic and political problems. In
any event, the Soviets, who contributed importantly to the
demand growth of the 1970s, may be less active buyers of
American grain in the future. The very poor weather in Russia in much of the 1970s is bound to improve. But regardless,
Soviet policy seems to be moving away from dependence on
the United States because of the cooling of relations between
the two countries and the threat of another grain embargo by
this country.

Another reason for expecting reduced demand for U.S.
agricultural products is that other countries with extensive
agricultural resources are becoming much more active in the
world grain export market. This is demonstrated in Table
5-3, which shows exports of corn, wheat, barley, sorghum,
and oats (collectively known as coarse grains) for selected
years in the last decade. Canada and Australia have become
particularly strong exporters of wheat, while Argentine
exports of corn have increased markedly.

Meanwhile, demand for agricultural products on the part
of the developing world may slow in the 1980s. The developing countries have lots of hungry mouths, but they are lim-

Table 5-3 Coarse Grain Exports for Selected Countries
(1000 Metric Tons)

	1973–1974	1976–1977	1978–1979	1980–1981
Argentina	8737	9917	11470	13885
South Africa	3436	2610	2903	4940
Australia	2485	2741	2603	3195
Canada	2720	4443	3851	6809
United States	40,669	50,295	56,910	61,800

DATA SOURCE: U.S. Department of Agriculture, Foreign Agricultural Service.

ited in their ability to buy, as was discussed earlier in this chapter. As a means of calculating the impact of the slowdown in worldwide economic growth on agricultural export demand, we constructed an econometric model linking dietary patterns and economic activity. Were world economic growth to slow by 1 percentage point in the 1980s, our analysis suggests that U.S. farm exports would rise about one-fourth as fast as the 8% annual rise recorded in the 1970s. For exports to rise more rapidly would require the opening of new markets, such as the People's Republic of China. But even in this best-case assumption, growth in agricultural exports would average only 4% per year. Thus, it appears that agriculture in the 1980s will more closely resemble the 1950s–1960s period of surpluses than the 1970s period. This means that agricultural prices should be far more stable.

Industrial Commodities and Manufacturers' Goods

Industrial commodities such as steel should also be in surplus. Consider how sluggish domestic demand and excess supplies are leading to intense international competition, with governments in Europe, the United States, and Japan all trying to figure out ways to dump unwanted steel production on each other without suffering penalties for doing so. Steel producers throughout the world are working at extremely low capacity; indeed, in this country capacity utilization rates have dropped well below the 50% mark.

As was discussed in Chapter 2, in January 1982 the steel trigger price mechanism that had helped protect our domestic steel industry was suspended. By May 1982 steel imports had jumped 35%. The reaction was the filing of a bevy of petitions for duty on the basis of alleged subsidization, with 85% to 90% of European Economic Community (EEC) steel exports to America covered by pending duty suits in mid-1982. And no wonder: American producers' list prices were $200 per metric ton higher than spot market prices on average at the time, while imports were coming in at prices roughly $100 per metric ton cheaper than the most deeply discounted American prices.

Petrochemical production is another area in which capacity is already ample but is being greatly increased by new facilities being built in less-developed countries, especially in the mideast, where petroleum inputs are plentiful and cheap and local consumption is limited. Consequently, supplies of petrochemicals for exports should remain excessive, and pressure on world markets will probably continue to be intense.

Intense competitive pressure internationally is also developing for manufactured goods. Japanese companies are producing IBM-compatible computer equipment, Airbus Industries has become a significant competitor of American airframe manufacturers, and auto assembly plants in less-developed countries, where labor costs are significantly cheaper, are becoming increasingly common.

In fact, the less-developed countries are likely to play an increasingly larger role in manufactured exports. The top tier of developing nations—e.g., Brazil, Korea, Taiwan, and Singapore—all of which the United States spent three decades helping to develop, are predominantly exporters of manufactured goods which are generally in competition with similar U.S. and European goods.

Of course, some may disagree with our conclusion about

worldwide surpluses, arguing that cartels may be formed to protect prices. In fact, we're now looking at worldwide economic conditions that are hospitable for cartel formation. The 1920s and the 1930s—periods when prices of raw materials were weak in relation to those of manufactured goods, when the underdeveloped nations producing raw materials had large balance-of-trade deficits, and when these countries were importing more manufactured goods than they were exporting raw materials—were the times when cartels were instituted in great numbers. There were cartels for tin, nitrates, jute, copper, and many other goods.

The missing ingredient at this time—and the reason why the likelihood of big cartel formation is rather low—is the sponsor: the key country which sets up, bankrolls, and polices a cartel from its inception. In the 1920s and 1930s the Dutch and British still had vast colonial empires and played that role. As a matter of fact, in the 1920s there was a speech delivered on the floor of the House of Commons by one Winston Churchill, in which he advocated a rubber cartel as a means of soaking the Americans in order to repay World War I debts owed to America. Now, except in the case of the Saudis with oil—and their dominance seems to be fading—we simply don't have such strong sponsor countries, and so the prospect of generalized cartel formation seems fairly limited.

There is an additional point to be made about cartels. While they are normally set up in response to falling prices, they usually do well only in periods such as the 1920s, when, after the 1920-1921 commodity collapse, prices stopped falling. Conversely, cartels often fall apart if demand and price weakness continue. Declining demand in the depression killed many of the cartels set up in the 1920s and early 1930s. This suggests that the noninflationary world we see ahead may not be hospitable for any new cartel that manages to get set up or even for the few remaining older ones. One might not want to bet on the success or even longevity of the tin cartel, for example.

The Strong Dollar

Another factor favoring the fight against inflation is a strong dollar, which is subjecting U.S. business to increased competition. As shown in Exhibit 2-6, starting in 1980, the dollar moved up in relation to the weighted market basket of currencies of our major trading partners. Part of the reason was rising U.S. interest rates, which attracted funds from abroad. But the dollar's strength probably resulted mainly from a correct assessment abroad of the results of the 1980 presidential election and its effect on U.S. economic policies. After all, for years foreigners have considered the United States a safe haven for both portfolio and direct investment. Previously, however, they had been deterred from investing here by U.S. inflation problems and the resulting weakness in the dollar's purchasing power in this country and in foreign exchange markets.

While the dollar may not move significantly higher than its mid-1982 levels, it could well maintain its strength despite the detrimental effect a strong dollar has on the U.S. trade balance by encouraging imports and discouraging exports. Foreign investors see the United States as a big market with solid prospects for long-term growth, in contrast to the inflationary government controls and political risks they see at home. Foreign direct investors also see the U.S. corporations they like to buy as cheap, and in a number of cases, such as chemicals, production costs are lower here than at home.

At the same time that foreign investors are likely to continue to buy dollars to make investments here, U.S. direct and portfolio investors may slow their investments abroad for many of the same reasons. This, of course, would reduce the demand for other currencies and thereby support the dollar indirectly.

Furthermore, it's far from clear to us that high U.S. interest rates are a major source of support for the dollar in anything but the very short run. Correlations between various countries' interest rate differentials and their exchange rates are rather weak. Indeed, when interest rates dropped sharply in the United States in the summer of 1982, the widely expected weakness in the dollar failed to materialize. Furthermore, to the extent that interest rate differences are significant, the continuing high real interest rates we expect in the United States may exceed those abroad in coming years and lend some support to greenbacks. Finally, even if the dollar is overvalued after all these considerations, including continuing anti-inflationary policy in Washington, it's still likely to remain so for some time. Currency movements tend to have considerable momentum; when a currency is undervalued or overvalued, corrections often are slow in coming.

A strong dollar will reduce inflationary pressures in a number of ways. As was noted earlier in this chapter, a strong dollar aids imports because the dollars the producer receives are worth more in his own currency. This usually results in some cuts in the producer's dollar price, which also puts competitive pressure on domestic producers of the same goods. A strong dollar can put pressure on U.S. importers as well. For instance, the recent collapse in the French franc made it possible to buy Japanese cameras in France and sell them in the United States at prices considerably below American dealers' costs. U.S. imports of goods account for only 8.9% of GNP, but they represent 24% of the goods component of GNP with which they compete. Consequently, some calculations suggest that the U.S. inflation rate has been reduced by 2 percentage points because of the recent strength in the dollar.

A strong dollar also helps restrain domestic inflation through its effects on exports. Many U.S. exports, such as computers, oil-field gear, and military hardware, are relatively insensitive to currency fluctuations. However, others are sensitive, and a strong dollar means higher prices in foreign currencies; this leads to fewer sales abroad by American producers. This in turn increases domestic supplies and puts downward pressure on prices in this country.

U.S. agricultural products are a clear case in point. The strong dollar as well as other factors caused international grain buyers to turn to cheaper sources such as Canada, Argentina, Australia, and Brazil. The resulting surpluses of U.S. grain have severely depressed prices here at home.

Deregulation

Another plus in the battle against inflation is deregulation. The reduction of government regulation has been proceeding apace in a number of areas. The relationship of this process to the easing of price pressures may perhaps be most easily seen in industries in which regulations had earlier fixed prices, restricted entry (thereby allowing prices to be fixed by the members of the "club"), or both. The airline, trucking, and brokerage industries are probably the most prominent examples of this kind of regulation and of what happens when it ends.

When airlines were first deregulated in 1978, the immediate reaction was a rash of special discount fares that offered consumers unheard-of low prices for the heavily traveled routes. At first, when the economy was still strong, it looked as though demand might respond strongly enough to this price cutting to keep the market pie big enough for all in the industry. Our analysis at the time, however, concluded that the sensitivity of air travel to fare levels was limited. Instead, the economic expansion then in full swing was moving many people, especially postwar babies, into the income range in which they could afford to travel by air. Our conclusion? Big trouble for the airlines whenever economic weakness pushed people back below that income threshold—and trouble there certainly has been. However painful this has been, though, it is the process by which inefficient excess competition is weeded out of the marketplace; the survivors learn how to control costs and keep prices down.

We recently saw an example of this firsthand when we traveled from New York to Washington, D.C., on a new, nonunionized airline. The young woman who took our tickets walked us to the plane, directed us to place our baggage—which we carried ourselves—in the rear of the plane, helped us board the plane, gave us the safety demonstration, and then got into the pilot's seat and flew the plane to Washington.

The trucking industry provides a second dramatic example of how deregulation can lower costs. Prior to the Motor Carrier Act of 1980, it had been necessary for anyone interested in engaging in interstate trucking to obtain operating authorities either from the Interstate Commerce Commission (ICC) or from other truckers having such authorities. The approval procedure was such that it was virtually impossible to obtain authority from the ICC without the agreement of existing truckers, since the latter could easily not only file protests against approval of a new competitor but also win those protests. This procedural system, combined with antitrust immunity granted to rate-making bureaus in the motor carrier industry, created a situation in which trucking companies, lacking competition, could charge rates well above true cost. In a study performed for the ICC in April 1980, *An Analysis of Rates and Costs in the Motor Carrier Industry*, we found that rates were 20% to 30% above their costs, including reasonable profit, in the industry. This was reflected in part in the huge prices of operating authorities traded in the open market—well into the million-dollar range.

To see the impact of deregulation on the industry, compare the value of Wilson Freight Co.'s operating authorities before deregulation as they were carried on the books in the 1979 annual report—$6.4 million—and their sale price in a 1982 auction—$565,000. Among the authorities involved was a Cincinnati-to-Atlanta traffic lane, bought 6 years previously for $2.45 million and sold for $6,000.

In the brokerage industry, commission rates were deregulated on May Day of 1975. The initial large-trade discounts from the earlier fixed rates were no more than 5% or 10%. "Nonevent," yelled Wall Street. But stock-exchange volume was then at relatively high levels. When volume declined sharply in the fall of that year, those bracing winds began to blow the leaves off that famous buttonwood tree, and discounts grew quickly to the 35% to 40% range.

These are only a few of the industries in which deregulation is occurring. Others include railroads, banking and financial services, investment banking, and telecommunications. Still others may follow.

One of the "fat" areas in any industry protected from the full blast of competitive forces tends to be labor compensation. Remember how each gigantic Teamsters settlement was followed immediately by ICC-endorsed increases in trucking rates? In fact, it is frequently in regulated or otherwise cartellike industries that strong unions tend to thrive. These unregulated industries which still exhibit cartellike behavior—autos and steel, for example—tend to be highly concentrated and to lack effective foreign competition, at least until recently.

To get an idea of the magnitude of union gains—which were then passed on to the relevant consumers—in regulated industries, it is worth noting that wages in the trucking industry in 1971 were 31% higher than they were for the private nonfarm sector as a whole, a differential that rose to 40% by 1981. In the auto industry, as shown in Exhibit 5-3, earnings of motor vehicle production workers were already 125% of the manufacturing average in 1958 and rose to 154% of the average by 1981. This occurred despite the fact that toward the end of the period, the domestic industry was being flattened by foreign competition.

In many regulated industries, but especially in trucking, the earlier cartellike control over their markets resulted not only in very high wages but also in huge pension funds. In the Teamsters' case, those funds seem to have attracted organized crime, and government allegations of misuse of funds are well known.

Control of these funds and other plums created by this cartellike situation may have been at the root of the struggle for control of the Teamsters several years ago between

EXHIBIT 5-3
Earnings of Motor Vehicle Production Workers as a Percentage of All Manufacturing Average. *(U.S. Department of Labor, Bureau of Labor Statistics.)*

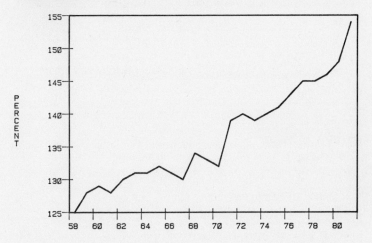

Jimmy Hoffa, the former head, and Frank Fitzsimmons, the then current head. It has recently been alleged by a former Teamster insider that Hoffa planned to kill Fitzsimmons in order to regain control of the union but that Fitzsimmons learned about it and had Hoffa killed first. (Fitzsimmons subsequently died of natural causes.) Assuming these allegations have merit, and considering the fact that the power Hoffa sought to regain was the result of the government-supported cartellike structure of the industry, it may be fair to say that Jimmy Hoffa was done in by government regulation.

Less inflation in wages, particularly union settlements that tend to set the tone for the whole wage structure, is of great importance to the inflation outlook because labor accounts for roughly 75% of all business costs. But while it seems clear from the figures just reviewed that there is a lot of excess to be cut from wages in industries which have been regulated and that increasing competition in these areas has put the handwriting on the wall, labor may take some time to see the light. We discussed the psychology that lies behind this sluggishness on the part of labor leaders in an article for the editorial page of *The Wall Street Journal* of January 21, 1982, and our description still seems apt today:

> Even when managements accept the reality of competition and the need to control costs once the price umbrellas are gone, union leaders are understandably reluctant. Many would probably prefer to see a continuing decline in their membership to announcing something like, "We've enjoyed a great cartel-like atmosphere for many years, but the party's over, boys, and we've got to take substantial pay cuts and work harder in order to meet competition." In the former case union leaders may preside over declining bailiwicks, but in the latter they risk being retired at the next union election.

A Change in Attitudes

Demographic and social changes in recent years also have tended to reduce inflationary forces. One aspect of this change is that as the general population gets older, it tends to move toward more conservative viewpoints. The postwar babies are aging and moving away from the radicalism of youth, becoming more cautious, and in general increasing their incomes and asset holdings. And improved economic status tends to move people to the right in both their political and their economic thinking. There's nothing that will make conservatives out of a people like giving them something to conserve.

There is also evidence that the concept of individual, as opposed to societal or governmental, responsibility is returning. Employers, partly because they can no longer pass on costs easily but also perhaps because of a basic change in attitude, no longer feel the necessity of granting every employee a cost-of-living increase just for being present. Instead, wage and salary raises are increasingly being linked to the employee's contribution to the firm's success.

Individuals also seem to be developing a renewed sense of personal responsibility, and the concepts of right and wrong, good and evil, seem to be reemerging. We even have a bona fide villain, J. R. of the TV series *Dallas,* who has become so famous that he has reached the apex of American culture—a cover picture on *Time* magazine.

A feeling of responsibility for the welfare of others also seems to be growing. It's too early to know for sure, but there is some evidence that even with the prolonged recession that began in early 1980, corporations and individuals are moving to fill the gaps left as the federal government disentangles itself from the social welfare area. People are beginning to realize that the government no longer automatically fulfills every social need.

These shifts toward less reliance on government and more responsibility by individuals and nongovernment organizations work to reduce government influence on the economy and, as a result, inflation.

Another sign of the shift from the "me" decade of the 1970s to a "we" decade of the 1980s is the change in Pepsi-Cola's advertising campaign in 1980. Pepsi is a major advertiser—the fifth largest spender on TV commercials in 1980, with $145 million in outlays—and prides itself on spending its dollars effectively and only after comprehensive research on the nation's orientation. The February 5, 1980, edition of *The Wall Street Journal* quoted Alan M. Pottasch, senior vice president of creative services for Pepsi-Cola Co., as saying, "Our commercials have reflected America. . . . We've held a cultural mirror up to life."

In early 1980, Pepsi dropped the self-centered "Have a Pepsi day" campaign in favor of one centered on "Catch that Pepsi spirit. Drink it in," which stresses togetherness. TV ads show such scenes as a young Texan who hires a skywriter to make a marriage proposal to his intended, a big league baseball player returning to his hometown triumphantly, and a European father reunited in America with his son and family. "If the seventies were the decade of self," said Mr. Pottasch, "the eighties will be a season for sharing, an era of emotion, relationships, and above all, family."

But perhaps the most crucial change in attitude should be the reversal of expectations of inflation. Just as inflationary expectations, once they had become ingrained in the national consciousness, became a self-fulfilling prophecy during the 1970s, so the end of inflation, once it takes hold, should ensure that successively lower inflation rates occur. If people don't expect prices of tangible assets to go up, they won't buy them; demand drops, and prices *don't* go up. If businesspeople expect inflation to stay under control, they'll wait to buy the raw materials until they need them instead of stocking up on them ahead of time.

Likewise, the self-reinforcing aspects of inflation discussed in Chapter 3 also will work in reverse to promote disinflation. Lower inflation will strengthen the dollar, which will reduce the price of imported goods, increase competition, and create lower inflation. Lower inflation will produce high saving, encourage investment and productivity, and hence lead to slower price growth. Lower inflation will reduce businesspeople's ability to pass on costs and lead to stringent cost control, passed on to the consumer in the form of lower inflation.

For those who are still skeptical about the possibility of lower inflation becoming a permanent feature of life, this self-reinforcing aspect of the end of inflation should be kept in mind. What we are seeing now is just the beginning; once expectations are reversed, the trend may snowball.

Given all these forces promoting ample supplies, healthy competition, and an end to the expansion of government's role in the economy and a resulting slower growth in the money supply, there seems little question that the nation will experience much lower inflation rates in the years ahead. Are we entering a period of true disinflation—a stretch of declining inflation rates that serve as a transition to an era of stabler and considerably lower rates—or will the trend go all the way to deflation, with prices declining on a widespread and prolonged basis?

Deflation seems unlikely, even though it used to be the rule in peacetime. That was before the 1930s, however, when wages could fall as well as rise, even though real wages usually rose, since wages rarely fell as much as prices. Nationwide sentiments against falling wages as well as the growth in the labor unions since the depression have made general declines in wages nearly impossible. Today, the only time wages get cut is when a company is clearly facing bankruptcy, and even then labor concessions may only amount to a slowing of compensation increases. Minimum wage laws, Social Security benefits, welfare, and unemployment benefits have also greatly reduced the likelihood of widespread wage reductions. The last three items have made people less concerned about layoffs, which as a result have replaced pay cuts as the mechanism for reducing labor costs. For the nation as a whole, labor cost accounts for over three-quarters of total costs. Consequently, if wages don't fall, the only way that overall prices can fall appreciably is for profits to be wiped out—and that suggests a 1930s-style economic collapse, which, as discussed in Chapter 9, is possible but not likely.

There is, however, a way in which at least modest deflation could occur without economic collapse, but increases in labor cost would have to be very small by recent standards. If productivity nationwide were growing at about its long-term trend rate of 2.5% per year and labor compensation were rising at a 1.5% annual rate, overall prices could fall 1% per year. This is not outside the realm of possibility, given the anti-inflationary forces we see in place.

Perhaps more likely is a return to inflation rates of 2% to 3%. When we talk about this range, which we have since 1975, most people respond, "That would be fabulous, but your numbers are far too low." In fact, the range is very high by historical standards. Forget that before the 1930s deflation during peacetime was the rule and consider the post-World War II period. As shown in Exhibit 2-1, between the Korean and Vietnam wars, a period not too dissimilar to the era of peace and stability that we assume lies ahead, both wholesale and consumer price indexes rose about 1% per year.

There have been, of course, many changes in the economy's structure since the last "peacetime" year, 1965. A number of them, as discussed in Chapter 2, added to inflation in the last decade by reducing productivity, exaggerating cost-of-living adjustments, giving the nation inflation by fiat, etc. But this chapter has spelled out how many of those inflationary factors have been reversed or even eliminated and how other anti-inflationary forces such as deregulation have developed. In any event, inflation rates of 2% to 3%, or 2 to 3 *times* the earlier norm, should more than account for any net inflationary structural shift since the mid-1960s.

This is obviously below the current consensus long-term inflation forecast of about 6%, a number that troubles us for two reasons. First, it suggests a much more rapid structural shift in the economy in the last decade than is likely to have taken place in a period that short. Second, even if 6% inflation were built in, it seems unlikely that the nation could, as the consensus believes, comfortably settle in at those rates and happily ride off into the sunset. The problem is that when consumers and businesspeople see a high inflation rate lasting for some time, they begin to believe that it will continue or speed up. Inflationary expectations heat up, and then a rush into real estate, collectibles, assets in the ground, etc., gets under way and soon becomes a self-fulfilling prophecy. In our opinion, 6% inflation on a sustained basis is above the trigger point for inflationary psychology, but 2% to 3% is perhaps below it.

Regardless of whether prices end up increasing slowly, holding constant, or decreasing modestly, one thing is clear: The ending of the inflationary atmosphere which has plagued the nation for decades will create a much different world, one that many people are ill prepared to face psychologically or financially. We'll examine this world in more detail and how we get there from here, but before doing so, we want to point out in Chapter 6 the numerous signs that suggest we are indeed at an inflationary peak.

The Peak of Inflation: Ten Clear Signs

6

Ever since high rates of inflation began several decades ago, forecasters have repeatedly called for its demise. But time and again those who bet on continued inflation profited handsomely, while those who expected it to end came out losers. Is it unreasonable, then, to ask what is so different this time around? What concrete evidence is there beyond what we presented in Chapters 4 and 5 that inflation has really peaked? The evidence is overwhelming in our opinion.

Indeed, we would argue that many of the classic signs of a major top are now present, signs which were not there at the numerous false peaks during the last two decades. Studies of previous investment and business cycle peaks show common characteristics, 10 of which now seem to be in place:

1. Everybody has gotten on the "inflation-hedge" investment bandwagon.

2. Speculations are seen as sure bets.

3. Enormous borrowing has taken place for speculative purposes.

4. Price rises of certain speculations have reached ridiculous extremes.

5. Attempts are made to separate the speculative and investment elements of assets.

6. Trading volume in speculative investment vehicles has risen to record levels.

7. There has been a frantic search for new speculations.

8. There has been an attempt to revive the old favorites, despite an obvious deterioration in the fundamentals.

9. Market action suggests that the peak is past.

10. The game in question—in this case, high inflation rates—is expected to continue forever.

Let us examine each of these 10 points in some detail.

Everybody's In

In the securities business, it is generally acknowledged that prices will continue to rise as long as new buyers keep coming into the market. When everyone who can be enticed is in the market, there are no more buyers left, only potential sellers. That is usually when the peak is reached, and all the risks shift to the downside. The "market" for expectations of inflation and the related inflation-hedge activities is probably no different from the market prevailing in the securities business.

One of the authors was personally involved in a vivid example of this several years ago as a member of a committee searching for a new rector at his local church. After an elaborate screening process, we narrowed the list to eight people and then made the first personal contacts by phone. With four of the eight clergymen, the first question wasn't, "What's the size of the parish?" or "How would you describe the spiritual life of the community?" but rather, "Can I own my own house or must I live in a church-owned residence?

I've simply *got* to invest in real estate and build up some equity." When the clergy's in, everybody's in.

The same is true for small investors who gamble their life savings on a throw of the dice. In *The Wall Street Journal* of January 30, 1981, in an article entitled "Many New Investors Have Modest Means but Large Ambitions," we learn that many investors have been speculating in Denver's "penny stock" market. David Fox, a 32-year-old salesman, says, "I bought one for 30 cents a share and sold it the same day for 94 cents." Mr. Fox concedes that he is taking large risks: "If you read the prospectuses, you wouldn't buy them. . . . But to me, investing is a hobby. It beats the roulette wheel, and if I get wiped out, I can still live."

This attitude apparently was widespread among many small investors. In the same article, Donald Kinsey, senior vice president of Dean Witter Reynolds, says that investors "see the stock market as Las Vegas East. . . . They go out and put their money on the table. They're definitely not risk-averse."

Another example of widespread participation can be seen in a story we recently heard from the publisher of a tax shelter publication. He told us in no uncertain terms that he became worried about the future of the shelter business when his piano teacher stated proudly that he had invested $5000 in that "hot, new R&D deal, Trilogy." Apparently, the teacher was delighted to have reached the ranks of those for whom tax shelters are appropriate investments.

Even more recently, we learned about tax shelters from the workers repairing the air conditioning system in our offices. It had been inoperative for 3 weeks in a sweltering summer heat wave while we were sweating out the final drafts of this book. These "experts" were overheard to say that oil deals are dead but that real estate shelters are coming back. Apparently their broker disagreed, however, or at least the telephone shouting matches during their prolonged coffee breaks suggested so. Aren't shelters supposed to make sense only for the very wealthy?

In some cases, fear of inflation or shortages resulting from inflation can cause people to take dramatic measures. In the August 15, 1979, issue of *The Wall Street Journal*, in an article subtitled "Heeding Warnings of Seers Like Howard Ruff, They Stock Food, Tools, Guns," we learn that a Dr. Oxford and a Mr. Papp

> Have put away a year's supply of food for themselves and their families and bought some gold or silver coins, which they think will come in handy if inflation destroys the value of paper money.... Dr. Oxford has installed and filled a 300 gallon gasoline storage tank on some farmland he owns. Mr. Papp has armed himself in anticipation of having to defend his emergency stores.

In addition, the popularity of what we call "inflation forever" books—those which promise to tell you how to profit from hyperinflation—are also indicative of an "everybody's in" peak. These books are meaningful because we have found in the past that a cluster of books on a particular financial topic or a best-selling book about investments invariably indicates a change in trend and thus a price drop in that investment form.

It is not so much that the author's original premise is wrong but rather that the popularity of the book indicates that everyone wants to get into the investment. In many cases, when the book was first written, the investment in question was undervalued and subsequently entered a big bull market. But as was mentioned earlier, when everyone is on board an investment vehicle, there's no one left to push the price up, and its price inevitably declines.

The classic example in the past was a 123-page book entitled *Common Stocks as Long-Term Investments* by Edgar Lawrence Smith, which was published in 1924, just as the great bull market of the 1920s was getting under way. Smith was an economist and investment analyst who had studied the record of bonds, stocks, and commodities from the end of the Civil War to 1923, and he came to the then revolutionary conclusion that stocks, not bonds, were the best long-term investments.

As commonplace as that may sound now, it represented a 180 degree reversal of the conventional wisdom of the time. Stocks were generally regarded as good speculations but certainly not as good long-term investments. Bonds, on the other hand, were considered an excellent place to put your capital for the long haul.

Smith's thesis attracted a lot of attention, and in the years 1924–1929, a host of Wall Street brokers carried his message to millions of Americans. But in an amazing example of irony, his book did not become a best seller until 1929. When you consider that the Dow plunged from its high of nearly 400 in 1929 to around 40 in 1932, the popularity of the book has to go down as one of the worst instances of investment timing on record.

The popularity of other best-selling investment books has also proved ill-timed. The seventh best-selling nonfiction book in 1968 was Adam Smith's *The Money Game*, which was a marvelously written book largely about stock speculation. As it turned out, 1968 marked the end of the great postwar bull market in stocks—the very year that the public's interest in stocks pushed the book onto the best-seller list.

Morton Shulman is another financial writer with a number of good investment calls to his credit. In 1979, Shulman published a book called *How to Invest Your Money & Profit from Inflation*, and it briefly hit the best-seller list. Shulman's advice can be summarized as follows: "Inflation is here—it's not going away. Get rid of paper investments. Buy equity. My timing may be good or bad, but I know that 5 years down the road, no one following this advice will regret it."

In 1980, Burton G. Malkiel's *The Inflation Beater's Investment Guide* was published. It makes the following statement: "The inflation rate in the 1980s is likely to be well above that of the past and [this book] shows you how to manage your money so as to cope with its ravages."

William E. Donoghue's *Complete Money Market Guide:*

The Simple Low-Risk Way You Can Profit from Inflation and Fluctuating Interest Rates, a best seller in 1981, aimed to capitalize on people's fears of inflation. Roger Bridwell's *The Battle for Financial Security: How to Invest in the Runaway 80's* was published in 1980 and had this to say: "An annual inflation rate of 20%—and perhaps 30%—will become a way of life, as it has in several other countries where, nevertheless, life goes on as usual."

Books on real estate also became the rage. *How to Become Financially Independent by Investing in Real Estate* by Al Lowry and *Nothing Down* by Robert Allen were also best sellers in 1979-1980. One day in 1980, we counted over 15 books on real estate in a local bookstore.

One book that particularly struck our fancy was *Winning with Money: A Guide for Your Future* by Beryl W. Sprinkel and Robert J. Genetski. Sprinkel is a monetarist and now Undersecretary of the Treasury in the Reagan administration. An advertisement in *The Wall Street Journal* of August 29, 1977, for the book carried this headline: "How You Can Protect Yourself from the Ravages of Inflation."

You Can't Lose

The second sign of a peak is the conviction that one just can't miss with speculative activity. In recent years, many people argued that speculation was a highly rational endeavor in a time of rapid inflation, and indeed, it paid off handsomely for those who were skillful at it. But there is *always* a rational reason for speculation, be it in the stock market during the 1920s, the South Sea bubble, tulip mania, etc. In the recent wave, normally conservative people were persuaded to take highly speculative risks with their life savings, activities they would never have contemplated in more normal times. The rationale this time around was basically that you had to speculate and be an aggressive risk taker in order to beat double-digit inflation.

Of course, there were other reasons for speculation that appeared particularly concrete. For example, the wild speculation in housing in some areas of southern California was based on the absolute conviction that environmental and zoning restrictions were severely limiting the number of houses that could be built in Orange County. With the continuing influx of new buyers, supply would never rise to meet demand, and so prices had to go up. As a result of this logic, people slept in their cars overnight to get in on the auctions that became necessary to allocate new housing developments.

It's all reminiscent of the Florida land boom of the 1920s, which sprang from the belief that "there's only so much land in Florida." Unfortunately for the speculators, there was quite a lot of it, and much of what they bought turned out to be under water.

This time around, speculation got so heated that housewives even got into the game and began trading puts and calls on their houses in southern California supermarkets. Also, timesharing vacation spots, which may go down as one of the most blatant inflation exploitation strategies, caught on all over the country. Under a timesharing arrangement, you don't own any physical property but merely acquire the right to rent an apartment in a resort area several weeks a year for many years in the future. The gimmick is that people are assured that their vacation costs will never go up, but the price of this assurance is high. Apparently, the sale of timesharing slots generates a lot more revenue for the developer than selling the apartment outright to one buyer.

European investors, known on Wall Street as typical buyers at market tops, were particularly avid purchasers of U.S. real estate. Indeed, we know of one real estate broker who handled many sales of cooperative apartments in Manhattan without ever meeting the buyers and without their ever seeing the apartments. In one memorable sale, a Greek tycoon bought a co-op for around $350,000, sold it a year later to a Spaniard for a $200,000 profit, and then with the proceeds bought another apartment from an Argentine. None of the principals involved in these sales ever met one another or saw the apartments they were buying and selling.

Indeed, one could argue that in terms of numbers of participants, the speculation in real estate has been as great as or perhaps even greater than that in stocks during the 1920s. At present, there are some 86 million houses in this country, of which 56 million are owned by the people who live in them. There are no accurate statistics, but clearly a good portion and probably a majority of these homeowners "speculated" to a certain degree in their houses. They traded up to a larger house, justified the expenditure of remodeling or additions, or bought second or third houses and condominiums on the basis of the widely held view that any investment in a house was bound to be rewarded. By contrast, there were only 1.4 million margin accounts for stocks in 1929.

For sheer excess, no speculation can beat the California pyramids, a variation on the chain letter scheme that swept California in the late 1970s and early 1980s. In order to enter one of these pyramids, a player had to put up $1000. Then, just as with a chain letter, the player had to find two other people to put up $1000 each. If each one of these people recruited another two players, and so on, the person at the top of the pyramid could easily collect $16,000 tax free.

In an article in *The Wall Street Journal* on May 29, 1980, David Peters, head of the fraud and forgery unit of California's Department of Justice, says this about the pyramids: "I've never seen anything like them. Nothing before has grown like this, and nothing seems to end it." The article goes on to say that some pyramid parties take in $40,000 to $60,000 a night from the newcomers. The article describes one particular party where a man named Ken "reminds the gathering that 'there isn't much else the small guy can invest in' to keep pace with inflation. 'This is people helping people. This is $16,000 tax free,' he says."

Certain pieces of advertising also are indicative of the

speculative impluse. The ad for Doug Casey's latest book, *Strategic Investing*, tells the reader that speculation is necessary for survival:

> How to overcome the fear of speculation. Successful speculators should emerge from the 1980s wealthy beyond their wildest dreams.... The virtually riskless way to get a 10 to 1 return on commodities.... The truth is that you have no choice but to speculate in this depression; the conventional, prudent wisdom will not help you take advantage of today's different and extraordinary investment opportunities.

A favorite ad of ours from the Chicago Board of Trade features a picture of Teddy Roosevelt, implying his support for Treasury bond futures, and states, "We think he'd be pleased to see the opportunity that exists today in T-bond futures contracts on the Chicago Board of Trade."

Another ad that has all the earmarks of peak psychology was taken by Citibank in *The Wall Street Journal* of November 7, 1979. In this double full-page advertisement, we read, "Art as an Investment: Private Banking Division Makes Two Inspired Moves." As it turned out, Citibank had recently hired Mr. Patrick Cooney, formerly on the staff of the Frick collection.

Citibank also made an arrangement with Sotheby Parke-Bernet to tap the auction gallery's expertise on behalf of the bank's clients—an ironic choice since Sotheby subsequently got carried away with the increase in its business that resulted from the speculation in art and antiques, overexpanded, and now, with the drying up of speculative activity, has been losing money and has been forced to retrench.

Unbelievable Borrowing

A third sign of a peak is the amount of money which has been borrowed for speculative purposes. In the later stages of a bull market, stock market analysts carefully watch the level of margin debt for signs of borrowing excess. Borrowed money can eventually inflate prices to a dangerous level, from which the fall can be quite dramatic in a credit crunch or bear market.

One classic case of excess borrowing occurred during the conglomerate phase in the late 1960s, when corporations acquired other companies for debt in order to increase their earnings per share. As a result of the debt burdens, the acquiring companies overextended themselves financially, and many were hurt during the 1969–1970 credit crunch.

The next craze financed with borrowed money was real estate, and a whole new industry sprang up to finance it: real estate investment trusts (REITs). Many of these trusts were run by unsophisticated managers who virtually threw money at properties, and when the 1973–1974 credit crunch occurred, many REITs were forced into bankruptcy.

But both these borrowing binges paled in comparison with the amount of money used to "speculate" in housing. The increase in mortgage debt on homes was $35 billion in 1974, $38 billion in 1975, $62 billion in 1976, $93 billion in 1977, $108 billion in 1978, $115 billion in 1979, and $83 billion in 1980. Between the years 1966 and 1971, some 16% of the capital raised by the nonfinancial sector of our economy was used to provide home mortgages. But by the late 1970s the figure had risen to more than 27%.

One analysis of these numbers suggests that much of the mortgage financing was not used for the construction of new homes but rather to finance the inflation in existing home prices. In the *Brookings Bulletin* (Summer 1980), Anthony Downs makes some interesting observations. In the 1950s, the annual ratio of total mortgage financing to the total cost of new home construction was over 66%. By the 1960s it had jumped to nearly 90%, and in the early 1970s it rose to 108%.

But in the years 1975–1978 the ratio was some 145%. Obviously, a good portion of this financing came from homeowners who obtained second mortgages in order to realize some of the gains in the prices of their homes.

Prices at Ridiculous Extremes

A fourth sign of an inflationary peak can be seen when the price advance of an investment has reached ridiculous proportions. Whenever it becomes too easy to make money by following a particular strategy, the latecomers are bound to receive a rude awakening. A good example of this was the surge in the median price of a new home, from $30,800 in 1970 to $80,100 in 1981.

The jump in prices for existing houses is larger, with many houses having tripled in value, to say nothing of certain extreme examples, such as co-ops in New York City and houses in southern California. In the mid-1970s, for example, the average price per room of a co-op in Manhattan was around $10,000, but it had climbed to $93,261 by October 1981. In California, many houses jumped tenfold or more in value in a little more than a decade.

A survey of the entire spectrum of tangibles by Robert S. Salomon Jr. of Salomon Brothers shows, however, that many other categories outperformed housing over the past decade. As shown in Table 6-1, the 10-year compounded rate of return ending June 1, 1981, was 30.8% for oil, 28% for gold, 27.3% for oriental carpets, 27.1% for U.S. coins, 23.5% for U.S. stamps, 22.9% for Chinese ceramics, 21.5% for silver, 16.8% for rare books, 15.4% for old masters, 14.6% for farmland, and 14.5% for diamonds. Indeed, with a 10.3% compounded gain, housing was near the bottom of the pack.

When compared with previous speculative periods, the degree of price appreciation for the tangible assets discussed above may be unprecedented. In the June 1981 *Investment Strategy*, Barton M. Biggs and Richard R. Schmaltz of Morgan, Stanley pointed out that the average yearly appreciation for stocks between 1921 and 1929 was 21.4%. It is interesting to note that five categories of tangible assets generated a higher return over the past decade than common stocks did during their greatest decade of speculation.

Table 6-1   Compound Annual Rates of Return
(For period ending June 1, 1981)

	10 Years, %	Rank	5 Years, %	Rank	1 Year, %	Rank
Oil	30.8	1	20.9	˙ 5	14.3	6
Gold	28.0	2	30.7	3	−13.9	14
Oriental carpets	27.3	3	20.9	6	−0.2	11
U.S. coins	27.1	4	29.7	4	−8.0	12
U.S. stamps	23.5	5	32.9	1	18.0	4
Chinese ceramics	22.9	6	30.7	2	36.5	1
Silver	21.5	7	20.1	7	−26.6	16
Rare books	16.8	8	13.8	11	18.0	5
Old masters	15.4	9	16.8	9	22.9	3
Farmland	14.6	10	14.8	10	9.7	8
Diamonds	14.5	11	16.9	8	0.0	10
Housing	10.3	12	11.6	12	8.1	9
CPI	8.3	13	9.7	14	10.0	7
Stocks	5.8	14	9.8	13	25.3	2
Foreign exchange	5.3	15	3.1	15	−17.3	15
Bonds	3.8	16	1.1	16	−9.6	13

All returns are for the period ending June 1, 1981, based on latest available data.

SOURCE: Salomon Brothers, New York.

Forget Investing: Concentrate on Speculating

A fifth sign of a speculative peak can be seen when the investment aspect is entirely taken out of an asset and all that remains is the speculative element. "Why bother with the dullness of an investment? Concentrate on the speculative fun," is the idea. We saw the first sign of this with the launching of the Chicago Board Options Exchange in 1973, which created an auction market for stock options, thereby attracting the public in large numbers.

In the late 1970s and early 1980s other speculative vehicles followed, such as futures in Treasury bonds, Treasury bills, Treasury notes, French francs, Mexican pesos, German marks, British pounds, Japanese yen, gasoline, heating oil, certificates of deposit, commercial paper, and Eurodollars.

A new height was reached in 1982 with the introduction of stock index futures. While some investors no doubt use these vehicles to hedge stock portfolios, the majority of trading volume apparently comes from pure speculation. At this writing, there are three stock indexes being traded: the Value Line Index at the Kansas City Board of Trade, the New York Stock Exchange Composite traded on the New York Futures Exchange, and the S&P 500 traded on the Chicago Mercantile. Combined daily volume on all three exchanges has recently been running around 20,000 contracts, representing nearly $1 billion of stock value.

In a semiannual survey of favored futures speculations, *The Wall Street Journal* of July 19, 1982, found stock indexes to be the third favorite choice after hogs and copper. When stocks are put in the same boat with hogs, pure speculation has reached an extreme.

But apparently, the speculators are still not satisfied, even with all the existing alternatives to choose from. Regulatory approval for another speculative vehicle, commodity and financial options, has recently been requested. Commodity options are like a stock option in that they have a fixed exercise price and mature within a specified period of time. It is probable that the first commodity options to be traded will be those on Treasury bills and other government securities. If all goes well, options eventually will be offered on many other financial instruments and commodity vehicles.

Unlike the futures market, where a sudden swing against one can produce enormous losses, the risk of options is limited to one's purchase premium. Therefore, many small investors who shied away from the unlimited risk of futures may be attracted to commodity options if speculative fever remains high.

Speculative Trading Volume at Records

A sixth way to detect a peak is to look at trading volume in the most speculative vehicles, which has risen dramatically in recent years. For instance, volume on the Chicago Board Options Exchange has jumped more than 600% in its 9-year history, and volume has increased more than 700% in the past decade at the Chicago Board of Trade and the Chicago Mercantile Exchange.

To be sure, the urge to speculate in commodities was such that by the end of 1981, there were 36 publicly offered commodity funds with assets totaling $400 million. Since the margin for commodities can be as low as 2 to 4%, these funds in effect have futures purchasing power amounting to between $10 and $20 billion, large enough to distort any market.

Futures speculation among individuals and other professionals may be even greater. An article in *Barron's* of April 5, 1982, carried an interview with a number of prominent economists and money market experts. It was amazing how many of them, by their own admission, were active in the futures markets for treasuries, foreign currencies, or gold.

Another illustration of the increase in trading and speculative activity is the large number of advertisements about the benefits of commodity futures trading. An investment in advertising is usually made only if it leads to increased business that at least pays for the ad, and so a large number of ads on a given theme suggest that the public is very responsive.

Merrill Lynch, Heinold, ContiCommodity, and others blanketed the newspapers in 1981 and early 1982 with full-page ads about their effectiveness in the commodities business. Merrill Lynch has frequently run an advertisement which has this boldface headline: "TO RISK OR NOT TO RISK. THAT'S NOT THE QUESTION." The Chicago Mercantile has run ads with the following big headline: "MAN DOES NOT LIVE BY STOCKS AND BONDS ALONE." And

Heinold Commodities has carried ads such as: "WHEN TRADING FINANCIAL FUTURES WAS A NOVELTY TO MANY PEOPLE, IT WAS A BUSINESS TO YOUR HEINOLD BROKER." Even the First National Bank of Chicago has taken full-page ads: "FROM CORN TO CATTLE TO T-BILLS TO SECURITIES, NO BANK COMMITS MORE MUSCLE THAN FIRST CHICAGO."

New Speculations Needed

Next on our list of sure signs of an inflationary peak is the frantic search for new winning speculations that occurs once successful speculators begin to realize that some of their standbys are petering out. One of the authors recently saw an example of this when several successful west coast real estate brokers said they were moving out of real estate and into tuna fleets and jojoba beans. Jojoba beans?

Yes, jojoba beans, which have all the elements of a classic speculation. They produce an oil to which are attributed marvelous properties. Supposedly, gasoline mileage can be increased by 25% when the oil is added to the crankcase, transmission, and differential of a car. And of course, it is just great as a hair restorer, a claim backed by the personal testimony of several of its proponents. Even the Indians, they claim, use jojoba for this purpose.

The jojoba obviously must have amazing investment potential. Its proponents declare that it is the "superbean of the future" and should return 200% profit annually within 10 years, although the oil is a bit expensive now—$65 a gallon.

Not to suggest that jojobas are just any rank speculation; they were even dignified by a front-page article on January 27, 1981, in *The Wall Street Journal*. The article stated that "no lesser authority than Jerome Smith Sr., the investment advisor credited with steering the Hunt brothers into silver, called jojobas 'the silver of the 1990s'." The article goes on to observe that backers say "jojobas are ripe for investment, and they are promising not only a hedge against inflation but mind boggling returns." Furthermore, the *Wall Street Digest*, an investment advisory service, recently picked jojoba after real estate and rare coins as one of the "10 best places to put your money now."

Promoters claim that a severe shortage of jojoba is the only thing that is preventing it from becoming a household word. The maximum amount of oil that is available today, they claim, is only about 500,000 pounds per year. To meet all the expected demand will require a world output of between 50 and 100 million pounds per year, they speculate. Backers rate the jojoba as "an estate builder, something you pass from generation to generation."

What makes this such a classic speculation and in our view a sure sign of the peak in inflationary expectations is the fact that the jojoba plant does not begin to produce at all until its third year and reaches full maturity only after 10 years. This delay, plus the fact that there are few cultivated jojoba plants in existence, obviously gives promoters and speculators plenty of time to put down their money, plant their jojobas, and dream about the tremendous returns that lie just a few short years down the road.

Another example of new speculative horizons can be found in the recent diversification efforts of Investment Rarities, one of the big promoters of collectibles and inflation hedges, whose annual sales rose from nothing in 1974 to $550 million in 1980. In an interview in *The Wall Street Journal* of May 27, 1982, James R. Cook, the company's 42-year-old founder, says that diversification means "being ready to go along with investors in whatever direction they may go." The *Journal* reported that "as part of its diversification, Investment Rarities has formed 'a personal security department' to advise gold and silver dealers, jewelers and other clients who worry about being victims of kidnapping and other possible crimes."

Finally, out of the search for new vehicles for speculation

has come the Merrill Lynch Phoenix Fund, which will invest in companies in financial difficulty that Merrill Lynch believes can rise from their own ashes. Companies selected for the fund will be those with poor earnings results or strained liquidity positions and will include corporations in various stages of reorganization. The minimum initial investment is $2500, but for individual retirement plans a mere $250 will do. Merrill Lynch apparently thinks there are lots of speculators left who will be interested in this new fund. The firm expects to raise $75 million to $100 million in its initial offering.

Bring Back the Oldies

An eighth sign of an inflation peak is the attempt to revive dead horses. Gold hit a peak of $875 an ounce in early 1980 and at this writing is selling for about half that amount—obviously a tremendous decline for anyone who bought it near the peak price. Yet recent ads in *The Wall Street Journal* trumpeted: "One of 1982s Strongest Investment(s). Gold at Spot." The ads go on to say: "The Wise Investor Knows When to Invest. Buy Low—Sell High—Buy Gold Now!" Furthermore, it said that "Gold has proven to be Man's Ultimate Hedge Against Inflation! How much will $100 in Paper Currency be worth in 5 years? How much will the same $100 in Gold be worth in 5 years! Many experts are predicting $1,000–$2,000 per ounce! Gold is a more valuable buy now than ever!"

The ad even shows imposing office buildings underneath the heading "Offices Coast to Coast." Apparently we are meant to think not only that gold is a solid investment but that the firm placing the ad is equally solid.

Furthermore, real estate promoters are also still plying their trade. We recently received in the mail a Call-o-Gram notifying the recipient of possible awards ranging from $1000 cash to a Hawaiian vacation. There was only one caveat. The recipient had to listen to "an informal presentation of Greenhouse and its outstanding recreational facilities, while visiting their luxury vacation resort." We were also told that this Call-o-Gram was not a land sales promotion.

Nor has Howard Ruff given up the ghost. In the July 16, 1982, issue of the *Ruff Times,* he told his subscribers that if he inherited $1 million, he would put $600,000 into silver, $200,000 into bonds, $100,000 into gold, and $100,000 into a money market fund. In another letter dated July 1, 1982, Ruff says, "All that I'm quite sure of is that the next cycle will be inflationary."

Market Action: Does It Tell All?

A glance at some of the major sensitive commodity indexes also lends credence to the view that inflation has peaked. Markets represent reality—not forecasts, hopes, expectations, or prophecies. Commodities are a useful barometer of economic activity or inflationary expectations because they are sensitive, and a little bit of buying or selling can have a dramatic effect on their prices, much more so than in the case of stocks and bonds.

A look at some of the sensitive commodity charts and commodity indexes shows that inflation appears to be receding, as is evident in the 13-week moving average of raw materials prices shown in Exhibit 6-1.

Indeed several technical analysts see no imminent recovery in commodity prices. In some cases recovery may be many years away, according to several commodity trading experts. Technical analysts who have spent years looking at chart formations suggest that many commodities have reached major tops. After looking at the chart for silver, one successful commodity trader said that it might not have a major bull market for 50 years. If that is true, renewed high rates of inflation do not appear to be a serious threat.

Other tangible assets appear to be following commodities downward. Table 6-2 shows the 1- and 10-year performance

EXHIBIT 6-1

Raw Industrial Materials Spot Price Index. *(U.S. Department of Commerce, Bureau of Labor Statistics; Commodity Research Bureau, New York.)*

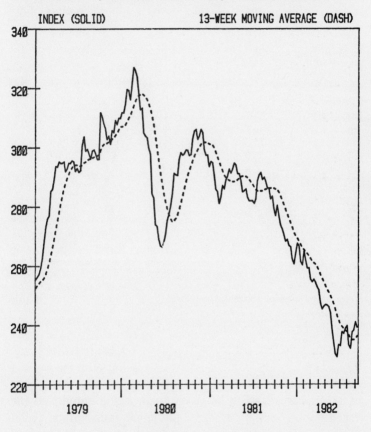

as of June 1, 1982, a year later than Table 6-1, for a number of tangible and financial assets, prepared by Robert S. Salomon Jr. of Salomon Brothers. It is interesting to note that oil, the number 1 performer for the 10-year period, had slipped to the number 3 position for the 12 months ended June 1, 1982. Likewise, U.S. coins slipped from number 2 to number 13, U.S. stamps from 3 to 9, oriental rugs from 4 to 11, and gold from 5 to 14.

Table 6-2   Compound Annual Rates of Return
(For period ending June 1, 1982)

	10 Years, %	Rank	5 Years, %	Rank	1 Year, %	Rank
Oil	29.9	1	21.2	4	6.3	3
U.S. coins	22.5	2	21.4	3	−27.8	13
U.S. stamps	21.9	3	26.6	1	−3.0	9
Oriental rugs	19.1	4	17.1	6	−16.2	11
Gold	18.6	5	17.3	5	−34.0	14
Chinese ceramics	15.3	6	23.7	2	−0.5	6
Farmland	13.7	7	10.7	9	−0.9	7
Silver	13.6	8	5.5	13	−44.5	15
Diamonds	13.3	9	13.7	7	0.0	5
Housing	9.9	10	10.0	10	3.4	4
Old masters	9.0	11	13.7	8	−22.0	12
CPI	8.6	12	9.6	11	6.6	2
Stocks	3.9	13	7.7	12	−10.5	10
Foreign exchange	3.6	14	1.6	14	−1.9	8
Bonds	3.6	15	0.6	15	11.4	1

All returns are for the period ending June 1, 1982, based on latest available data.

SOURCE: Salomon Brothers, New York.

Inflation Forever

A tenth sign of an inflationary peak is the conviction that inflation will remain at very high levels indefinitely. This is manifested in the recent popularity of zero or very low coupon bonds. Unlike current coupon bonds, which normally pay interest semiannually, these issues are sold at discounts, and the investor gets most or all of the return in the form of capital gains at maturity. Furthermore, these bonds cannot be called at anything less than the maturity price, and so there is no way short of default for the issuer to reduce the financing costs, even if interest rates decline.

It is true that zero or very low coupon bonds have been

issued at slightly lower interest rates than those for market rate bonds because investors like the idea of locking up the recent record yields with no worry about reinvestment should interest rates drop before the bonds mature. Nevertheless, the saving in interest costs to the issuers seems trivial compared with the risks they face. If inflation and interest rates decline sharply, the issuers will be faced with interest costs that far exceed the amounts they can pass on in a non-inflationary environment.

On to the Ridiculous

Finally, to go from the sublime to the ridiculous, now even racehorses are called an investment. In an article in *The Wall Street Journal* of March 18, 1982, which is headlined "Runaway Inflation Makes Horse Racing an Investor Sport," a racehorse promoter was quoted as follows: "This is where you shoot the moon. It's where the excitement is, the sizzle. My God, if you go through life nursing every nickel, it's not for you."

Major banks apparently thought the underlying fundamentals of racehorses so attractive that many of them are now making loans to thoroughbred horse breeders. One executive at European-American Bank, according to an article in the March 11, 1982, issue of *The Wall Street Journal*, "already manages $17 million in loans to horse investors . . . (and) by the end of year . . . the portfolio should grow to $50 million." The executive said that "the bank 'is adding New York bank savvy' to an industry that was never exposed to it before."

If inflation is peaking, it will come as a shock to most Americans, the majority of whom are prepared for its continuation. The clash between continued inflationary expectations and an administration that was elected to eliminate inflation could create some severe shocks. In fact, the risks are predominantly on the downside, as we shall explain in Chapters 7 and 8.

Inflation's End: Bang or Whimper?

7

In Chapter 3 we explored the distorting effects of government-created inflation—the behavior that resulted when people became convinced that inflation would probably continue to increase and would certainly last forever. Furthermore, in Chapter 6 we saw the extremes in speculative behavior that followed—extremes that suggest that the nation is unlikely to change its attitude toward inflation easily and that few will voluntarily give up on what they consider a risk-free and immensely profitable strategy. As human beings, people seldom quit while they're winning; they normally play till they lose.

We saw in Chapter 4, however, the growing disenchantment with inflation, the correct association of government activity with this plague, and the voter response culminating in the conservative sweep in the 1980 election. In Chapter 5 we examined the anti-inflationary reductions in government spending and monetary growth that are likely to result and the multitude of other anti-inflationary factors now on the scene.

We have, then, two very basic but different forces at work in the economy. The same nation that attracted so many players in the inflation game has also elected a government that is dedicated to changing the rules. We must not be enjoying the game, or we're plain schizophrenic. In any event, the nation's expectations of inflation and the new government's policies and other anti-inflationary forces are in direct conflict, and this may make the transition to a less inflationary economy a rough one.

Of course, the inflationary forces may win. The nation may decide that the price of eliminating a major inflation is too great. "Inflation was tough, but getting out of it is unbearable," many may reason. Indeed, at this writing, at the beginning of the 1982 congressional campaign, many Democrats and some Republicans are beginning to balk at the President's and the Fed's no-deviation approach to eliminating inflation. Interestingly, few Democrats except Tip O'Neill and Teddy Kennedy are advocating a return to New Deal-type programs, and the party as yet has no real alternative program. Nevertheless, many Democrats and others believe that the administration's attitude and the recessionary medicine of high interest rates being administered by the Fed may well result in considerable losses for the conservatives in November 1982.

If so, Washington's economic policy may shift toward easier credit and the same old antirecessionary fiscal stimulation. The President himself probably wouldn't reverse gears; he appears to be a determined and unflappable man. Like President Ford, however, he may lose virtually all the initiative and revert to being a vetoer of stimulative measures. The nation, however, seems to like offensive, not defensive, presidents; like Ford, Reagan may see his influence sink to extremely low levels.

Meanwhile, speculators, having once again seen Washington chicken out of the inflation-control game, would surely redouble their earlier activity, convinced even more than in the past that there's no way of losing in the wonderful game of inflation. Real estate, collectibles, assets in the ground, etc., would probably all surge in price as a speculative binge even greater than the one we've just left commenced. Even though the Fed might be more accommodating, the burden of financing a spectacular climb in the Federal deficit coupled with credit demands that almost by definition would exceed any available supply would undoubtedly push interest rates to new highs. Interest rates would also be pushed up because investors remain so concerned with the inflationary effects of monetary and fiscal stimulus that they would probably respond to an easy economic policy by dumping not only stocks but also bonds. This, of course, would be a rational expectations reaction of the sort discussed in Chapter 4. The dollar would collapse, adding more fuel to the fires of renewed and skyrocketing inflation, and gold might easily exceed its earlier peak of $875 per ounce.

In short, the nation would enter a speculative blowoff that would probably be choked by unbelievably high interest rates and followed by an even worse financial and economic collapse than it now faces. Alternatively, the nation's economic framework would be changed and America would go the way of the typical Latin American banana republic in which speculation and inflation become the dominant forces, replacing productive work and investment. In other words, we're saying that expectations of inflation at this writing are still alive and well and ready to resume very active duty if the anti-inflationary heat is turned off. Obviously, this is not an appetizing prospect.

Short of a complete reversal in the nation's orientation, however, another round of inflation seems unlikely. Indeed, quite the opposite, largely because the Fed now believes that the nation wants what the Fed itself has desired all along: control of inflation. Ironically but not surprisingly, the Fed had read recent political developments including the 1980 election results much more clearly and rapidly than Congress. The policy of tight credit and high interest rates that started before that election has continued and is now approaching its third birthday, despite the recession and financial problems that have resulted. In the past, attempts to squeeze out inflation by tight credit were abandoned at the first hint of economic weakness.

Congress, in contrast, has yet to deal with near-runaway growth in federal spending. The budget compromise reached in the summer of 1982 raised taxes by about $100 billion over 3 years but would cut spending only about $30 billion. Yet even after these measures, the administration, in its 1982 midyear review, estimated the fiscal 1983 budget deficit at $115 billion, far below most private estimates.

In summer 1982, the Fed did not appear convinced that expectations of inflation had yet been laid to rest, and the monetary authorities also had a strong desire to avoid a rerun of their 1980 experience. After the imposition of credit controls in the spring of that year, consumer spending collapsed because people were scared, patriotic, or both. Remember when some cut up their credit cards and mailed the pieces to Washington? After that, the Fed panicked and allowed interest rates to collapse, with the bank prime rate dropping from 20% to 11%. However, much to the Fed's dismay, the economy and inflationary behavior came roaring back in the second half of 1980, with the players more convinced than ever that the Fed lacked the conviction to end the inflationary party.

Subsequently, the Fed's attitude apparently became that it "never again" would back away prematurely from the inflation problem; it now appears determined to convince even the most ardent speculators that inflation, like crime, does not pay. Conversations with a senior Federal Reserve official in June 1981 demonstrate this determination.

At that time, this official predicted that the Fed would keep credit tight and interest rates high until the nation became completely disabused of expectations of inflation. He also said that the inflationary atmosphere was so deeply ingrained that it would take at least a year to do the job and that in the meantime, high interest rates would keep the economy in recession and virtually kill the savings banks and savings and loan associations.

Every attempt would be made, he suggested, to merge the weak thrift institutions with strong ones, but clearly there wouldn't be enough strong ones to go around. Consequently, Congress and the administration would finally have to allow the large commercial banks to buy failing thrifts. Those banks would be interested in doing this as a way of getting around the current prohibition on interstate branching. Other business failures might occur, he believed, but he hoped that they would be contained.

The Fed's suspicions that expectations of inflation are far from dead are probably well founded. The problem is that few people believe that what the nation has been going through since 1980 is anything but a typical business cycle. In the last 2 years, that attitude has led to the stubborn belief that just as in a typical business cycle, the economy can never be more than about 6 months away from the beginning of a recovery, which will soon return things to business as usual, i.e., more double-digit inflation, successful speculation, etc. The conviction that nothing has really changed has resulted in the loss of untold billions of dollars by investors, speculators, and businesspeople.

The truth is that we are in anything but a typical cycle. One of the principal reasons for this is the Fed's determination, for the first time in decades, to eliminate inflation, almost regardless of the consequences. This means, for example, that real estate speculators must be convinced that conditions aren't going to return to "normal." Many speculators, particularly in southern California and other areas of recent exuberance, still believe that they can outwait the Fed, that interest rates must decline sharply and soon, and that the good old boom times will then return. The first thing that many home builders plan to do when mortgage rates decline sufficiently to revive their markets is rebuild their profit margins by raising prices 15% to 20%. That action may be justified for the individual home builder, but collectively it is inflationary.

In the early summer of 1982, many industrialists also held a similar view. Not that they were sitting on their hands, of course. The recession created an urgency about cost control the like of which we have never seen, and those who have observed the scene for much longer than we have tell us that they haven't seen cost-control efforts of the present magnitude since the depression.

Fierce domestic and foreign competition is making it impossible to pass on such items as high interest costs, rapidly rising labor costs, and above-market materials costs that stem from long-term fixed-price contracts. Incentives are being offered to induce older employees to resign or retire. High-ranking "cost-containment" executives at the corporate level are "assisting" division level management in finding opportunities to cut costs. Production lines are being eliminated, plants closed, and entire business lines dropped.

Current cost-control efforts in American industry are indeed mighty, but thus far many of them are more temporary than permanent and suggest that businesspeople believe that the economy will soon return to normal. Advertising and travel budgets are being slashed or virtually eliminated, but certainly some of these costs will be restored later on. Old and obsolete plants are being mothballed but not put to the wrecking ball, as would be expected if stringent cost controls were viewed as a permanent necessity. A number of corporate jets are being grounded "for the duration," but few are being sold. These business attitudes bother the Fed because they suggest that businesspeople are still not convinced that the inflationary climate and their long-term ability to pass on costs have changed.

The Fed is probably even more worried about American labor, which is even less convinced than businesspeople that any long-lasting change in the inflationary climate has occurred. Despite the great number of layoffs and the financially precarious position of many employees, organized labor remains blasé.

Over 200,000 auto workers have been laid off—about a third of those employed in peak years—yet the wage and benefit settlements with Ford and GM early in 1982 suggested no substantial labor concessions. Both settlements were calculated to increase compensation 17% over their 2½-year lives. Had the old and generous contract been continued, the 2½-year cost increase would have been 24%—a difference of only 7%.

Concessions of 7% over 2 ½ years, or roughly 2% per year compounded, don't strike us as meaningful in an industry that is being devastated by imports and in which sticker prices of new cars are so high that they make potential buyers' hearts stop. Furthermore, even these meager concessions were barely accepted by GM workers, with only 52% voting in favor.

Not only did these new pacts fail to close the $8-an-hour, or 40%, labor-cost disadvantage in relation to Japanese automakers, they hardly addressed productivity-robbing absenteeism or restrictive work rules. The hope at GM was to make progress in these areas at the local plant level, but this hope has been largely unfulfilled. Labor cooperation has been significant only at plants threatened with closing.

This same attitude exists in airlines, farm equipment, forest products, and rubber—indeed, throughout American industry. The only time labor seems to provide meaningful cooperation is when the business is threatened with extinction, and not always then.

Consider the steel industry as another case in point. One hundred thousand steel workers, or about 40% of the industry's work force, were on layoff in mid-1982, and the industry's operating rate was running at 42%. Nevertheless, the steel workers rejected the companies' offer, which would have provided some wage increases, even though average employee costs are about $23 an hour, or $10 an hour higher than steel wages among the Japanese competition.

Consider the plight of the farm equipment manufacturers. Despite the ghastly condition of industrial and agricultural equipment, fierce price competition, and money-losing operations, in the summer of 1982 Allis-Chalmers was unable to win union agreement for a 2-year wage freeze and renegotiation of labor contracts. The troubled rubber industry settlement in April 1982 was hardly better, calling for no concessions from labor and for compensation increases estimated to exceed 20% for the next 3 years, following hikes of 50% over the previous 3 years.

Labor cost increases are a long way from noninflationary levels, but the Fed probably is even more concerned about what may happen to labor costs if the economy revives any time soon. In their settlement with the trucking industry in early 1982, the Teamsters did recognize the industry's current plight, but they failed to acknowledge that deregulation had permanently eliminated the industry's cartellike ability to enjoy high revenues and pay labor costs far above competitive levels.

The Teamsters' settlement allows the union to reopen contract talks after April 1, 1984, if economic conditions in the industry improve. In the United Auto Workers' (UAW) concession-granting contract with nearly bankrupt International Harvester in May 1982, there is a provision that allows the UAW to reopen the contract whenever worldwide pretax profits from continuing operations exceed $300 million in any two consecutive quarters—hardly the route to rebuilding the company's financial strength if it survives.

The United Auto Workers at Chrysler went even further, however. The company did finally show a profit in the first half of 1982, but almost all of it resulted from the sale of its defense business. Nevertheless, the UAW reopened contract talks in July 1982 with the objective of pushing up wages to the levels of GM and Ford, irrespective of the still precarious health of the company. Marc Stepp, a UAW vice president, was quoted as saying in The Wall Street Journal of August 5, 1982, that "It's up to Chrysler how they would handle" the higher labor costs that would result from wage increases.

Until labor unions' expectations of inflation are modified and wage demands become much more moderate, the Fed seems likely to continue its course of maintaining relatively high interest rates and providing only enough credit to accommodate real growth or inflation but not both. The Fed's strategy is to squeeze out inflation gradually and have it replaced by sustainable recovery and expansion.

As noted, the Fed is well aware of the financial risks that its strategy involves. In a way, the monetary authorities seem to view themselves as tragic heroes in a classical Greek drama. They realize that they are probably doomed, but they take actions that seal their fate. Despite the risks, the Fed feels that it has no choice.

The monetary authorities cling to the hope, however, that they can avoid financial disaster, in other words, that inflationary expectations can be extinguished before self-feeding financial disaster sets in and pushes the financial structure off the cliff.

This brings us to another reason why we are in anything but a normal business cycle. The risks of a disaster are much greater than in the past. Tremendous vulnerability has developed in the past decade as corporations and individuals have borrowed to the hilt, reduced their saving rate, and sold stocks and bonds to raise funds for speculation in tangible assets. They believed that their tangible assets were hard because they had been appreciating faster than inflation and that their debts were soft because they could repay them with much cheaper dollars. Now the reverse is true. High real interest rates have made debts rock-hard, and tangible assets have become soft in price as well as illiquid as their markets have dried up.

In other words, in making the shift to a relatively inflation-free environment, the nation is not starting from a favorable or even neutral position but from one of extreme financial vulnerability. Costs can no longer be passed on easily, whether it's an individual's borrowing costs that can no longer be absorbed by the capital appreciation of his or her real estate or a corporation's costs on the loans used to finance the takeover of a natural resource company whose sales and earnings are declining. Obviously, if an individual or business can't pass on its costs, sooner or later it runs out of money, and more important, even its bankers eventually find out.

Thus, a financial crisis is an alternative route to the elimination of inflation, and the possibility of one occuring looks
uncomfortably high. A financial crisis of sufficient magnitude
could speed up the whole process, convincing everybody
much more quickly that the inflation game is over. The economy might then commence recovery sooner, but probably
from a much lower level of activity than if the anti-inflation
education of the nation were more drawn out. Also, interest
rates would probably fall more sharply under the financial
crisis scenario than they would with a drawn-out transition.

A substantial financial shock, however, might well cause
interest rates to rise first—before the rapid fall commenced
as a mad scramble for liquidity unfolded. This occurred in
the early 1930s, as shown in Exhibit 7-1, a period that we
don't see as an exact parallel to present times but as the only
example of severe financial difficulties in the modern era.

Perhaps even more interesting, the graph shows that the
quality differentials on bond yields widened immensely in
the early 1930s as investors began to fear for the solvency of
lesser-quality companies. U.S. government bond yields rose
about 1 percentage point but Baa bond yields jumped about
5 percentage points, and the spread did not return to pre-
crisis levels until World War II. This suggests that today's
financial risks are not adequately reflected in current yield
spreads.

Regardless of whether the end of inflation comes through
more of the gradual squeezing-out process we've seen so far
or by means of a financial shock felt nationwide, the whole
transition process will probably take a number of years to
complete, perhaps until the end of the decade. (In fact, we've
labeled this long period as the *transcession,* since it is a combination of a transition from a high to a noninflationary climate and a series of recessions by which the transition is
made.) Individuals and businesses have been very successful
at inflation-inspired speculation for a long time. Consequently, losses that are heavy enough to change their views
will probably create a different and certainly a cautious attitude for many years. Conversely, if caution does not become

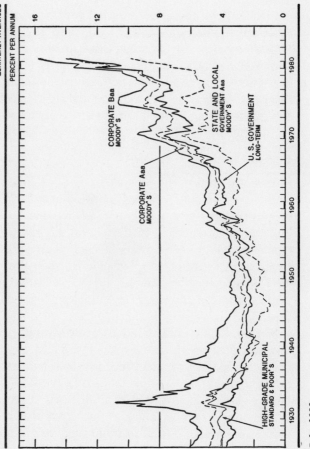

EXHIBIT 7-1

Long-Term Bond Yields. *(Board of Governors of the Federal Reserve System, 1980 Historical Chart Book, Washington, D.C.)*

QUARTERLY AVERAGES

PERCENT PER ANNUM

CORPORATE Baa
MOODY'S

CORPORATE Aaa
MOODY'S

STATE AND LOCAL
GOVERNMENT Aaa
MOODY'S

U. S. GOVERNMENT
LONG-TERM

HIGH-GRADE MUNICIPAL
STANDARD & POOR'S

July 1982

widespread and long-lasting, inflation will probably not be eliminated.

Of course, we already have seen a number of financial problems in the past several years, but all have been contained and have not had many ripple effects. We're all familiar with the difficulties at Chrysler, First Pennsylvania Bank, the Hunt silver operation, International Harvester, Massey-Ferguson, numerous savings banks and savings and loan associations, Braniff, Drysdale Government Securities, Penn Square Bank, many small businesses, etc. But as the inability to pass on costs gets worse, more and more companies will reach the precipice of financial collapse. Thus, the odds of an uncontainable financial problem are obviously high.

Into the Mud?

In fact, the odds of a financial collapse are being increased by the combination of three factors that may well succeed in driving the economy, and with it the financial structure, right into the mud. The first of these mud-aimed pile drivers is monetary policy. After years of backing away prematurely from credit restraint, the Fed is hanging in there and may well overdo tight credit. Second, conservative strength in Washington and concern over ballooning federal deficits are leading to significant tax increases and even some election-year spending cuts which will probably put considerable downward pressure on the economy. Third, a great deal of weakness may develop in the private sector as a result of financial problems, disillusionment over falling prices of tangible assets, excessive debt at high real interest costs, etc.

The nation may be facing a classic case of fighting the last war. Monetary and fiscal restraints are well intentioned but may be coming much too late and may prove to be overdone, driving an already faltering economy into the quagmire. Let's keep this in mind as we examine some of the private sector's financial risks in Chapter 8.

Apocalypse Now?
The Risks of a
Financial Collapse

8

As we saw in Chapter 6, continued expectations of inflation are still widespread among the populace. Several decades of increasing inflation have caused a major shift in attitudes about debt, liquidity, and the inevitability of continued price increases. If inflation were suddenly to end, all those who are betting on its continuation would find themselves in desperate straits. Indeed, the winding down of inflation could produce a major shock for the whole financial system.

In surveying the economy, there appear to be a number of vulnerable areas, any one of which could bring on a crisis. But given the interconnection of the financial system, they collectively pose more risks than at any time in the past 50 years. We have identified 14 potential problem areas: commercial banks, corporate liquidity, commercial paper, money market funds, financial markets, municipalities, households, commercial real estate, agriculture, protectionism, LDCs, OPEC, domestic energy, and thrift institutions. Let's take a look at each one.

Commercial Banks: A Growing Number of Bad Loans

One of the authors always had the yen to own a commercial bank. He continually observed how his banker friends and their spouses came back with great midwinter tans after attending an American Banker's Association convention in an exotic tropical location and promptly got ready to leave on the next one.

He also knew several owners of small Texas banks, and they really had it made. They had good correspondent relationships with other small banks, lending money to each other as if they were next of kin and at interest rates well below prime. Why beat your head against the wall as an economic consultant when commercial banking seemed so inherently profitable that it could support all these sorts of activities and still show credible earnings?

However, things started to go wrong for the banks, and the idea of owning one lost its appeal. The activities of Bert Lance in several Georgia banks before he went to Washington led to so much tightening of the rules that it took a lot of the fun out of small banks, even in Texas. Of course, the trend toward statewide, and eventually nationwide, banking is allowing many small bankers to sell out and retire in comfort. Still, the problems for the remaining commercial banks continue.

The recent recession and the slowing of inflation have hit with a vengeance. During all those lush years, the banks believed that everything would be fine so long as they lent money at a decent spread over their cost of funds. As long as inflation continued, there was no reason to worry about bad loans. Quite the contrary, a company might be going down the tubes in real terms, but there was little incentive to call a bad loan and throw the borrower into bankruptcy. Not only would the write-off be embarrassing, inflation would probably bail out the borrower sooner or later as inflation-caused underdepreciation and inventory profits created enough cash flow to pay off the bank. It worked beautifully, but commercial bankers, working with their spreads and strictly in nominal dollars, had little understanding of how their willingness to keep extending what were clearly very shaky loans really amounted to bets on continuing high inflation.

This attitude may have made some sense during a period

of inflation, but it is highly inappropriate when inflation slows or ends. Indeed, if a company can't pass on costs today, why should it be able to do so tomorrow? It will be poorer then, and the prudent approach for lenders is to blow the whistle on all those bad loans. It doesn't make sense to throw good money after bad, but sometimes the prudent strategy isn't an easy one to adopt. Pressures to keep companies alive with more credit are intense.

Even the cautious bankers are finding themselves in enormous difficulty, however. The switch from high and accelerating inflation to disinflation has come so very suddenly that even many conservative bankers are having trouble adjusting fast enough unless they already understood the role of inflation and anticipated its end. The real nub of the banks' problem is this: Inflation bailed them out of a lot of inherently bad loans, but if inflation ends, all those chickens will come home to roost, and maybe in one big flock. Problems that could have been handled satisfactorily if they had been written off one by one as the difficulties actually occurred can be much more disruptive when corrective action is postponed and they all must be faced at the same time.

Let's look a little more closely at the banking picture and the dimensions of the problem. As was pointed out in Chapter 3, the banks' liability structure has become more exposed to fluctuations in interest rates in recent years. First, corporate money managers became more sophisticated and insisted that excess balances be "swept" each day into some type of "earning" asset, such as CDs and repurchase agreements. Second, consumers began shifting their idle balances from checking accounts to NOW accounts and 6-month money market certificates.

The banks, however, had a great deal of pricing flexibility and were able to insulate themselves effectively against the increase in interest rates. Their strategy was to reduce the maturity of their loans and thus respond more quickly to a jump in interest rates. For instance, between 1977 and 1982, commercial banks reduced the average maturity of their short-term business loans from about 3½ months to about 1½ months. Intermediate-term construction loans did lengthen from about 11 to 13 months on average, but the portion of such loans made on a floating basis doubled, from 25% to 50%. And the percentage of long-term business loans with floating rates rose from about 50% to 70%. Thus, on balance, the banks were able to force their customers to bear an increasing portion of the interest rate risk.

But their strategy was a two-edged sword. Once corporations and other borrowers had the interest rate risk, it greatly increased the strains in the business world. As the rising cost of bank funds was quickly passed on to business borrowers, earnings deteriorated, pressures on corporate liquidity mounted, and credit quality inevitably declined. In effect, banks had been substituting credit risk for interest rate risk. As high real rates began to take their toll and fading inflation and recession made cost pass-through nearly impossible, it was only a matter of time before the inflationary excesses of the 1970s affected the banks, too, through mounting loan write-offs.

Ominous signs surfaced in 1981, when nonperforming—that is, problem—loans jumped 40% after falling for the prior several years, according to the Federal Reserve. The deterioration no doubt persisted into 1982, and just how severe the repercussions can be was aptly illustrated in summer 1982 by the collapse of the relatively obscure Penn Square Bank of Oklahoma City.

Penn Square epitomized the way inflationary psychology can destroy sound lending procedures. Energy prices were expected to keep rising at exponential rates, and thus oil and gas reserves were seen as an excellent collateral for loans. It was no surprise that eager young lenders were able to find eager energy producers who wanted money to explore for oil. As a result of aggressive lending policies, the bank's loan portfolio had grown to $323.5 million by March 31, 1982, more than 3 times its level at the end of 1980.

Many others were also eager to get in on the energy bandwagon. Thus, Penn Square had no difficulty finding a lot of other banks and financial institutions around the country, such as Chase Manhattan, Continental Illinois, and Sea First Corp, to join the fun.

When the energy shortage turned to a glut in 1981 and gas and oil prices dropped, the crash was inevitable. Loans that appeared more than adequately collateralized at $8 per thousand cubic feet of natural gas suddenly looked precarious as prices dropped to $5 per thousand cubic feet. And falling prices made it difficult, if not impossible, for thinly capitalized producers to meet the interest payments on all those loans which shouldn't have been made in the first place. This is as fine an example as we know of how commercial bankers built a house of cards on the shifting sands of inflation and realized it only when the tide of deflating energy prices swept away their frail foundation.

Another important lesson of Penn Square is that it pointed out the highly integrated—and vulnerable—nature of the nation's financial system, through which strains can be transmitted rapidly from a seemingly isolated incident to the entire economic system. The thrifts and credit unions with large paper holdings of Penn Square stood to lose up to 20% of their uninsured deposits. And major commercial banks participating in the $2 billion of loans purchased from Penn Square incurred losses totaling several hundred million dollars.

Penn Square contributed to only a handful of insolvencies among the smaller institutions. But how many more such episodes can the financial system stand? How many more surprises will it take before lending institutions begin testing the limits of their capital resources? These are important questions because Penn Square could be indicative of long-term problems with the banking industry.

The loan situation is just as bad if not worse on the international scene, where loan growth by U.S. banks has been particularly aggressive. For example, at the end of 1980, over

30% of the $1.1 trillion in assets of those U.S. banks with any foreign operations represented foreign-based lending. What's more, about the same proportion of their net income was derived from foreign lending activities. With unsteady worldwide economic conditions, a large foreign exposure can only compound the deterioration in the quality of bank loans.

A good example of the problem is the $25 billion external debt of Poland. With their economy in a shambles, the Poles had little chance of paying the interest on their debt in 1982, much less the $10 billion principal due to all western banks. No doubt benefiting from the experience of U.S. borrowers, the Polish government hoped to "restructure" its debt, in other words, request the banks to forgo most of the scheduled principal payment and lend Poland a good chunk of the funds needed to "pay" the interest due.

Why would the bankers even consider such a proposal? Simply because such an agreement would postpone the eventual day of official default, with all the implications for loan write-offs and deterioration of earnings.

Another example of international loan problems is the exposure to Mexico, a country in truly desperate financial straits, to which U.S. banks have lent $20 billion to $30 billion. Indeed, in summer 1982, Grupa Industrial Alfa S.A., Mexico's largest privately owned company, was forced to suspend interest payments on its $2.3 billion of bank debt. Alfa had already suspended principal payments on its debt in April 1982. One can only ask whether such loans ever will be repaid.

In addition, the financial crisis in Mexico in the summer of 1982 resulted in highly disruptive controls on the Mexican peso, the nationalization of all Mexican banks, and a general collapse in foreign and domestic confidence in the country and its government. Emergency loans through the IMF and other forms of international financial support became necessary, and at this writing any feasible long-run solution of the country's financial difficulties is far from obvious. In the final analysis, it may be necessary for the United States to sustain Mexico financially in order to keep its relations with its southern neighbor from deteriorating to frightening levels that might even entail the threat of a communist takeover.

In any event, it is clear that the advent of considerable oil revenues allowed the Mexican government to borrow extensively in international markets to finance extremely rapid growth through a wide variety of projects. The assumption was that oil prices would continue to rise rapidly enough to make it possible to service these debts from oil revenues. With the decline in world oil prices, however, it became painfully clear that the Mexican bet on high inflation, especially in oil prices, was a bad one.

Corporate Liquidity: The Lowest in Postwar History

As we have seen, the banks have shifted interest rate risks to their customers, thereby weakening the finances of the business sector. Indeed, corporate liquidity is currently in the worst financial shape since World War II. Part of the problem stems from the double taxation of dividends and the deductibility of interest on debt, which encouraged business to leverage its balance sheet, particularly in the inflationary 1970s, when negative real interest rates made debt look "cheap," as illustrated in Exhibit 8-1. As a result, very few CEOs could pass up the attraction of borrowing money.

The result of this borrowing binge was a steady deterioration in debt to equity ratios for business firms, from an average of around 0.85 in the mid-1970s to about 1.05 in 1981. In that period, corporate debt nearly doubled to $1.2 trillion. One of the most troubling aspects of the increase in debt was that much of it was of a short-term nature. As shown in Exhibit 8-2, the ratio of short-term debt to long-term debt climbed steadily upward, from 0.40 in the mid-1960s to around 0.70 in the early 1980s.

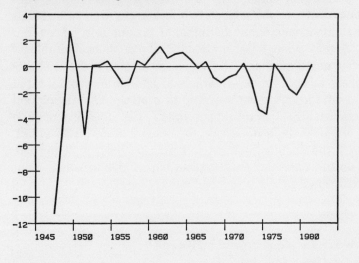

EXHIBIT 8-1
Real After-Tax Interest Rates, AA Corporate Bonds. *(Moody's Investors Service, Inc.; U.S. Department of Commerce, Bureau of Economic Analysis; A. Gary Shilling & Co., Inc.)*

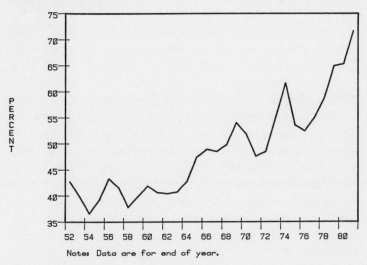

EXHIBIT 8-2
Ratio of Short-Term Debt to Long-Term Debt, Nonfinancial Corporate Business. *(Board of Governors of the Federal Reserve System, Flow of Funds Accounts.)*

Note: Data are for end of year.

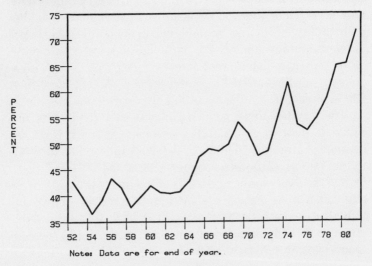

This heavy reliance on short-term financing posed a number of potential problems. First, as short-term interest rates fluctuate, so do borrowing costs, interest rate coverage, and profitability. Since the direction of interest rates was generally upward, the large interest payments continued to eat away at corporate profits and contributed to the erosion of short-term corporate asset holdings as well.

Second and potentially more dangerous is the fact that short-term debt must constantly be rolled over. In an environment of increasing concern over credit quality, a corporation could find it difficult to roll over existing indebtedness.

This deterioration in liquidity has been reflected in the rating agencies' evaluation of credit quality. In both 1980 and 1981, there were more credit downgradings than upgradings by Moody's and Standard & Poor's. In 1980 and 1981, S&P made 39 and 47 increases, respectively, in bond ratings and 44 and 62 downgradings. During the same 2-year period, Moody's increased ratings for one electric utility in 1980 and one in 1981 while downgrading 13 in 1980 and 6 in 1981.

One doesn't have to look very far for other examples of deteriorating corporate liquidity. One striking illustration is the number of business failures, which has soared, as shown in Exhibit 8-3. Indeed, in the first half of 1982, failures hit the highest level since the depression of the 1930s. In the first several months of 1982, business failures occurred at an annual rate of 80 per 10,000 companies, according to Dun & Bradstreet. This figure was 30% higher than the comparable 1981 rate and is not far from the rate of 100 per 10,000 companies achieved in 1933. Clearly, the small businesses are the ones that are suffering the most. They are usually undercapitalized and are least able to survive an extended period of depressed business conditions.

In the past, many a faltering firm was able to go to its friendly banker and obtain a "restructured" loan that would tide the company over until the next inflationary surge. However, as was suggested earlier in this chapter with regard to problem loans, bankers are beginning to see the full impli-

EXHIBIT 8-3
Business Failure Rate per 10,000 Concerns.
(*U.S. Bureau of the Census,* Statistical Abstract of the U.S.
1981 *and* Survey of Current Business, *May 1982.*)

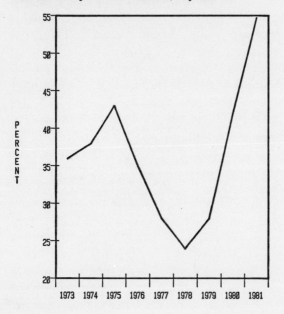

cations of a fundamental slowdown in the rate of inflation:

1. Prices are no longer rising rapidly enough to bail out marginal companies.

2. Loans to meet interest payments, interest payment stretchouts, and generally lax credit standards all have the effect of building up a backlog of postponed defaults and bankruptcies that is only beginning to show up in the statistics. Thus, firms that fail to streamline operations, eliminate unprofitable product lines, close inefficient plants, and otherwise cut costs will find their bankers no longer accommodating.

Commercial Paper: Is Another
Penn Central Scare Possible?

The rapid buildup in corporate short-term credit demand we have described brought with it enormous growth in the commercial paper market. Such borrowings by industrial firms had risen from $14 billion in 1977 to almost $60 billion by the summer of 1982, equivalent to about 15% of the value of commercial bank loans to business.

A lot of that growth has come from the 200 new industrial issuers who have flocked to the market since 1977. Attracted by the convenience, flexibility, and lower costs relative to bank loans, many firms shifted to the paper markets when high interest rates made borrowing in the bond market unattractive. They represented not only medium-size firms but also a number of foreign companies, neither of which were well known in the marketplace.

Of course, not all firms are able or, in the case of some secretive foreign firms, willing to obtain the top ratings that many investors are demanding. Yet this didn't stop many lower-rated firms from borrowing in the paper market. They were still able to tap the marketplace at a reasonable cost so long as they obtained third-party backing for their paper, such as letters of credit, irrevocable credit agreements, or insurance company indemnity bonds. It should be noted that this kind of third-party backing is quite risky.

While the investors in commercial paper evidently have become much more quality-conscious and the quality of paper has improved, risks no doubt remain. It is always possible for even a top-rated firm to fall into difficult financial straits. Furthermore, with banks under their own pressures, some investors might question the usefulness of backup credit lines with the banks should economic problems become severe enough.

Indeed, bank holding company paper accounted for about 15% of the total in 1981, or about $27 billion. A problem at a bank or banks could cause a drying up of funds for other banks, thereby exacerbating any liquidity problem.

Money Market Funds: The Threat
of a Redemption Stampede

The ramifications of any industrial or banking collapse would almost certainly be amplified by the arrival of a new investor in the commercial paper market: the money market fund. Nearly one-third—almost $60 billion—of the funds' total portfolio was invested in commercial paper as of April 1982.

One of the troubling aspects of money funds has been their phenomenal growth. Since their inception in 1973, the number of funds has grown to 200, and total assets at this writing exceed $220 billion. Such rapid growth in any new and untested industry is serious cause for concern and raises the specter of some kind of shakeout.

What could go wrong? There are a number of possible alternatives. For example, an overly aggressive fund manager could place heavy bets on an interest rate forecast—a risky venture under any circumstances but particularly so in the extremely volatile markets of late. Extending maturities in anticipation of lower rates would backfire if rates rose and the fund was locked into lower yields. Conversely, shortening maturities in anticipation of rising rates would reduce the fund's return if rates dropped unexpectedly. In either case, the fund's return could lag behind that of the competition, and thus it might face a liquidity squeeze if shareholders suddenly tried to redeem their money.

That is exactly what happened in 1980 to Institutional Liquid Assets, a large Chicago-based fund. In the summer of 1980, the fund extended its average maturity to almost twice that of the industry, only to see short-term rates shoot upward. As its yield lagged behind the market, Liquid Assets' institutional shareholder base moved to higher-yielding competitors, net sales turned to net redemptions, and the fund rapidly shrank from about $1.5 billion in assets to a little over $1 billion.

Faced with the prospect of a run on Liquid Assets, Salomon Brothers and First National Bank of Chicago, the fund's marketing agent and adviser, respectively, came to the rescue. Through a combination of above-market securities purchases and a rebate of management fees, the fund was able to resume paying a competitive rate, halt redemptions, and avert a possible collapse.

Other things can also go wrong at money funds. Given the funds' large holdings of commercial paper and CDs, credit problems in these areas could quickly spread to the money market funds.

Indeed, recurring episodes such as Chrysler, International Harvester, Braniff, Drysdale Government Securities, and Penn Square Banks could lead to a crisis in consumer confidence and widespread redemptions of money fund shares. It certainly would not take much to get the ball rolling. Even if only one fund were to experience losses, the resulting publicity could cause a redemption stampede. Most money fund shareholders are concerned with yield, not risk, and appear to be blissfully unaware that there is no capital reserve to be offset against loan losses. Also, the shareholders of money funds generally view the money fund industry as homogeneous, and a problem fund, no matter how localized, could lead to mass redemptions.

It is easy to see how this could happen. Let's say the First National Bank of Cabbageville is writing off huge losses on its portfolio of farm loans, which it was aggressively booking before the bumper cabbage crop confounded all the forecasters. In Peoria, a wealthy shareholder in the AAA money fund reads about this in his local paper but can't remember whether it was First or Second of Cabbageville that he's seen among AAA's CD holdings in the last quarterly statement. Anyway, he's already thrown the statement away. He does recall, however, that he can pick up the phone, dial an 800 number, and have his money wired to him or transferred immediately to AAA's new U.S.A. fund, which invests entirely in government securities. He heads for the nearest phone, and soon millions like him are following suit.

Another problem with the money funds is that many of the largest ones are sponsored by brokerage firms. In effect, the broker's name is on the door and the firm's reputation is at stake. It is likely that if problems were to develop with such a fund, the sponsor would try to stand behind its subsidiary. That could raise questions among investors about the financial strength of Wall Street, further aggravating any crisis.

Of course, not all money market funds are created equal. Some invest only in securities of the federal government, which are generally considered essentially risk-free. The difference in yields between these government-only funds and money market funds that also hold CDs and commercial paper has run only about 1%, which strikes us as very small considering the differences in quality and the fact that most investors in money market funds are not looking to run any risk with their capital.

In fact, one of the authors felt so strongly about this risk problem and the yield differences that in March 1980 he transferred all cash reserves for his family and business accounts and in the accounts of two churches he looks after from conventional to government-only funds.

Since then, many other investors have done the same. In June 1981, there were 16 of these funds with $6 billion in assets. One year later, there were 46 such funds, 26 of which had been formed since the beginning of 1982, with assets of almost $20 billion. Of course, funds which own only federal government and agency securities still represented only a small portion of total money market funds. In mid-1982, they accounted for only about 10% of the total of over $220 billion.

Regardless of the source of trouble, money funds' instant-redemption feature, one of the major selling points, could become a serious liability if the all-important confidence factor collapsed. But let's assume that any redemption "stampede" is slow enough to enable funds to wind down their portfolios. What happens to the money? As suggested above, it may find its way into a government fund or directly into Treasury bills or other government securities or into NOW accounts or mattresses. The money will stay in the system, but it still may not be available to those who need money most, even if the Federal Reserve were to flood the banks with liquidity. A liquidity crisis can quickly evolve into "every man for himself," with lenders reluctant to share their hoard of liquidity with others or unwilling to throw good money after bad. More important is the loss of confidence in financial institutions, which, as in the 1930s, could take years to rebuild.

Financial Markets: Speculative Excesses Could Cause a Panic

The financial markets and Wall Street are also vulnerable to a financial panic. Indeed, the nation almost had one in 1980, when plummeting silver prices pushed the Hunt brothers to the brink. The securities firm of Bache Halsey Stuart Shields Inc., the Hunts' principal broker, was rumored to be the subject of huge margin calls and capital trouble, although the Federal Reserve came to the rescue in time. But Wall Street and public confidence were severely shaken by the fact that two individuals of such enormous wealth could have problems meeting their financial obligations.

Another scare occurred with the Drysdale Government Securities fiasco in 1982. Because of an accounting quirk, Drysdale was able to obtain the use of interest-free funds through a complex transaction in the market for repurchase agreements. The firm used the funds to speculate on interest rates and guessed wrong, and when the debacle was over, Drysdale Government Securities was out of business, Chase Manhattan had to write off $160 million, and the Federal Reserve had to pump liquidity into the government securities markets as firms became increasingly reluctant to position securities or deal with many less well known, undercapitalized Treasury dealers. It was a striking example of how an isolated incident can quickly spread and curtail liquidity in the nation's capital markets.

Indeed, developments were occurring so fast as this book was in its final stages of preparation that we had to update the text almost daily for new financial disasters. For instance, the dust had hardly settled on Drysdale and Penn Square, when Lombard-Wall, Inc., and Lombard Wall Money Markets filed for bankruptcy, freezing hundreds of millions of dollars in government securities transactions as well as causing concern about more than $100 million in secured liabilities.

Another risk is a forced liquidiation of assets by financial institutions, which could cause considerable problems. The basic problem is that bond portfolios have suffered tremendous losses, but the losses have not showed up in many earnings statements because most financial institutions do not mark bonds to market as they do stocks but carry them on their books at the higher purchase prices. Let's use the property and casualty industry as an example. Underwriting losses were $6 billion in 1981, but good investment results of $6.9 billion that year provided an offset.

But suppose the bond market drops sharply so that investment results are poor and at the same time a major hurricane causes even bigger underwriting losses. Stocks and short-term asset holdings may not be adequate in some companies to meet cash needs, and so bonds would have to be liquidated. This, of course, would cause those bonds which were sold to be marked to market, which would cause the difference between their market and higher book values to be written off against earnings and reserves. This could cause considerable problems for the companies involved and greatly reduce the ability of these companies to underwrite insurance.

Another vulnerable area is speculation in the futures markets, particularly financial futures. An article in *Barron's* of June 14, 1982, entitled "Speculative Pulse: Financial Futures Set It Leaping" points out the magnitude of the excesses in this market. Some high rollers in Hong Kong reportedly trade "500–1000 T-bond contracts at a time," in effect a bond position worth $50 to $100 million.

The article goes on to quote one observer who estimates

that there may be 400,000 to 600,000 speculative accounts in financial futures. Trading volume certainly suggests that there is a lot of speculation going on. In 1977, when financial futures trading began, volume was about 1 million contracts a year. By 1981, volume had jumped more than 25-fold. One speculator, according to the article, calls his broker every 4 minutes throughout the trading day. Another trader claims to have been so successful that he calls himself the "Jean Dixon of the bond market."

The vulnerability in all this is the potential for a sudden and surprising shift in interest rates, not an unknown occurrence in this volatile age. We have just spoken of the dangers of problems at the money funds, the commercial paper market, and banks. Given the fact that margins in those financial futures are so low (2 to 4%), what would happen if a sudden scramble for liquidity caused overnight money rates to shoot up to, say, 20 to 30%? The bullish speculators would probably be locked into their positions for a number of "limit-down" days. For all but the wealthiest and most liquid speculators, this could well spell financial ruin. If some speculators were unable to make good on their losses, futures trading firms handling the business might be dragged down too. This could well cause a chain reaction similar to the Hunt fiasco, but this time around the problems might not be contained so successfully.

Municipalities: Will Defaults Throw the Market into Turmoil?

Municipalities are another weak link in the economy. The reduction in the top tax rate for individuals from 70% to 50% and competition from the tax-free All Savers certificates have put upward pressure on borrowing costs. Few municipalities can afford the 10% to 14% interest costs on new debt to replace the old issues that are maturing, and raising new money is not always easy.

This is occurring at a time when municipalities face severe budget problems. There has been a slowdown in economic activity and, in many cities around the country, an end to the commercial construction boom. In addition, reduced federal grants-in-aid, the growing pressure to take over phased-out federal government programs, and a flattening out of real estate values and associated property tax gains have all cut into state and local government revenues. At the same time, a cap on tax increases exists because of voter resistance and the potential for a further exodus of businesses and jobs to more favorable economic climates. All in all, municipalities are being crushed in a vicious vise. While many municipalities are trying to adapt, it remains to be seen whether they can do so fast enough to avoid defaults.

This threat is all the more real because of the municipal market's growing dependency on the individual investor. Back in the 1960s and 1970s, commercial banks often bought between 60% and 100% of the new issues. However, because of heavy loan demand; new devices for sheltering taxable income, such as leasing subsidiaries; and from time to time a lack of taxable income to shelter, banks have backed away from the municipal bond market. In 1981, commercial banks bought only about 15% of all newly issued tax-exempt bonds while individuals bought 74%, compared with 19% in 1980. In addition, the fire and casualty companies, traditionally heavy purchasers of tax-frees, have suffered sizable losses, reducing profits and their need for municipal bonds as well.

Relying on any one investor group is dangerous, particularly if it's the individual investor. As New York City's plight indicated in 1975, fiscal problems can put a damper on investor interest in municipal securities. At best, investors would demand a sharply higher risk premium, as they did in the wake of the New York affair. At worst, they would leave the market altogether. With individuals as the major support for the market now and with credit problems potentially worse than in 1975, defaults could easily mount if the bond and money markets became closed to many municipal borrowers.

Households: Falling Tangible Assets Pose Big Problems

Just like corporations, households took off on a huge borrowing spree in the 1970s, building up an enormous mountain of debt. This raises the question of how susceptible the nation's consumers might be to an economic or financial shock and what effects such an event might have on other parts of the economy.

Household borrowing has typically occurred in cycles, as ·shown in Exhibit 8-4. What is noteworthy about the decade of the 1970s is the sharply higher rate of net borrowing relative to personal income compared with the prior two de-

EXHIBIT 8-4
Household Borrowing (Change in Consumer and Mortgage Debt) as a Percentage of Disposable Income. *(Board of Governors of the Federal Reserve System, Flow of Funds Accounts; U.S. Department of Commerce, Bureau of Economic Analysis.)*

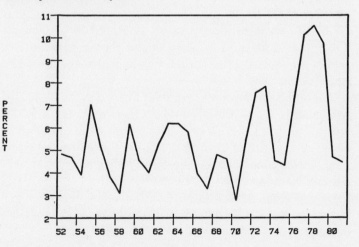

ades. For instance, the cycles of the mid-1970s and late 1970s peaked at about 8% and 10%, respectively, while the peaks of earlier cycles tended to range between 5% and 7%. Note also that when the 1970s cycles did turn around, they bottomed out at rates noticeably higher than those of earlier cycle bottoms. As a result, the ratio of outstanding debt to income, which had plateaued in the 1960s, began to rise again in the 1970s, as discussed in Chapter 3.

However, this latter burst of expansion can be explained by the postwar baby boom generation's coming of age, or at least borrowing age. Indeed, the 1970s was a period of rapid expansion of the population aged 25 to 44. This is the age of household formation, house buying, and the accumulation of durable goods that go along with setting up house and raising a family. Moreover, with high income expectations, people in this age group tend to be confident of the ability to repay debt out of future income growth. Thus, a large part of the buildup in household debt must logically be attributed simply to the rapid growth of a high-debt-propensity age group.

The problem, then, is not so much the magnitude of the borrowing but what was being done with the proceeds. As noted in Chapter 3, there is every indication that households participated along with everyone else in the inflationary excesses of the times.

A big part of the shift can be attributed to the housing boom that occurred as inflation made a larger, more expensive house look like the perfect risk-free investment and an excellent inflation hedge.

The problem arose as climbing interest rates combined with soaring house prices to make it more and more costly— and risky—to play the game. The nature of the problem is depicted in detail in Table 8-1, where the "affordability" of new houses is calculated. The table shows that the ratio of the median house price to the median income rose to about 5.0 in 1981 from the 4.0 range of earlier years, indicating that house prices easily outstripped the gains in spendable income.

Table 8-1 Affordability of New Homes
Costs of Home Ownership (Conventional Mortgage) Compared to Median After-Tax Household Income

Year	Median New Home Price (Conv. Mtg.)	Median Household Income After Tax,* $	Ratio of Home Price to Median Income	Mortgage Rate, %	Mortgage Payment (25% down, 30 years), $	Mortgage Payment as a percentage of Median Income*
1964	$21,300	N/A	N/A	5¾	93.23	N/A
1965	22,700	N/A	N/A	5¾	99.36	N/A
1966	24,400	N/A	N/A	6¼	112.69	N/A
1967	26,600	6,207	4.29	6½	126.10	24.4
1968	28,500	6,646	4.28	6¾	138.64	25.0
1969	30,400	7,091	4.29	7¾	163.36	27.6
1970	30,800	7,477	4.12	8¼	173.55	27.9
1971	31,900	7,805	4.09	7¾	171.42	26.4
1972	31,600	8,245	3.83	7½	165.73	24.1
1973	35,200	9,006	3.91	8	193.72	25.8
1974	38,000	9,461	4.02	9	229.32	29.1
1975	43,900	10,236	4.29	9	265.95	31.2
1976	48,000	10,891	4.41	9	289.67	31.9
1977	53,400	11,574	4.61	9	339.22	35.2
1978	61,300	12,800	4.79	9½	385.97	36.2
1979	70,300	13,980	5.03	11¼	513.66	44.1
1980	76,900	14,930	5.15	14	685.15	55.1
1981	80,100	15,995	5.01	16¾	843.24	63.3

*Median after-tax income is calculated by multiplying median household income by the ratio of total disposable income to total personal income.

SOURCE: Federal Home Loan Bank Board; U.S. Bureau of the Census; Federal Home Loan Bank Board, Office of Economic Research; Board of Governors of the Federal Reserve System, *Federal Reserve Bulletin.*

Of course, most people don't pay cash but take out a mortgage. As suggested, the surge in mortgage rates, plus the higher house prices, substantially raised the proportion of household income needed to meet the monthly mortgage payment. Not only does this reflect the unaffordability of housing, it also indicates the potential financial strain on house buyers.

Back in the 1960s, the average family spent some 25% of its income on the average mortgage payment. This figure rose to 30% in the mid-1970s but recently catapulted to 63%. The combination of rising house values and higher mortgage rates was just too much for the average family to afford. Note that these figures don't even include such factors as utility bills and local real estate taxes, both of which can be substantial. It's no wonder the consumer is feeling the pinch.

If housing prices fall, some players could be hit hard, e.g., those who leveraged themselves by taking out second mortgages and using the proceeds to buy other tangible assets. To the extent that these people were betting on inflationary income gains to ease the burden of steep mortgage rates, an end to inflation will produce severe financial strains.

To add insult to injury, many homeowners have begun to feel the effects of a major downward correction in housing prices. Since the mid-1960s, it is evident from work we have done that an ever-widening gulf has opened up between actual house prices and the price that could be expected on the basis of construction costs. That gap reached as much as 15 to 20% in 1980, as shown in Exhibit 8-5.

Not surprisingly, the inevitable correction soon began. House prices, which rose at an annual rate of 9.5% from 1970 to 1980, rose only 4% in 1981 and were rising at only 1.3% in early 1982.

Moreover, even these prices are likely to be optimistic estimates of market value. Because of the use of creative financing, where the seller offers a submarket mortgage, actual sales prices are probably down on the order of 10 to 15%.

EXHIBIT 8-5
Home Prices as a Function of Construction Wages, Interest Rates, and Building Materials Prices. (*U.S. Department of Labor, Bureau of Labor Statistics; A. Gary Shilling & Co., Inc., estimates.*)

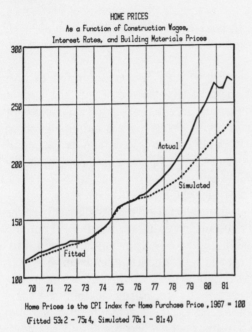

HOME PRICES
As a Function of Construction Wages,
Interest Rates, and Building Materials Prices

Home Prices is the CPI Index for Home Purchase Price , 1967 = 100
(Fitted 53:2 - 75:4, Simulated 76:1 - 81:4)

Furthermore, the assumption of mortgages was effectively eliminated in 1982, when the U.S. Supreme Court voided the California Supreme Court's 1978 Wellenkamp decision to prohibit the enforcement by state-chartered S&Ls of due-on-sale clauses written into mortgages. The following example indicates the seriousness of that decision.

Suppose a family buys a house in 1977 at $53,400, the average then, using a standard 30-year mortgage with the then current 9% interest rate and a 20% down payment. The family pays the mortgage for 5 years and then puts the house on the market in May 1982. What is the value of the 9% mortgage to a prospective purchaser of the house? If current mortgage rates are 15%, every $10,000 of house value is worth $3,500, based on our calculations. Thus, the total benefit to the purchaser is about $14,000.

If the prospective borrower were unable to assume the 9% mortgage, his or her perception of the value of that house might change a lot. Indeed, rather than being worth $88,000, today's average, the house might sell at only $74,000, or some 16% less.

With the resurrection of due-on-sale enforcement and the squeezing of the speculative price-cost gap, the end of the spiral in housing must affect the financial strength of many households. As house equity values either vanish or fail to keep up with anticipation, perceived wealth and liquidity could deteriorate. Indeed, households may become "house-rich but cash-poor."

The combination of high debt, high interest rates, declining inflation, and eroding values of tangible assets leaves households in a vulnerable position. Further economic weakness resulting in higher unemployment, layoffs, and income losses could push debt-income ratios from tolerable to critical, and delinquency rates could skyrocket. Debt-weary, cautious householders may begin to increase their savings, further dampening business activities and accelerating the financial strains on business firms and financial institutions.

The Growing Surplus of Commercial Real Estate

As was pointed out in Chapter 3, investors loved commercial real estate during the late 1970s. It regularly racked up 20% to 30% total returns per year, and the party looked like it would never stop. Indeed, many complained at the time that the problem was a lack of available properties. Availability of properties is still a problem today, except that it's one of excess rather than shortage. Indeed, many developers who built space on speculation are now willing to foresake all their equity just to get out from under the debt burden.

As usual, the journey from boom to bust was quick. In 1979–1980, prices were at their peaks, profits were fat, vacancies were scarce, and rental rates were high and rising. This sounds exactly like the kind of environment in which an investor and a developer should get together and put up some new construction—which is exactly what happened. While other forms of capital formation—equipment spending and residential construction—were collapsing in the double-barreled recession, commercial construction climbed onward and upward.

Now the new construction is ready. What kind of market does it confront? In a word, terrible. Vacancy rates in many major cities are triple or quintuple what they were when the new wave of construction was initiated. In its quarterly survey of office vacancies for the period ending June 30, 1982, Coldwell, Banker found a 7% vacancy rate nationwide, up from 5.4% at the end of March and the highest since June 1978. Coldwell, Banker sees this as "largely supply-induced, the product of a national boom in office building development of historic proportion." Some cities are showing a surprising jump in vacancy rates: San Diego, 19.8%, up from 2.5% in March; San Francisco, 3.4%, up from 0.8% in March; Washington, D.C., 3.9%, up from 0.2% a year ago; and Denver, 2.1%, up from 0.9% in March.

Disbelief and surprise are widespread among owners of new buildings, many of whom refuse to lower rents. But owners of existing buildings have already done so, and as a result the rent gap between the two has increased to its widest level ever. Renters have responded by filling old space, making even more uncertain the prospects for owners of new buildings.

Recent purchasers of existing buildings are being hurt also. They are finding that expiring leases cannot be renegotiated with the kind of inflationary increases that had been anticipated. Worse yet, rents must be renegotiated in a very weak market, creating a classic case of declining revenues and high embedded costs.

Finally, many pension funds that invested in commercial real estate when they thought that it was a fabulous inflation hedge are seeing their sweet dreams turn into nightmares. Many that had invested in insurance company–sponsored pools that purchase commercial real estate did not realize fully that their funds could not be withdrawn at will. The fact hit home in the summer of 1982, however, when Prudential Insurance's PRISA was unable to meet over $100 million in withdrawal requests because of the lack of liquidity in its commercial real estate holdings.

Agriculture: In the Worst Shape since the Depression

The huge run-up in farmland values in the late 1970s, which was discussed in Chapter 3, is another source of potential vulnerability. For several years land prices kept soaring even though farm income actually declined. Although the inevitable correction in farm real estate values was postponed by the inflationary psychology of the late 1970s, it was not canceled. The long-delayed downturn in land values finally got under way in 1980.

Problems began when bumper harvests in 1978–1979 resulted in a huge buildup of grain stocks just as the Carter administration imposed an embargo on grain sales to the Soviets in retaliation for their invasion of Afghanistan. At about the same time, interest rates began skyrocketing in this country as a consequence of the change in the Federal Reserve's operating procedures.

The grain embargo was eventually lifted by the Reagan administration in 1981; while the embargo did not cause the Soviets any great hardship, it did cause them to realign their trading strategy so as not to be too dependent on any one source of supply.

The impact of the embargo on the American farmer was

more serious, particularly from the psychological standpoint. The speculative psychology affecting the farm economy in the 1970s was founded on expectations that farm prices and farm incomes would keep on rising because of increasing worldwide demand for agricultural products and a seemingly secure and stable international market in an atmosphere of détente, with the United States as the principal supplier. However, the grain embargo damaged those expectations, not because the sales were lost to the Soviets but because of uncertainties regarding the stability of the international market and the future actions of the U.S. government with regard to grain sales and prices.

While the embargo removed some speculation from the market for farmland, downward pressure on farm income because of excess supplies aggravated the situation. The embargo contributed indirectly to this by causing the Soviets to reduce their dependence on the United States and seek alternative supplies from Argentina, Canada, and elsewhere. But another cause was reduced purchases by LDCs, which were in a cash bind because of the second round of oil price increases in 1979–1981.

Farmland prices have already reacted somewhat to these pressures, with some surveys indicating declines in land prices of about one-third from their peaks. Moreover, we believe that they are still vulnerable to further correction.

Farmland, or any real estate for that matter, is unlike liquid, homogeneous, and constantly traded assets such as stocks. Consequently, owner attitudes toward market prices are quite different. If someone owns GM stock that was bought 10 points above the market, it's very difficult to deny that investor's loss. Every time the investor looks at a newspaper or a brokerage house quote machine, the facts are clear.

Real estate is different—neither liquid nor homogeneous. The owner of 100 acres that isn't selling at his asking price can easily deny the facts. It's a bad time of the year, or the broker is lousy, or investors have temporarily deserted that area, he can reason. Of course, sooner or later reality must be faced, but the risk is that by the time one owner finally decides to sell at whatever the market will bring—perhaps because of pressure from creditors or plain discouragement—many others have reached the same conclusion. The result can be a wholesale exit which so depresses prices that other sellers are also pulled into a vicious downward spiral.

The victims of declining land values and farm income include not just farmers but also equipment dealers, companies involved in the manufacture of equipment and structures, and even agricultural banks that have lent heavily to farmers. Weakening land values are adversely affecting farm wealth and thus farmers' ability not only to finance the purchase of new equipment but to pay back outstanding loans on existing capital goods.

This is evident from Exhibit 8-6, which shows the ratio of farmers' total debt to total assets, including and excluding land. With land values increasing steadily over the post-World War II period, the ratio remained relatively flat, thus giving the impression that farmers were indeed a conservative lot. However, this flatness was induced by rising land values. If one excludes land from the asset base, the ratio has

EXHIBIT 8-6
Farm Sector Debt-to-Asset Ratios.
(U.S. Department of Agriculture, Economic Indicators of the Farm.)

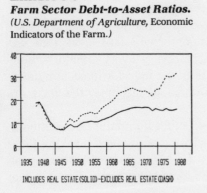

INCLUDES REAL ESTATE (SOLID)—EXCLUDES REAL ESTATE (DASH)

had a very sharp run-up. Now, with land values actually falling, the conservative level of the aggregate debt-asset ratio may quickly shoot up and become a significant impediment to taking on additional debt.

As long as this condition continues, farmers will be unwilling, if not unable, to make capital investments, and the farm equipment industry will remain depressed. With that industry currently operating at about 50% of capacity and many of the smaller companies already having filed for bankruptcy, the pressure on the larger companies will remain intense and in some cases perhaps insurmountable.

This is not to suggest that all farm equipment companies will join the ranks of White Motor, which filed for bankruptcy in 1980. Nevertheless, International Harvester and Massey-Ferguson have already posted a long string of losses, and Deere too would have lost money in the first part of 1982 were it not for gains from its finance and insurance units.

A classic example of what can go wrong in farmland is provided by the case of Eugene Smith, a farmer in Lebanon, Indiana, whose boom/bust exploits were described in a front-page article in *The Wall Street Journal* of March 11, 1982.

Apparently, Smith was very adept at the leverage game. He started off by acquiring farmland with a small down payment. Then, as inflation boosted the value of the land, Smith borrowed against the capital appreciation to buy more land. The *Journal* reported that over the past decade, Smith acquired 10,000 acres of farmland and rented another 4000 acres. In the process, he went into debt to the tune of $30 million.

This strategy worked so well for Smith that he took it upon himself to lecture to farmers all over the country about the benefits of leverage, advocating 80% debt and 20% equity. Indeed, Smith was so successful that he was featured in a *Business Week* article in 1977 as the prototype of a new breed of successful, wealthy farmer. One of the authors recalls that article well. What Smith was doing seemed to indicate one of two things. Either he would end up in bank-ruptcy or our forecast of the forthcoming demise of inflation would be grossly in error.

Unfortunately for Mr. Smith, his financial problems are weighing heavily upon him now. In the *Journal* article, it was reported that he "is selling his two dozen tractors, firing the hired hands, padlocking his barns. Eugene Smith is on the verge of financial ruin."

Protectionism: Is a Trade War Brewing?

Another area of potential vulnerability relates to the impli-cations of recent worldwide sluggish growth and excess capacity and the prospect for more of the same. Despite the worldwide recovery from the 1974–1975 recession, unem-ployment in the United States and Europe remained above the level experienced prior to that slump, as was mentioned in Chapter 5. The downturn that began in 1980 and still per-sists has put further pressure on unemployment, with the result that joblessness in most countries is now well above the 1974–1975 peaks and higher than at any time since the 1930s.

This problem of persistently high unemployment has cre-ated a growing pressure for exports in all countries and for more protection for local industries. Unfortunately, though, there's only so much worldwide demand to go around, and so every country can't export its unemployment to some other nation, especially when global demand is weak. The clash between desire and reality has resulted in an increase in protectionist sentiment in recent years, which threatens to grow into an all-out trade war if global economic weakness persists.

In the United States, for example, steel trigger prices were introduced in 1978 to ensure that foreign steel, partic-ularly Japanese steel, would be priced competitively with steel produced in this country.

In Europe at about the same time, import restrictions were introduced against U.S. petrochemicals, plastics, and textiles, all of which had the advantage over home-produced goods because of the relatively low prices of U.S. feedstocks. Meanwhile, Japan has not shown much inclination to step up its purchases of imported goods and has persisted in its tendency, along with many developing countries, to cut prices to expand exports.

Virtually every country has long been critical of Japan's aggressive foreign trade practices. As shown in Table 8-2, Japan and the other four largest exporters among the nonoil developing nations have indeed been aggressive. In 1979, for example, the share of world exports garnered by these five countries was actually higher than it was in 1975, while the shares of the United States and Europe were lower. Since the onset of the global slump in 1980, the group's share has jumped even further. Meanwhile, the shares of the United States and Europe increased only slightly and were still below the 1975 level.

Given this state of affairs, the United States and Europe have finally started to get tough with the Japanese. Indeed, Europe complained bitterly in 1981–1982 about Japanese penetration of its market, while Japan was maintaining non-

Table 8-2 Percentage Shares of World Exports

	1975, %	1979, %	1981, %
Japan	7.0	6.7	8.2
Brazil	1.1	1.0	1.3
Korea	0.6	1.0	1.2
Taiwan	0.7	1.1	1.3
Singapore	0.7	0.9	1.1
Total	10.1	10.7	13.1
United States	13.5	11.9	12.7
Europe	4.5	2.3	2.5

SOURCE: International Monetary Fund, *International Financial Statistics Yearbook*, 1981 and July 1982 issue.

tariff barriers on shipments of autos and machine tools into that country. Whereas Japan's purchases of manufactured goods from abroad represent only 32% of its imports, manufactured goods represent 44% of Europe's imports and 55% of those for the United States.

Animosities between the United States and Europe have grown as well. The International Trade Commission found that domestic specialty steel producers are being hurt by imports from Europe and alleged that European countries are subsidizing steel operations and thus allowing their steel companies to sell their products in the United States at unfairly low prices. The Europeans then charged that the duties were too harsh and warned that retaliation might be taken against U.S. exports of food, textiles, and other products. As of the summer of 1982, these issues remain unresolved, and both sides appear to be well entrenched in their positions.

This trend toward restraint of trade is indicative of the change in attitude toward foreign competition that has occurred in the United States in recent years. To be sure, throughout most of the post-World War II period, the attitude of this country was personified by the "golden rule," which implied that we would open our doors to foreigners' goods in the hope that they would follow our lead. Our discovery that other countries did not follow our lead, combined with the prolonged recessionary problems of the early 1980s, led the American people and Congress to decide to change course.

Now the theme in Congress is "reciprocity," which means that America's trading partners must open their countries to U.S. exports or America will close its doors to theirs. The protectionist sentiment embodied in this switch is so strong that even though the administration is resisting the reciprocity doctrine for fear of touching off trade wars, it is being forced to compromise with the growing protectionist elements of Congress.

The growing protectionist sentiment is exemplified by several bills recently introduced in Congress to expand U.S.

export opportunities. Specifically, both the Senate and the House have overwhelmingly approved a measure that would extend the Webb-Pomeraine Act of 1918. In its original form, this law allowed merchandise companies to band together for purposes of exports, with immunity from antitrust prosecution with respect to price fixing and quotas. The new law extends the exemptions to service companies, including bank holding companies as well as merchandise companies. Interestingly, Japan has long used trading companies and has been heavily criticized for it in the United States and in Europe. Now the United States is following the same path.

Some of these actions clearly resemble the trade wars of the 1930s. It is interesting to note that the tariffs of 1930 were erected by people whom we now regard, at best, as too stupid to realize that their actions were detrimental to trade overall and, at worst, as absolutely evil. They simply didn't understand that protection does nothing but reduce every country's economic activity and employment. Jude Wanniski in *The Way the World Works* claims that a primary cause of the depression was the enactment of the Smoot-Hawley tariff, which imposed a huge increase in duties on 20,000 items. He even makes an interesting case that the stock market crash in 1929 occurred in anticipation of that infamous act of 1930. Human nature apparently does not change, however, and now we are seeing legislative officials reacting to similar circumstances in similar ways.

LDCs: Caught between Falling Revenues and High Debt Burdens

A rise in protectionism among developed countries would increase the already enormous problems of the developing nations. The export earnings of the developing countries are primarily generated by trade with the industrialized world, and so any reduction in trade as a result of protectionism is bound to have an impact on the developing world.

But even without protectionism, these countries are in desperate shape. For one thing, many developing countries depend on a few export commodities for foreign exchange. In most cases these commodities are primary products, which are very sensitive to external factors beyond the countries' control. For example, weather is a vital factor for countries whose main export is agricultural commodities, and the business cycle in the developed world is crucial for the exporters of industrial materials.

The worldwide recession has depressed commodity prices dramatically. As shown in Exhibit 8-7, commodity prices, excluding oil and precious metals, fell about 15% in 1981 after increasing about 10% in 1980 and 16.5% in 1979. These declines have been broad-based as well, and so almost all developing countries have suffered declines in export earnings. Metals prices fell about 14% in 1981; prices

---

EXHIBIT 8-7
World Export Prices (line) versus Crude Oil Prices (dash).
Includes All Commodities except fuel. *(International Monetary Fund,*
International Financial Statistics Yearbook, 1981 *and July 1982 issue; American*
Petroleum Institute, Basic Petroleum Data Book, Petroleum Industry Statistics,
vol. 1, no. 3, section VI, Table 11.)

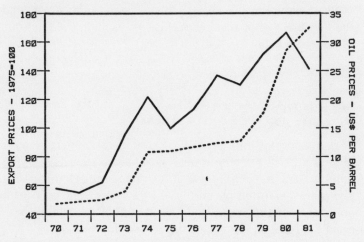

of coffee, cocoa, and tea fell about 22%; and sugar prices declined about 37%.

For some countries, the declines in commodities are aggravating already troubled economies. For example, Malaysia has had to close about 160 of its 850 tin-mining operations. But recession and low prices are affecting even well-managed economies, such as that of Chile. In recent years, Chilean economic policies have been influenced greatly by the Chicago school of economic thought. By imposing strict monetary discipline on the economy, in the past 9 years Chile has gone from a deteriorating economy with high inflation to one characterized by a balanced budget, reduced inflation, and economic growth that has outstripped the rest of Latin America. Largely as a result of these policies, Chile's debt relative to GNP actually declined.

Nevertheless, Chile provides a good example of the problems faced by a single-commodity exporter. It depends on copper exports for half its foreign exchange. Not only has world copper demand dried up in the face of recession, copper prices have fallen nearly two-thirds from their 1980 peak level. As a result, in the first 6 months of 1982, unemployment in Chile increased to nearly 20%. More serious economic problems, particularly related to Chile's deteriorating ability to repay its foreign debt, appear on the horizon.

The LDC's problem is particularly acute in the current environment of world economic weakness because even during the previous expansion, the developing world was unable to build up any financial muscle. For example, as shown in Exhibit 8-8, between 1968 and 1973 the LDCs exhibited a more rapid growth in exports than in imports, but since 1973 exports and imports have grown at essentially the same 18% annual rate in nominal terms. This has made it difficult for the developing world to accumulate foreign exchange reserves.

The primary factor behind the LDCs' inability to build up a cushion has been their exposure to energy imports and the

---

EXHIBIT 8-8
Export and Import Values of Nonoil
Developing Countries. *(International Monetary*
Fund, International Financial Statistics Yearbook, 1981
and July 1982 issue.)

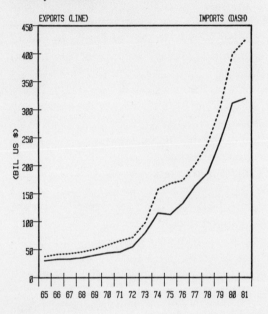

severe impact of sharp rises in oil prices in the 1980s. Let's put this in perspective. Before 1974, the world's nonoil developing countries spent only about 8% of their export earnings on oil imports. But after the first oil shock, about 23% of the developing countries' export earnings went to pay for oil. After the second shock in 1979, oil import payments absorbed more than 30% of the group's export earnings.

While this vulnerability to foreign oil destroyed the balance of payments of the developing world, OPEC surpluses grew mightily. For example, OPEC had a current account surplus of $6 billion in 1973, but it rose to $67 billion in 1974. Between 1975 and 1977 the surplus remained above $30 billion, but then it climbed to nearly $115 billion in 1980 before dropping back to $71 billion in 1981.

What happened to all this money? Instead of acquiring direct investments in developing countries, OPEC chose to acquire bank deposits in the west. Thus, the banking system became flush with liquidity, and it proceeded to recycle these "petrodollars" back to the deficit (i.e., LDC) countries.

This was all well and good for a time in that the process contributed to world economic growth in the 1970s. However, the debt load of the developing countries grew steadily, as did the banking system's exposure to political and economic turmoil. Since that first oil shock in 1974, the external debt of the nonoil developing nations has increased at an astounding rate. The total debt of nonoil LDCs currently stands at about $525 billion, up from only $90 billion 10 years ago. Note that these figures do not include the $90 billion owed by the Soviet bloc, e.g., Poland's $27 billion, Romania's $10 billion, and Yugoslavia's $10.5 billion.

Table 8-3 shows the growth rate of the external debt of selected nonoil LDCs. It is interesting to note that Brazil has the largest amount of outstanding debt, which has grown nearly fivefold since 1973. The debt buildup has been even more rapid among some countries with extensive petroleum resources. Nigeria and Venezuela, for example, have seen their external debt rise nearly 500% and 300%, respectively, over the 1973–1980 period.

Not only has the absolute size of the external debt of this group of countries increased, but as Table 8-4 shows, debt has increased dramatically relative to their GNPs. For example, of the 18 countries listed in the table, 15 had a higher ratio of external debt to GNP in 1980 than they did in 1973. Zaire's debt exposure is by far the greatest, while Portugal's and Thailand's debt exposure has shown the largest increase.

At the same time that debt relative to GNP was increasing, the relative size of the interest payments necessary to

**Table 8-3   External Debt of Selected
Developing Countries**
(Billions of U.S. Dollars, Disbursed Only)

	1973	1976	1980
Argentina	2.8	4.4	10.3
Brazil	12.6	28.5	54.9
Chile	3.2	4.5	9.6
Colombia	2.3	2.9	4.8
Greece	1.5	2.4	4.5
Ivory Coast	0.6	1.2	4.3
Malaysia	0.7	1.6	3.1
Mexico	5.6	15.9	33.5
Morocco	1.0	2.3	7.1
Nigeria	1.2	0.8	5.0
Peru	1.4	3.7	6.2
Philippines	1.9	3.9	8.4
Portugal	0.7	1.3	5.1
South Korea	3.8	7.3	16.7
Taiwan	1.1	2.4	4.7
Thailand	0.9	1.6	5.6
Turkey	3.0	3.8	14.9
Venezuela	1.5	3.0	10.9
Zaire	0.9	2.9	4.2

SOURCE: *World Debt Tables*, Document of the
World Bank (EC-147/80, Table 1-a; EC-167/81).

service that debt also increased. Along these lines, a recent
survey indicates that debt service in 1981 for all nonoil
developing countries amounted to $175 billion, or roughly
half the current account balance of payments of those
countries.

What has happened basically is that with the slowdown
of the world economy over the past few years, foreign
exchange earnings have slipped, and as a result many countries have had to borrow simply to meet their interest payments. Soaring interest rates have also added to the problem.
The same survey found that the nonoil developing countries
paid back $144.7 billion in 1981 but borrowed $145.2 billion.

Table 8-4   Principal Debt Ratios for Selected Developing Countries

	1973		1976		1980	
	Debt/ GNP	Interest/ GNP	Debt/ GNP	Interest/ GNP	Debt/ GNP	Interest/ GNP
Argentina	6.8	0.5	7.8	0.5	15.4	1.2
Brazil	9.3	0.5	12.1	0.7	16.6	1.9
Chile	27.0	0.4	39.0	2.2	18.0	1.8
Colombia	19.1	0.8	16.4	0.8	13.2	0.9
Greece	9.2	0.5	10.2	0.8	10.9	1.0
Ivory Coast	25.0	1.2	25.7	1.4	41.9	3.0
Malaysia	9.7	0.6	15.0	1.1	13.6	0.9
Mexico	11.5	0.7	24.5	1.7	20.0	2.4
Morocco	16.1	0.7	20.1	0.7	40.1	3.5
Nigeria	7.0	0.2	1.9	0.1	5.5	0.4
Peru	14.4	0.9	26.0	1.4	33.7	3.0
Philippines	8.3	0.3	11.9	0.5	18.2	1.0
Portugal	6.1	0.2	8.6	0.3	21.4	1.9
South Korea	26.8	1.7	24.9	1.4	28.2	2.3
Thailand	4.2	0.2	5.0	0.3	11.4	0.8
Turkey	13.1	0.4	8.5	0.3	23.7	1.0
Venezuela	9.4	0.6	9.4	0.4	17.9	2.0
Zaire	32.3	1.2	68.6	1.5	78.5	2.9

SOURCE: *World Debt Tables*, Document of the World Bank (EC-167/81).

With external debt becoming increasingly burdensome, debt rescheduling among the developing countries has been commonplace. Besides Mexico and Poland, Romania, Bolivia, Costa Rica, Liberia, Madagascar, Nicaragua, Senegal, Sudan, Turkey, and Zaire are just some of the countries which have been unable to make their debt service payments on time over the past several years. By making increasingly generous concessions so that countries could avoid defaulting on their obligations, many banks have pushed themselves close to the legal limit of what they may lend to any borrower. Meanwhile, at the same time that LDC export earnings are under pressure because of the worldwide business downturn, the huge OPEC surplus of 1980–1981 is dwindling rapidly because of declining oil prices, falling worldwide energy demand, and an acceleration in spending within OPEC countries to finance their own development. The result is that there are fewer petrodollars to recycle at the very time when the LDCs have to borrow more just to service their outstanding debt.

Economic realities are now forcing the banking system to become more selective in its lending policies. In fact, according to the Bank for International Settlements, new lending to non-OPEC developing countries in the first quarter of 1982 fell to $3 billion, down from $17 billion in the prior 3-month period. In any other circumstances, this might be construed as a very healthy development. But in the current environment of falling commodity prices and weak demand, a slowdown in lending is putting the developing countries in a precarious position.

As if the noose on the developing world were not tight enough, the Reagan administration has moved to reduce LDC dependence on the industrialized world. In a recent speech in Cancun, Mexico, Reagan rejected the notion of redistributing income from the developed to the developing world. He also indicated that he would push for significant changes in the operation of the World Bank and the International Monetary Fund.

The intent of this action was to put a lid on the issuance of paper reserve assets (SDRs) because the administration felt the creation of such assets in the current economic environment would prove inflationary. Along these lines, the administration has also hinted that it may reduce its contribution to lending agencies that assist developing nations. This presumably would force these agencies to focus on the world's poorest nations, leaving the others to borrow in the private capital market.

It can be said that loans to sovereign foreign countries are different from loans to domestic corporations because the lenders cannot easily foreclose, regardless of a borrowing country's financial plight. This may be true, but the LDCs' constant need for additional funds means that the problem is not just one of inducing the lenders to continue existing loans but, more important, of inducing them to pump in new funds as well. Consequently, the risk of defaults is real. The increasingly widespread financial problems in a number of LDCs have not only made it extremely difficult for them to obtain the external funds needed to continue operating but have also made lenders reluctant to extend credit to other developing countries that are still creditworthy. Furthermore, credit and prospective problems in these countries may badly impair the world financial community's confidence in its major banks and other lenders to LDCs.

In the final analysis, it will probably fall to the U.S. government and the governments of other strong industrialized countries to keep the LDCs afloat financially, both to preserve the integrity of large commercial banks and to prevent world financial chaos. One can speculate that the strong countries' roles as financiers of the LDCs could broaden so that they would exert much wider influence over them. Furthermore, if worldwide protectionism becomes the rule, the relationships might even reach the point of resembling what in the nineteenth century were "spheres of influence."

The huge exposure of international banks to defaults by less-developed countries is but one more chink in the armor of the world's financial system.

Will OPEC Fall Apart?

Another area of financial risk lies in the possible breakup of the OPEC oil cartel. With the worldwide recession and energy conservation weakening demand and with high prices encouraging alternative supplies, OPEC production was pushed down from 30 million barrels a day in 1979 to between 18 million and 19 million barrels a day early in 1982. Even that, however, was insufficient to contain the oil glut, and so for the first time, OPEC imposed a quota system limiting its total crude oil output to 17.5 million barrels a day.

One of OPEC's earlier strengths was its lack of quotas,

since setting defined limits on individual countries' output encourages arguments over allocations, cheating, and mutual distrust. It didn't take long for that to happen, and by the summer of 1982, intense pressure was being brought to bear on Saudi Arabia, the OPEC leader and the country that had reduced output the most. Led by Iran, the Saudis' archrival, many OPEC members began to insist that the share of production should be governed by financial need and population, not just by oil reserves and historical production levels. If adopted, such a plan would imply further substantial cuts for the Saudis and production increases for Iran and others.

The root of the problem is that many OPEC countries, such as Iran, Venezuela, and Nigeria, have large populations and have engaged in massive economic development programs. Nigeria, which epitomizes these problems, is building oil refineries, petrochemical plants, a huge steel mill, and a railroad among other costly facilities. With recent oil price weakness, Nigeria's output of 1.3 million barrels a day barely covers two-thirds of the annual projected expenditures. Oil provides 95% of the country's export earnings, and continued political stability hinges on the government's ability to spread the oil money around.

However, Nigerians quickly became accustomed to the good life that oil payments brought and are having difficulty adjusting to the restraints imposed by the combination of excessive spending and weak oil prices. Even worse, their once-flourishing agriculture has atrophied, while the country has squandered its oil money on imported food and luxury goods in addition to impractical industrialization projects.

Overall, the big spending habits of Nigeria and many other OPEC countries and the weak oil prices in the last several years have reduced the oil cartel's total current account balance from a huge surplus of nearly $115 billion in 1980 to a deficit of perhaps $15 billion in 1982, according to estimates of the Organization for Economic Cooperation and Development (OECD). The big importers among the OPEC countries—Iraq, Nigeria, Iran, Algeria, Venezuela, Indonesia,

Gabon, and Ecuador—registered an "unsustainable" current accounts deficit of $30 billion to $40 billion in the first half of 1982, the OECD reported. All but two or three OPEC countries are now borrowers on balance.

As a result, the obvious tendency of these producers will be to step up production in order to at least maintain foreign exchange earnings, thereby adding more supplies to an already overburdened market. The situation could be further exacerbated by rising production in non-OPEC countries such as Mexico, which has boosted exports to the United States to help prop up a plummeting peso.

Of course, the Saudis could continue to permit others to increase their production by cutting their own output further. Nevertheless, at some point, even the patient Saudis are likely to decide that enough is enough and cut prices and flood the market in order to punish the cheaters. If that happens, OPEC will no longer be an effective cartel.

Interestingly, a number of earlier cartels ended in this fashion. A study of cartels all the way back to ancient Greek times that we did a number of years ago (and which, incidentally, led us to predict the demise of OPEC as early as 1975) revealed many examples of cartels that broke up when the leader got tired of accommodating the cheaters and fringe producers. Given the fact that OPEC oil now sells for over $30 per barrel but costs only several dollars a barrel to extract from the ground, a collapse of the OPEC cartel could push world oil prices down sharply.

However, it is probable that U.S. oil prices may hold up better. In the name of fostering domestic self-sufficiency, but in reality to protect the North Slope and other "minor" U.S. investments, Washington would probably quickly impose an import quota system or duty. A duty would be the logical choice because it would simply transfer revenues that had been going to the OPEC countries to the U.S. Treasury and help reduce the federal deficit. Additional revenues would also help offset the declines in revenues from the windfall profits tax that are already taking place as oil prices fail to keep up with the inflation rates that form the basis of the tax. What might the oil price support level be? It's hard to say, but we're told that the North Slope begins to get into big financial trouble at about $25 a barrel.

What are the financial risks if the OPEC cartel collapses? Assuming the United States imposed an import duty or quota system, domestic and imported oil prices would probably equalize and remain considerably above world prices, which is how things were when the nation had a quota system in the past.

Japan, on the other hand, which has no domestic energy investments to protect, would benefit from the low international prices. Therefore, one effect would be to increase the energy cost component of U.S.-produced goods in relation to imports and further increase the risks of protectionism.

This would be a mild threat, however, compared with the effects of the likely declines in the currencies of the United Kingdom and other North Sea oil producers and the probability of defaults on international loan payments by many OPEC countries and non-OPEC oil producers such as Mexico. The effects on the money center banks and other heavy lenders to those lands could be devastating.

Domestic Energy: Overextended and Unprepared for Hard Times

If OPEC falls apart, our domestic energy industry will obviously be hard hit, particularly in view of the exuberance discussed in Chapter 3. This euphoria was exemplified by the growth of domestic oil and gas drilling activity from about 27,000 wells in 1973, prior to the first oil shock, to over 80,000 wells in 1981. Accompanying this burst of activity was a new mentality. Energy price stability, if it ever occurred, would be only temporary, and prices would move up forever. Given this rosy view of oil prices, the consensus expectation in the industry was that drilling and exploration could only increase. Forecasts of 90,000 to 96,000 well completions per year by the mid-1980s were fairly commonplace.

Such expectations seemed rather outlandish to us as long as a windfall profits tax was imposed on oil prices and drilling costs continued to rise. Even if market prices stabilized in 1982, as shown in Table 8-5, the price per barrel of oil after adjusting for the windfall profits tax and for inflation would actually decline—the second such decline in as many years. Moreover, just to keep the inflation-adjusted net price to producers on a gradual upward trend beyond 1982, the market price of oil would have to rise to nearly $50 per barrel by 1985, a 50% increase in 3 years.

Given the earlier bullish mentality, the outright decline in oil prices in 1981–1982 came as a shock. As a result of a major inventory reduction by the major oil companies in an environment of weak demand, prices actually declined by about $4 to $6 per barrel from the offical OPEC benchmark. As if this were not enough of a problem, interest rates remained high, and the recently enacted cuts in tax rates reduced the attractiveness of investing in drilling programs.

The result was an across-the-board retrenchment which affected the major oil producers as well as the smaller inde-

Table 8-5 Oil Price Path
($ per barrel)

	Oil Price, $	Net to Producer, $	Deflated, $
1979A	12.51	12.51	7.68
1980A	21.19	21.19	11.94
1981A	31.77	22.24	11.48
1982	31.77	22.24	10.74
1983	36.00	25.20	11.50
1984	42.00	29.40	12.61
1985	48.00	33.60	13.65

SOURCE: American Petroleum Institute, *Basic Petroleum Data Book*, vol. 1, no. 3, section VI, Table 1: A. Gary Shilling & Co., Inc., estimates.

pendent exploration and production companies. Whereas initial estimates were that the "majors'" exploration and production budgets would increase about 18% in 1982, they actually ran about 9% higher than the 1981 level. The cuts instituted by the independents were even more severe because the independents are much more dependent on outside financing.

Indeed, when prices were rising, it was a fairly common practice for the independents to spend 2 or 3 times what they generated internally. However, when energy prices fell and estimates of reserves were marked down rather than up, the sources of outside financing needed to fill this gap dried up. Thus, in those instances where cash shortages became acute, the results were either the forced sale of properties or outright default.

Such forced sales became so commonplace that many properties in Texas and Oklahoma were reportedly being sold in mid-1982 at 25% discounts from prices 12 months earlier. Meanwhile, lenders are getting nasty. In a June 24, 1982, article in The Wall Street Journal, it was reported that the First National Bank in Dallas took possession of Condor Drilling Company's rigs when the company could not meet its debt service payments on a $10.5 million loan.

The upshot of all this was a downturn in drilling rigs in operation. As reported by Hughes Tool Co., the rig count peaked at about 4500 in December 1981 and numbered about 2900 in mid-1982, a 36% decline, which devastated the oil-service and equipment industry. Cancellations of outstanding orders mushroomed in response to the slowdown, as the double and triple ordering of components of 1980–1981 evaporated. Not surprisingly, the used equipment market was reborn, where prices ran only about 30% of that for new equipment and discussions about selling perfectly serviceable equipment at scrap metal prices were not unheard of.

The domino effect on secondary industries or suppliers became gruesome as well. The market for tubular goods has dried up, and some experts estimate that shipments would fall about 25% in 1982. Meanwhile, established companies such as Hughes Tool and Dresser Industries have had to furlough more than 10% of their production workers.

Of course, the effect of the slowdown on the many recent entrants to the industry was even more severe. Activity for such companies has practically dried up because customers returned to their traditional, established sources of supply.

The downturn was obviously a rough one for the industry since it was so unexpected. However, the key question remains: How much worse can conditions get if the economy remains soft, energy demand stays depressed, and energy prices remain under pressure? The answer is that the impact could be devastating on those highly leveraged independent operators who paid top dollar for producing properties.

In such a situation, additional bankruptcies of independent drillers and even some larger companies may occur. Among larger companies, Dome Petroleum seems the most likely candidate. Dome is Canada's largest oil company in terms of assets and ranks third in oil production. But as a result of past overexuberance, it has over $7 billion in debt and currently spends about $100 million monthly to pay interest on debt and dividends on preferred shares. Not surprisingly, rescheduling of this debt has become necessary.

As rigs and equipment are sold off, further pressure will be exerted on the used equipment market, and as prices for used equipment drop, orders to the service and supply end of the industry will deteriorate further. For those supply companies whose entire customer base is energy-related, an additional consolidation will follow weakness in drilling. Meanwhile, more diversified companies will undoubtedly suffer earnings pressure as their energy divisions suffer losses or profit declines.

Finally, of course, bankruptcies among drillers and suppliers will affect the financial institutions that have been major lenders to the industry. Dome, for example, owes Canada's five largest banks 40% of their total equity and reserves. As a result, banks that have lent to Dome have had their credit ratings reduced.

Thrift Institutions: Why Merging the Strong and the Weak May Be Throwing Good Money after Bad

We have saved the most obvious financial problem—the thrift institutions—for last. Indeed, among all the nation's financial institutions, it is the thrift industry—savings and loan associations and mutual savings banks—that was most severely affected by the high level of interest rates.

As was discussed in Chapter 3, over the decade of the 1970s the thrifts experienced a doubling in the proportion of their deposit liabilities tied to market rates of interest, ending up with an 80% ratio in 1981. Indeed, the popular 6-month money market certificates, which were introduced in mid-1978, had grown to almost $175 billion by mid-1982, as shown in Table 8-6, and accounted for about one-third of total S&L deposits.

The thrift regulators hoped these new deposit investments would slow the erosion of thrift deposits that arose as the inflationary 1970s produced negative real passbook savings. Table 8-6 shows that this hope was realized. Total deposits rose a relatively small $7.6 billion over the 1978–mid-1982 period, but it took increases of $173.6 billion in money market certificates, $114.1 billion in 2½-year certificates, and $40 billion in jumbo certificates (those over $100,000) to do the job. Obviously, these high-cost deposits were simply replacing low-cost passbook money, and the net result was a considerably higher cost of funds for the savings institutions. Exhibit 8-9 shows the thrifts' actual cost of funds along with the maximum permissible passbook rate. At the beginning of the 1970s, the industry's average cost of funds was hovering near 5%, the maximum permitted on the then

Table 8-6   Savings and Loan Deposit Flows
($ Billions)

Year	Money Market Certificates	2½-Year Certificates	Jumbo Certificates	Total Deposits*
1978	+42.9		+ 2.4	+13.3
1979	+81.7		+13.0	+15.0
1980	+54.0	+49.0	+12.1	+10.7
1981				
Jan	+ 7.0	+ 2.9	+ 0.8	+ 0.6
Feb	+ 5.0	+ 1.3	+ 0.8	+ 0.9
Mar	− 0.1	+ 2.5	− 0.4	− 2.1
Apr	+ 0.3	+ 2.0	+ 0.9	− 4.6
May	+ 6.1	− 0.2	+ 1.4	− 0.1
June	0.0	+ 1.5	− 0.1	− 5.8
July	+ 2.4	+ 0.4	+ 1.3	− 5.5
Aug	+ 1.5	+ 6.2	+ 0.5	− 3.3
Sept	− 4.7	+ 9.3	+ 1.1	− 3.8
Oct	−12.6	+ 9.5	0.0	− 1.6
Nov	− 5.5	+ 5.6	+ 0.3	− 1.5
Dec	− 2.4	+ 4.8	+ 1.1	− 1.7
1981	− 3.0	+46.0	+ 7.7	−25.3
1982				
Jan	− 0.3	+ 5.0	+ 1.9	− 0.1
Feb	+ 2.0	+ 3.6	+ 1.1	− 0.8
Mar	− 0.3	+ 5.3	− 0.2	− 1.3
Apr	− 1.3	+ 3.4	+ 0.4	− 5.2
May	− 2.4	+ 1.8	+ 1.5	− 0.3
	− 2.0	+19.1	+ 4.7	− 6.1
1978–1982 cumulative total	+173.6	+114.1	+40.0	+ 7.6

*Net new deposits received.
SOURCE: Federal Home Loan Bank Board, Release, "Savings and Loan Activity."

dominant passbook savings accounts. But by 1981, the cost of funds had more than doubled to almost 11%.

The soaring cost of funds soon collided with the sluggish return on the thrifts' major asset, mortgages. The bulk of the industry's $500 billion in mortgages outstanding in 1981 had been put on the books prior to the sharp escalation in interest rates of the late 1970s. Thus, even though mortgage rates shot

EXHIBIT 8-9
Savings and Loan Associations. *(Federal Home Loan Bank Board, Office
of Economic Research; Board of Governors of the Federal Reserve System,
Federal Reserve Bulletin.)*

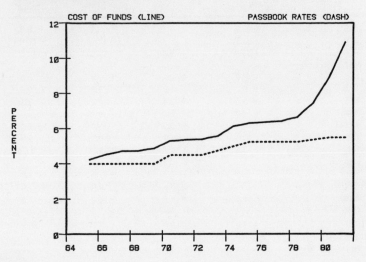

up to 14% and 15% in the 1980s, these rates applied only on
the new mortgages that were made, which were few in number because the high level of interest rates discouraged borrowers. Thus, portfolio turnover slowed markedly, further
dampening spreads.

To compound the problem, repayments began to decline
as well. Existing mortgage holders were reluctant to sell their
houses at depressed prices, especially if they had a cheap
mortgage, only to have to turn around and pay a sharply
higher mortgage rate on a new loan. In the 1977–1979 period,
thrifts were averaging over $100 billion per year in new
mortgage activity. By 1980 and 1981, mortgage activity had
slowed to about $60 billion per year, a drop of 40%.

The thrifts were in a clearly untenable balance sheet pos-
ture for an era of rising rates and negative yield curves:
short-maturity liabilities and long-maturity assets. Because

of this severe balance sheet mismatch between assets and liabilities, the thrifts' spread between portfolio yields and the cost of funds plummeted, turning negative by 1981.

In these circumstances, it is hardly surprising that thrifts' earnings deteriorated markedly. The net return on the assets of the nation's savings and loan associations fell from a 1977–1979 average of about 0.75% to a thin 0.13% in 1980, which is the lowest in over 15 years.

In the northeast and the midwest, net returns actually turned negative in 1980, a phenomenon which spread nationwide in 1981. Indeed, at this writing, the spread between mortgage portfolio yield and the cost of funds is a negative 1.05%. With a little over $500 billion in mortgages on the books, that spread meant the thrift industry was chalking up over $5 billion in annual losses, equal to about 16% of its net worth at the beginning of 1982.

The industry's fundamentally weak capital position makes it even more vulnerable to shocks from other parts of the economy. Many thrifts were as beguiled by the energy boom as the folks from Chicago and New York and purchased a large volume of CDs from Penn Square Bank. Thus, when Penn Square Bank went under, a number of thrifts had to take sizable losses. No doubt there are still many questionable assets lurking on the thrifts' books—the inevitable consequence of the pursuit of earnings.

Present losses don't mean the thrifts are collapsing yet. But if the losses continue, the industry's net worth may fall to 2% of total assets—a level deemed critical by thrift regulators—in about 3 years. Note, of course, that we are using an industry average here. Many individual thrifts are in much worse shape.

The situation is even worse for the nation's mutual savings banks, which are concentrated in the northeast. Banks in New York City and Boston had particularly rough going in view of the tough competition for savers' dollars in these areas and the usury ceilings imposed on New York banks until recently. Also, these institutions typically experience a slower portfolio turnover because houses in the area are bought and sold less frequently than in other parts of the country. That means that mortgages at these institutions aren't repaid as often, and thus the portfolio is slow to reflect market interest rates. These combined problems were so great that by 1982, the New York State superintendent of banks was encouraging the state's weaker banks to close unprofitable branches and look for stronger merger partners.

For a number of thrifts, time—and capital—has simply run out. In 1981, 200 thrifts went out of existence, and the pace picked up in 1982. The list of thrifts merging with stronger institutions includes the New York State Bank for Savings, West Side Federal Savings and Loan, Greenwich Savings Bank, Washington Savings and Loan in Miami, and First Savings and Loan.

The list continues to grow. In 1982 the Federal Home Loan Bank Board estimated that 80% of the nation's savings and loan associations were losing money and were candidates for mergers. In fact, the Federal Savings and Loan Insurance Co. (FSLIC) watch list of troubled thrifts got to be so long that the agency stopped referring to it for fear of raising public concern.

The FSLIC's solution to the problem, in most cases, was to encourage mergers. Outright liquidation was to be avoided whenever possible, because it might scare depositors in other thrifts and would require dipping into the FSLIC's reserves. Those resources are only about $7 billion, and the FSLIC was apparently worried that nervous depositors might notice that the fund was shrinking fast and, despite $100,000 of insurance per account, launch a major run on the thrifts in order to claim their funds before the insurance pool ran out.

As an inducement to get a strong thrift to merge with a weak one, the FSLIC generally agreed to guarantee a minimum profit for the weak thrift. Thus, the FSLIC's contingent liabilities have jumped sharply. The worry is that smart analysts or depositors will add up the cumulative total of such guarantees and conclude there is little, if any, money left in the reserve. One could make an analogy to those companies which tried to improve their balance sheets by leasing—an off-balance-sheet item. That worked for a while, until Wall Street got smart and started capitalizing leases on the balance sheet. How long will it be before the same happens to the FSLIC?

Taken together, all these areas of vulnerability consitute an environment of greater risk than the nation—and possibly the world—has seen for half a century. As we shall see in Chapter 9, this period of time corresponds uncomfortably closely with the frequency of the Kondratieff wave, an economic cycle that suggests we are about due for a major financial crisis.

The Kondratieff Wave: Will It Repeat?

9

It is particularly unnerving that the financial risks discussed in Chapter 8 are in evidence during a period when the Kondratieff wave, the 50-odd-year economic cycle, is scheduled to begin its down phase. The disconcerting similarities between the signs that normally accompany the peaks in this cycle and the signs that we see around us now suggest that the risks discussed in the last chapter should not be downplayed or ignored.

The Kondratieff wave is named after the Russian economist Nikolai Kondratieff, who correctly predicted big problems for the capitalist countries in the 1930s. But he made a strategic blunder by suggesting that the capitalist world would survive. The reaction of the Russians was predictable, and Kondratieff spent the rest of his career in Siberia.

The Kondratieff wave holds that capitalist countries have consistently been subject to a 50- to 60-year cycle of extended growth and decline, commodity price peaks and troughs, and rising and falling interest rates. After studying more than 100 years of data on commodity prices in industrialized countries, Kondratieff found that after a long period of expansion, approximately 24 years, a long decline ensued, lasting anywhere from 23 to 35 years. Kondratieff described the wave this way:

> The upswing of the first long wave embraces the period from 1789 to 1814, i.e., 25 years; its decline begins in 1814 and ends in 1849, a period of 35 years. The cycle is, therefore, completed in 60 years.
>
> The rise of the second wave begins in 1849 and ends in 1873, lasting 24 years. ... The decline of the second wave begins in 1873 and ends in 1896, a period of 23 years. The length of the second wave is 47 years.
>
> The upward movement of the third wave begins in 1896 and ends in 1920, its duration being 24 years. The decline of the wave, according to all data, begins in 1920.*

If one assumes a typical down wave lasting 23 to 35 years, the fourth up cycle probably began in the late 1940s or early 1950s, precisely when the postwar economic and stock market boom started. If we arbitrarily pick 1950 as the year the postwar economic expansion began, then 24 years of economic growth would put the next peak in 1974. It is ominous, to say the least, that the worst recession in 30 years struck in 1974, accompanied by sharply declining stock and commodity prices.

Actually, many people who were only slightly familiar with the long wave thought that 1974 was the beginning of another depression, based on Kondratieff's theory. But a strict interpretation of the long wave indicates that a gradually declining plateau exists for 8 to 10 years before the depression actually occurs.

Indeed, Kondratieff divided the economic decline into two phases: a primary plateau followed by a decade or so of gradual decline, which he called "secondary prosperity," and then a depression. His work showed a peak in 1814 and a gradually declining plateau through 1819, a peak after the Civil War and a gradually declining plateau for 10 years and a peak in 1920, with the great depression beginning 9 years later.

The Long Waves in Economic Life, Readings in Business Cycle Theory, American Economic Association, Blakiston, Philadelphia, 1944.

Adding 8 or 10 years to 1974, we get 1982 or 1984 as the likely target date for the beginning of the next depression.

Let's examine some of the characteristics of the up and down waves as identified by Kondratieff:

1. Commodity prices peak with a certain amount of regularity, invariably coinciding with an expensive war. In the first long wave, commodities topped out around the War of 1812 and continued to decline until 1843. After the end of the Civil War, commodities peaked again and kept dropping through 1896. In the next cycle, commodities hit their peak after World War I in 1920 and dropped until the late 1930s. Note that each commodity cycle top coincided with a war: the War of 1812, the Civil War, and World War I.

2. Wars recur with regularity in both the up and down cycles and have a number of similar characteristics. The upswing wars are typically highly emotional ones, partially because of the tension which accompanies an expanding economy. These wars appear toward the end of the upswing, as the populace and the government become adventuresome. But the wars soon become expensive because they can't be won easily and end up being highly unpopular.

As examples, consider that the Civil War, World War I, and the Vietnam war all started with a "crusader" spirit. The Civil War, for instance, began as a fight to free the slaves. In the beginning days of World War I, American soldiers marched off to war to "make the world safe for democracy." The rationale for the Vietnam war was to prevent falling dominoes in southeast Asia and to stop the spread of communism.

The enthusiasm for all three wars quickly evaporated, and they became highly unpopular. We are all familiar with the draft riots of the Civil War, the May Day riots in 1919, and the enormous unpopularity of the Vietnam War. It is interesting to note that the time span between these wars also fits the 50-year pattern: The Civil War came 49 years after the War of 1812, and World War I began 53 years after the

Civil War. Consistent with the pattern, the Vietnam war started 51 years after World War I.

Coincidentally, there is also a pattern of wars at the trough of the down wave. Such wars are typically short and inexpensive and in general don't create a lot of problems. The first trough war was the Mexican War, which started in 1846, only 3 years before the start of the next upswing. The second trough war, the Spanish-American War, began in 1897, 51 years after the Mexican War and 1 year after the second down wave ended. The third trough war, the Korean war, started 53 years later, right at the beginning of the upswing.

3. Protectionism and isolationism appear consistently during the Kondratieff down wave. As pointed out by James B. Shuman and David Rosenau in *The Kondratieff Wave*, "in the years after the peaks, when declining prices activated the downward spiral, when both business and labor felt the pinch, public attitudes swung towards restrictive imports." For instance, after the first Kondratieff cycle peak, tariffs were increased in 1816 and again in 1828—sometimes called the "tariff of abomination."

In the second down cycle, tariffs were raised once again. The McKinley Tariff Act of 1890, the Wilson tariff of 1894, and the Kingley tariff of 1897 were blatantly protectionist, according to Shuman and Rosenau.

The next cycle also had its protectionist legislation, which came in the form of the Smoot Hawley Tariff Act of 1930, involving more than 20,000 items as was mentioned in Chapter 8.

Whether protectionist legislation actually led to the depression or not, the "beggar-thy-neighbor" policies that governments pursued in the 1930s certainly made matters worse. As world economies slumped at that time, many nations tried to put off the day of reckoning by exporting their problems to some other country. Currencies were devalued to make exports more competitive, and the wealthy nations, particularly the United States, stopped extending credit to the less-developed ones. This caused financially weak nations to default on their loans, which exacerbated the U.S. banking crisis and worsened the deflation and depression. The reaction to the crisis by the wealthy nations was to balance their budgets, reduce welfare payments (particularly in Great Britain), and increase interest rates, thereby accelerating the downturn.

4. The decades of gradual decline, or "secondary prosperity," have similar characteristics. First, the recession which occurs at the peak turns out to be the severest recession of the whole up cycle and has a huge inventory correction as its base. Second, after that recession is over and the secondary prosperity begins, people erroneously expect "a return to normalcy," to repeat a popular phrase of the 1920s.

As a case in point, the 1920–1921 slump, a classic inventory recession, was the most severe downturn of the up cycle that began in 1896. The ensuing period of secondary prosperity, the 1920s, was seen by many as an attempt to return to the earlier boom years, but for agriculture and real estate, most of the 1920s was a disaster.

5. Agriculture is particularly hard hit during the down wave, which is what occurred after the War of 1812, the last two to three decades of the nineteenth century, and the two decades after World War I. Apparently, the peak in farmland comes well before the peak in other real estate.

6. During the beginning of the upswing, the production of gold increases, presumably as commodity prices boom and economic activity picks up. But gold production declines during the down phase, probably because there is less demand for it.

7. During the down waves, a number of important discoveries are made, but they aren't commercially exploited until the beginning of the next upswing.

8. Intermediate swings exist within each long wave. In the case of the upswing, years of growth and prosperity predominate, while in the downswing, years of declining activity are more frequent.

A final characteristic of the peak of the upswing, at least in this country, can be found in political scandals, presumably because prosperity encourages graft and political chicanery. For instance, toward the end of President Grant's second term, several years after the primary peak of the upswing in 1873, his secretary of war, William W. Belknap, and Orville E. Babcock, his private secretary, were involved in graft scandals.

Shortly after the peak of the next upswing, President Warren G. Harding died suddenly amid rumors of scandal in the Veterans' Bureau, the Office of the Alien Property Custodian, the Justice Department, and the Department of the Interior. Harding's death spared him the exposure of the Teapot Dome scandal and the dismissal under humiliating circumstances of his secretary of the interior, Albert B. Fall, and his attorney general, Harry M. Daugherty. History has dubbed Harding's administration one of the most corrupt in our nation's history.

Little needs to be said about Watergate and the resignation under fire of the two top officials of the land, except to point out that it occurred around 1974, the probable peak of the recent Kondratieff upswing.

Some analysts argue that the Kondratieff cycle is misleading this time around for two reasons: (1) Commodity prices rose uncharacteristically to new highs in the late 1970s (the declining plateau), and (2) stock prices did not rise nearly as much as they did in the 1920s.

One could rebut these arguments by pointing out that the plateau period is one of intense speculation; as we have discussed already, the 1970s showed more speculation than any period since the 1920s. This time, the speculation occurred in tangible assets, such as commodities and real estate, instead of stocks.

There are two possible explanations for this speculative shift. First, after the 1929 crash, the government moved to prevent excessive speculation in stocks by raising margin requirements, scrutinizing insider trading, requiring corporate financial disclosures, etc. However, real estate and commodities became freewheeling areas where newcomers could gamble with little or no money down.

Second, this upswing was characterized by an enormous increase in the government's share of the economic pie and a gradual acceleration in inflation. It is not surprising, then, that fear of inflation reached such an extreme that the speculation occurred largely in tangibles while earnings and stock prices suffered.

Finally, many commodities, such as copper, corn, cotton, and sugar, either made "double tops" (in the mid-1970s and early 1980s) or failed to rise to a new high in the late 1970s. Thus, commodity prices may well have peaked, perhaps not right on schedule but closely enough to fit in with the cycle.

Of course, some people reject the concept of a long economic wave because it implies a lack of free will on the part of industrial economies that is hard for most Americans to accept. Another criticism is that Kondratieff offered no rational reason for these long economic waves. To those who rely heavily on reason, the existence of a long economic wave, no matter how convincing historically, is hard to embrace without a rational basis.

Interestingly, Jay W. Forrester, a professor at MIT, may have come up with a rational explanation for the long wave. In a nutshell, Forrester believes that under- and overinvestment in capital goods is the major factor in the long economic wave. For example, after the last depression there was a great shortage of capital goods, which subsequently required a long period of investment catch-up.

Says Forrester in an interview with *Fortune* magazine in January 16, 1978:

After the Great Depression and World War II, every aspect of capital plant was inadequate. Consumer durables, housing, office buildings, factories, transportation systems, and schools were old and inadequate. To rebuild the depleted capital stock in a short time, like 20 years, construction rose to a rate higher than would be needed in the long run to compensate for depreciation. And when adequate capital plant had been created, a time that may have occurred in the 1960's, tremendous forces existed to sustain the process of capital accumulation. The result has been an unbalancing of the system, with too much capital and too much debt. Eventually, momentum falters as capital plant becomes more and more excessive. It is probable that enough capital plant now exists to sustain output for at least a decade with little additional investment.

It is interesting to note that Forrester believes that business can prepare for the down wave by focusing on the long-term prospects for technological innovation. In the *Fortune* article he says that

> managers should try to lay the ground work for a future compatible with the next long wave of capital creation and the new technological infrastructure that replaces the present one.... Those who correctly look across into the next technological upswing will be the ones who lay the foundations for success. Those who look across incorrectly and back the wrong vision of the future will be in difficulty.

Another possible explanation of this 50-year cycle that may not be as whimsical as it sounds relies on the observation that human nature changes very slowly over time, if at all. Therefore, people with similar background experiences react to like circumstances in similar ways. This explanation notes that it takes about 50 years for everyone who remembers the last trip through the meat grinder to die or retire. Therefore, only after that length of time are people likely to repeat their mistakes.

What are the chances that the Kondratieff cycle will recur in the 1980s? It is disturbing, to say the least, that many of the signs of this 50-year cycle are currently in evidence. The nation had a major inventory-building phase in 1974 which was very similar to the one in 1920–1921. There also has been a period of intense speculation and a gradual decline for the last 8 years, accompanied by expectations of a return to prosperity, just as in the 1920s. There probably has been a peak in commodity prices, and in the Vietnam war there occurred an expensive and unpopular war that began nearly five decades after World War I.

Protectionist sentiment is growing quickly, and financial problems are more serious and widespread than at any time in the past 50 years. Wealthy nations are again trying to export their problems. Less-developed countries are defaulting on their loans, and international banks are increasingly unwilling to extend further credit. The United States, in particular, is keeping interest rates high, cutting government spending, and attempting to balance the budget. Farmers are in severe trouble, and farmland prices have peaked, once again ahead of other real estate prices. Finally, there has been a burst of new technology, such as bioengineering, fiber optics, and satellite communications, which may require decades before commercial application. All in all, it is not wise to downplay the significance of these recurring trends.

If we are in another down wave of the Kondratieff cycle, what can a businessperson, investor, or farmer expect? First, we might expect recessions to last longer and be more severe than the postwar experience; recoveries may be shorter and less ebullient. Second, farming and agriculture should experience extremely depressed conditions for many years. Third, a tough economic climate may prevail through the year 2000 and possibly beyond. Fourth, the bases of the next great fortunes will stem from the technology discovered during this down wave. Remember, however, that the commercial application and the profits may not arrive for several decades.

An Assessment of the Risks: Where Do We Come Out?

The minefield of financial risks reviewed in Chapter 8 and the similarities between the current strained economy and past predepression phases of the Kondratieff wave certainly make one wonder whether we're about to experience a rerun of the financial collapse of the early 1930s. Furthermore, the "gold bugs" tell us that there is no way that inflation and the resultant financial excesses can be eliminated without widespread defaults that simply wipe the debt slate clean.

As we've discussed, there are many similarities. For example, the stock market speculation of the 1920s has its counterpart in the excesses of tangible asset buying of the past decade. True, the speculation in real estate and collectibles may have been less intense, but the fact that it was more widespread and the illiquidity of tangibles relative to stocks may more than make up for this. The heavily leveraged stockholder may have been decimated when he couldn't meet margin calls and was sold out in 1929, but at least there was a functioning market in which to sell. That's hardly true of the extremely thin markets for tangibles that exist today.

There are, however, big differences between now and 1929, or so say a number of observers. We've all heard the list, parts of which make sense while others don't. For instance:

- The service sector accounts for two-thirds of employment today, compared with one-third in 1929, and service jobs are less cyclical than those in goods-producing industries. (But don't airline pilots and cabin attendants ever get laid off?)

- Within that service sector, government employees at all levels now account for about 20% of the total nonfarm job holders versus 10% in 1929, and government employees never get laid off. (Then what is President Reagan trying to do in reducing the size of government?)

- Compared with 1929, income taxes are big now—the counterpart of a big government—and so sizable cuts could be used to stimulate a collapsing economy this time. (But didn't they recently raise taxes in Washington?)

- The Fed would certainly not allow the money supply to fall by one-third as it did in the depression, which, according to monetarists, was *the* cause of that debacle. (Even if the monetarists are right, would the Fed know just when to shift gears from the current policy of restraint to one of all-out ease?)

- International cooperation has now replaced the trade wars and beggar-thy-neighbor policies of the 1930s. (Then what about all the protectionism we see around us?)

- In stark contrast to the 1929 era, there is now an infinitely stronger desire to prevent major institutions from failing. (But doesn't the administration believe that the nation has had too many bailouts and that the right to fail is part of economic life? As noted in Chapter 3, haven't many people responded to the assurance of government bailouts by stepping up their level of speculation, apparently to maintain a constant level of risk?)

- Many households now have two or more wage earners, compared with very few in 1929. Consequently, if one is laid off, some income still continues. (But didn't many of those second and third job holders go to work simply in order to *maintain* family purchasing power that was being eroded by inflation?)

Maybe the usual list of differences between now and the late 1920s isn't all that comforting, although there are some meaningful differences. Government-backed insurance on virtually all types of deposits, unemployment insurance, welfare benefits, and agricultural price supports fall into this category. What these programs basically do is maintain income in the face of economic adversity, and that has been the whole thrust of the last 50 years' reaction to the depression. But could concentration on these programs amount to fighting the last war?

Maybe the source of weakness this time won't be a cumulative and self-feeding decline in income, but rather something else. How about a lack of willingness to spend money even though income is adequate? The nation is very good at getting money into people's hands but has had little experience getting them to spend it. That wasn't the problem to be solved in the depression, when people who lost their jobs had virtually no income. A crisis of confidence in this country could suddenly make big savers out of consumers and businesspeople and depress economic activity quickly and severely.

The Reagan administration, at least back in its "supply side" days, wanted more saving, but not this much this fast. The nation had a hint of what might happen in 1980, when credit controls were imposed and consumers, out of fright, patriotism, or both, cut up their credit cards, mailed the pieces to Washington, and went on a saving spree. Their rate of saving out of take-home pay rose from 4.9% in the first quarter to 6.2% in the second, an increase of only 1.3 percentage points. Spending, of course, dropped the same 1.3 percentage points, from 95.1% of take-home pay to 93.8%. Yet because consumer spending accounts for over 60% of GNP and because people acted almost overnight, the decline in the spending rate was the principal reason why real GNP fell at a 9.9% annual rate in the second quarter, the largest quarterly decline since the depression.

That weakness passed quickly, but let's step up to an example of depression-class, saving-induced weakness. Suppose housing prices collapse in southern California. Perhaps those who thought they would outwait the Fed throw in the towel and call their real estate brokers one morning to tell them to sell their houses for whatever the market will bring. Given the degree of leveraged speculation in southern California housing, the financial losses could be substantial for speculators and their lenders, and the effect could quickly spread coast to coast.

Even people in Dubuque who had no intention of buying or selling a house in the foreseeable future could react rather meaningfully. Like people throughout the nation, they probably have been spending their take-home pay freely because they consider their houses as large and automatically growing savings accounts that can take care of any rainy days.

When these folks hear about the housing collapse in southern California on the evening TV news and then recall that several neighbors or friends have been having trouble selling their houses or recently sold them at losses, their attitudes may change. Saving may become extremely popular. A saving rate increase of only 3 or 4 percentage points and a comparable decline in the spending rate could depress the economy severely; lead to substantial layoffs, capital spending cuts, etc.; and perhaps touch off a string of other financial problems.

In sum, the financial risks to the economy appear considerable. "Depression" is a loaded word that conjures up misleading images of soup kitchens and apple sellers. Nevertheless, if the economy ends up experiencing a decline that is not only more severe than the standard recession but also different in character—a decline that might even be labeled a depression—we will not be surprised.

Of course, economic weakness of this severe a character does risk a panicked response from Washington, leading to massive monetary and fiscal stimulation. Nevertheless, a rapid return to a strong economy and runaway inflation would not be likely. People as disillusioned and cautious as they would be after that degree of punishment—people who would have suffered huge declines in tangible asset values while still retaining their crushing debts—would be unlikely to rush to borrow available funds, regardless of how low the interest rates, or to spend much of any tax cuts or other forms of fiscal stimulation. As noted, the government can provide income, but it's much more difficult to get people to spend it if they're scared.

In any event, with or without this severe a decline in business activity, the ending of inflation should produce a crop of winners and losers quite different from those of the recent past. We'll examine this list in Chapter 10.

The New Scoreboard: Some Winners but Many Losers

10

The end of inflation, no matter how it comes about, may be enormously disruptive. Indeed, if people fully understood the risks, they probably wouldn't be so enthusiastic about trying to end it. Fortunately they don't, because the only alternative is continually rising expectations of inflation and eventually an even worse collapse or a deterioration into a Latin American type of economy in which productive work and investment lose out to speculation in existing tangible assets.

In any event, as was suggested in Chapter 7, whether inflation ends smoothly or roughly in the short run, the process probably will not be completed for a number of years. Just as the inflationary head of steam took decades to build, the cooling of the boiler and the aftermath of any explosions that may occur in the process will take some time to complete.

Lenders and Borrowers

In the meantime, who will the winners and losers be if inflation does end? In a general sense, firms and individuals with little if any debt should benefit, as should savers, because of lower income tax rates and high real, or inflation-adjusted, interest rates. Conversely, highly leveraged borrowers will be in trouble and won't be able to pay back in cheaper dollars. Furthermore, lower personal income tax rates mean that more of the interest rate will be borne by the individual and less by Uncle Sam.

Those who are heavily in debt and have used their borrowings to purchase tangible assets could be faced with high real rates and declining asset prices. As the collapses in silver and some other commodity prices have demonstrated, tangible assets are highly illiquid. When there is a rush for the exit, the door is often too narrow for everyone to get through without some people being bruised or even trampled.

Highly leveraged businesses locked into high borrowing costs by private placements or other means may have trouble passing these costs through to their customers. Some insurance companies and other lenders may have to "voluntarily" reduce their interest returns on these instruments in order to keep their borrowers alive. Obviously, these lenders, as well as commercial banks, could be in trouble if financial difficulties become widespread.

By the same token, concern over the quality of commercial paper and bank certificates of deposit could favor money market funds that invest exclusively in U.S. government securities. Conversely, funds that invest heavily in commercial paper and bank CDs may be less attractive.

Also, anyone who took out an expensive mortgage in recent years is probably a loser. If interest rates drop, the mortgage could be refinanced, but refinancing usually involves a considerable amount of expense.

Another loser will be leveraged buy-outs, a popular strategy of recent years in which a private investor group buys a company with a small amount of their own capital and large amounts of borrowed money. If inflation ends, the dollar value of corporate tangible assets will be reduced at the same time that high real interest costs will make debt burdens hard to carry. Of course, those who specialize in arranging these deals will also face tough times.

Financial Assets and Tangibles: The Roles Will Be Reversed

An end to inflation and any further downward slump in prices of tangible assets would make the whole array of commodities, collectibles, and real estate anything but attractive. Of course, those who make a living in those businesses, such as real estate brokers, art dealers, and art auctioneers, would suffer.

Weak commodity prices would also hurt the less-developed countries that are heavily dependent on commodity exports as well as commodity cartels, such as those for tin.

Furthermore, in a continued recessionary environment, commodity prices would probably be more influenced by their industrial uses than by speculative appeal. Oil is certainly no exception, despite the efforts of the OPEC cartel, which, as was pointed out in Chapter 5, looks increasingly weakened by excess supply and falling demand.

Substantial declines in oil prices would, of course, create great financial difficulties for OPEC countries as well as for other oil-exporting nations such as the United Kingdom and Mexico. Even worse, economic problems in oil-producing countries, which have huge external debts to the banks, could easily lead to a crisis of confidence in the international banking system, as was discussed in Chapter 8. Lower oil prices would also invalidate much of the huge joint venture investment in petrochemical plants, refining, and pipelines made by the international oil companies, OPEC and other oil-producing countries.

An end to inflation in general, and weak oil and metal prices in particular, would be an unpleasant shock to corporations that recently took over companies with large tangible asset holdings after borrowing heavily at high rates to do so. Cases in point are du Pont's purchase of Conoco, U.S. Steel's acquisition of Marathon, Sohio's takeover of Kennecott, Dome Petroleum's takeover of Hudson's Bay Oil and Gas, Hecla Mining's acquisition of Day Mines, Occidental Petroleum's purchase of Cities Service, Allied Corp. and Continental Group's takeover of Supron Energy, Atlantic Richfield's purchase of Anaconda, Standard Oil of California's investment in 20% of the stock of AMAX, Hiram Walker's purchase of oil and gas properties from Denver oilman Marvin Davis, the takeover of Texas Gulf by Elf Aquitaine, and the purchase of St. Joe Minerals by Fluor.

Any company that ran down liquidity during 1976–1982 is also likely to be a loser. As inflation ends, liquidity and financial strengths will offer considerable competitive advantages. Thus, those companies that played the inflation game may wish that they had saved their liquidity for a rainy day.

An end of inflation as well as the reduction in the top tax bracket from 70% to 50% could reduce the appeal of tax shelters, particularly since the investment potential in real estate, cattle, or other tangible assets is so limited.

Housing prices would decline in a noninflationary environment. Furthermore, renting a house may make more sense than buying. For those who do buy, smaller houses may be the new wave.

Commercial construction would also be hurt if inflation ended, because hotel, office building, and shopping center owners would be faced with high carrying costs and excess capacity. Farmland would also feel the effects of inflation's demise, as would farm income and sales of farm equipment and supplies.

Most financial assets, led by quality stocks and bonds, will be clear winners once any difficult transition period is behind us. An economy with little inflation and less regulation, where the government ceases to be the leading growth industry, with the action shifted to the private sector, should be much more hospitable for equities than has been the case since the early 1960s.

An end to inflation and a drop in interest rates imply a long bull market in the price of quality bonds. U.S. Treasury obligations should be standouts since they have the triple advantage of being the nation's best credits, being highly liquid, and being essentially free of call provisions that can limit capital gains. The prices of low-quality bonds, however, could be depressed by financial problems and concern over bankruptcies.

As financial assets prosper, so should pensioners and others with relatively fixed incomes. This is one of the clearest ways in which the longer-run implications of inflation control are favorable for the lower-income segment of the nation's population.

In any event, investment strategies that emphasize preservation of capital and risk probably will dominate investment management for the rest of the decade. The losses associated with ending inflation are likely to be so traumatic that speculating and risk-oriented strategies will fall out of favor. The same obviously holds true for speculators who can't adapt to the changing times.

Competitive versus Inflation-Related Areas

Inflation has covered a multitude of corporate sins, and firms that have relied on marking up their costs will surely suffer. Materials producers who have little control over their prices and therefore can't pass through their costs easily are likely to be in a depressed condition for some time to come.

Newly deregulated industries whose cost structures are way out of line with competitive levels will also have problems, at least initially. Included here may be trucking, banks and financial services, rails, investment bankers, telecommunications, and airlines. As was discussed in Chapter 5, these industries are being hit with a double whammy: the shift from regulation and competition, and the recession and the ending of inflation. Unions in newly regulated industries would suffer since competition and consolidation tend to depress wage gains. As we shall discuss in Chapter 12, however, these industries should do much better after any consolidations are completed.

Industries such as steel were not regulated but had the same lack of cost control because they were concentrated domestically and lacked strong import competition until recently. With intense foreign competition and a strong dollar likely to continue, however, these industries will face the challenge of significantly reducing their labor and other costs, barring worldwide protectionism.

Companies or industries with long-term, fixed-rate supply contracts may also be hurt. Not only would these companies be burdened with excess supplies of many commodities that may be in surplus, but the cost of getting out of contracts could be enormous.

Conglomerates often thrive in periods of inflation, since they can use financial leverage to buy everything in sight, with little concern over what those newly acquired businesses actually produce. If inflation ends, however, it will be a different story, and high-cost financial leverage may come home to roost. In addition, without inflation to facilitate the passing through of costs, areas of a conglomerate, or any business for that matter, that produce marginal profits and are subsidiary to the main businesses may no longer make sense.

Also, the levels of trading activity in financial and commodity futures markets may be slowed as a result of more stable economic and financial conditions. Slower volume would clearly hurt many commodity brokers that have high overheads and need large volume to ensure profitability. Also, the plethora of newsletters emphasizing short-term trading would suffer if volatility ended.

Merger activity should also be reduced greatly as stock prices jump sharply and corporate America remembers well the mistakes of the recent natural resource merger mania and no longer feels the need to speculate to beat inflation.

State and local governments may suffer because of reduced funds from Washington, voter resistance to offsetting tax increases, and other factors discussed in Chapter 8. Employees of local governments would no doubt feel the pinch, as would companies that derive considerable business from municipalities. Of course, the federal government bureaucracy will also lose out if our basic thesis is correct. Those who have kept ahead of inflation because their incomes are indexed to an overstated CPI will also do less well if inflation ends.

The new environment should not present overly big difficulties to firms that are already in highly competitive areas, especially areas in which price declines are a normal phenomenon. High-technology industries such as semiconductors, telecommunications, and computers may fall in this area. Other winners would include firms that already are low-cost producers and those making proprietary products whose prices need not reflect any saving as a result of weak prices of raw materials.

Without an inflationary atmosphere to facilitate the pass-through of costs, firms that can expand volume while controlling overhead and costs of purchased materials may have a good profit potential. The U.S. auto industry may fall into this category if it gets its labor costs under control.

Another winner will be specialized, continuing education. With the growing need for more productive work skills, more people probably will be enrolling at trade schools, night schools, and other specialized education centers. On the other hand, people are less likely to change jobs in the tough period ahead, and so executive recruiters could get hurt.

Firms oriented toward productive investment should also do well, and those which develop creative new products may thrive. Thus, research and development and those involved in it should benefit. Venture capitalists may also profit. It should be remembered that capital investment would be aided by government tax and policy changes as well as declining interest rates.

Effects of a Continuing Strong U.S. Dollar

Since early 1981, the U.S. dollar has shown remarkable strength, and it is likely to maintain a high level in relation to other currencies. Consequently, U.S. tourists traveling abroad should continue to find bargains, a dramatic change from the discouraging costs of travel that existed in many foreign countries in the late 1970s. Importers and consumers of imported goods would also benefit, assuming no serious protectionism develops, as would users of internationally traded commodities, which would remain depressed in dollar terms.

Companies that do a large export business will be hurt because of the strong dollar and fierce international competition. Other losers will be basic industries and other businesses that must compete against foreign imports.

Dollar-denominated debts may also represent big problems for some foreign countries. Mexico is a standout in this area. Another example is the Italian auto producer, Fiat, which has indicated that its total debt increased by the equivalent of $320 million in 1981, solely as a result of the dollar's strength.

A strong dollar would also tend to dampen enthusiasm for investing in foreign markets, particularly those with a heavy emphasis on natural resources, such as South Africa, Canada, and Australia.

Finally, the past investment benefits of foreign automobiles and foreign-produced collectibles would be absent with a continuing strong dollar. Foreign autos retained their value well during the 1970s, as pointed out in BMW, Honda, and Mercedes-Benz ads, because the dollar fell against the German mark and the Japanese yen. But if the dollar is stable in relation to those currencies, the price support will no longer exist.

The same is true for the "collectible" aspect of items like French wines. These wines were a good investment in the 1970s, partly because of poor harvests and increased interest in collecting but also because the dollar was weak against the French franc. Now that the dollar has risen strongly against the franc and the "collectibles" era appears to be over, the reverse may be true.

Other Winners and Losers

Some other winners and losers should also be mentioned. Publications often do well only if the markets they serve are prospering. Along these lines, those publications which emphasize instant gratification, speculation, real estate, or government regulation probably will have difficult times. Also, the growth in advertising should slow as continued cost pressures restrain corporate ad budgets. Advertising firms as well as all publications and media that sell advertising could be adversely affected.

Finally, the trend toward deregulation should hurt regulation-oriented lawyers and Washington consultants and lobbyists. Even more important, those who expect continued government bailouts may be disappointed. By the same token, those who are by nature more self-reliant will find themselves better able to cope with the new era.

In any forecast, there is a certain amount of uncertainty. But in looking over the winners and losers, there is one clear winner that is so obvious, so unquestionable, and so inevitable that we would be remiss if we didn't mention it. Given the continued difficult transition period ahead, it is hard to see how economic consultants can fail to thrive.

We have made a list below of some of the winners and losers if inflation ends. For many of the winners, we assume the difficult and perhaps lengthy transition period is already behind us.

The Winners

- Savers
- Businesses with little or no debt
- Quality stocks and bonds
- Producers of proprietary products, where competition will not erode pricing power
- Low-cost producers
- Venture capitalists
- Research and development
- Efficiency and quality control experts
- Entrepreneurs
- Companies that derive profits from increased volume rather than higher prices
- New products and those with the talents to develop them
- Pensioners and others on fixed income
- Marketing and production people
- U.S.-made automobiles
- Conservative investment practices
- The U.S. dollar
- Strict family budgeting
- Specialized education, continuing education for professional people, and trade schools
- Consumers with low debts, high savings, and productive jobs
- Renters
- Money market funds backed by U.S. government securities
- Importers
- U.S. tourists abroad
- Consumers of imported goods
- Users of internationally traded commodities

The Losers

- Individuals and businesses heavily in debt
- Municipalities
- Art auctioneers
- Real estate and commodity brokers
- Commodities and commodity producers
- Housing speculators
- Farmland investors
- Investors in hotels, office buildings, and shopping centers
- Producers of farm equipment
- Collectibles, objets d'art, antiques, and their dealers
- Previous buyers of tangible asset-rich companies
- Investment letters which stress trading and speculation
- Publications geared toward instant gratification
- Luxury, foreign-made automobiles
- Non-U.S. government money market funds
- Publications oriented toward real estate speculation
- French wines and other foreign-produced "collectibles"
- Foreign investments with an emphasis on natural resources
- Companies that earlier bought their stock and ran down liquidity
- International commodity cartels
- Countries with high external debts denominated in U.S. dollars
- Noncompetitive businesses that were shielded from competition by inflation
- Undercapitalized businesses
- Advertising activity

- Bureaucracy, corporate staffs, overhead, and staff functions
- Regulation-oriented lawyers and publications
- Unionized labor in previously regulated industries
- Washington consultants and lobbyists
- Creative finance people
- Conglomerates
- Merger and acquisition specialists and activities
- Arbitrageurs
- Those who were overindexed to inflation
- The federal government
- Newly deregulated industries such as airlines and trucking (initially)
- Many tax shelters
- Firms that merely mark up costs
- OPEC
- The United Kingdom, Mexico, and other non-OPEC oil exporters
- Executive recruiters
- Those who rely on government bailouts
- Companies with long-term, fixed-rate supply contracts
- Leveraged buy-outs and those who specialize in them
- Joint venture partners of OPEC countries
- Employees of local governments
- Businesses that depend heavily on municipal spending

A New Business Strategy: Eight Key Elements

11

The death of inflation means that American business will be operating in an entirely different environment. Whether overall prices increase slowly, remain stable, or fall gently, the old inflation-oriented strategy of borrowing to the hilt, investing heavily in tangible assets, and marking up costs as they pass through the system will no longer work. A new strategy will be required if sales are to be translated into meaningful earnings.

Elements of the new winning strategy would include:

1. Ruthless and permanent cost control
2. Orientation toward volume expansion
3. Adaptation to continuing high real interest rates and a much narrower spread between short- and long-term interest rates
4. Maximization of long-term performance, not short-run profits or financial manipulation
5. Avoidance of tangible asset plays
6. Realization that deregulation will continue and government bailouts are at an end

7. Recognition of continuing aggressive import competition and difficult conditions for U.S. exports
8. Paramount emphasis on financial strength, even at the expense of market share gains

As noted in Chapter 7, American business has been cutting costs vigorously. In fact, in the summer of 1982, announcements of job terminations were so frequent that our favorite newspaper seemed to have a daily layoff page. Furthermore, these cost-control measures have begun to be effective. Nationwide nonfarm productivity climbed at a 2.3% annual rate in the second quarter of 1982 and, more significant, rose 2.6% in the first quarter, when one would have expected the very weak economy to seriously depress output per worker-hour.

Nevertheless, many cost-cutting measures have appeared more temporary than permanent; they have often concentrated on variable costs—travel expenses and production worker payrolls—but not overhead costs such as obsolete plants or management staff.

This temporary approach to cost containment is completely consistent with the conviction of most business executives that inflation is far from dead, despite the fact that the rate of price increase has declined much faster than most had believed possible. A Harris poll conducted in June 1982 for *Business Week* magazine revealed that a majority of business leaders believed that inflation would surge again within a year and that few were factoring long-term stability into their plans. Furthermore, most executives felt that the decline in inflation rates was not due to any basic structural change but rather was the result of the deep recession. This also suggests that they see only a temporary abatement of inflation, since recessions don't last forever.

It was also clear in mid-1982 that the first thing many real estate developers, manufacturers, and other businesspeople planned to do as soon as a recovery arrived and sales picked up was to raise their prices to rebuild profit margins. While such price increases may seem perfectly justified individually, collectively they add up to inflation. Even more important, their intentions also reveal a conviction that an inflationary atmosphere in which marking up costs is the way of life will soon return.

Permanent Cost Control Is Essential

But the end of inflation that we predict almost *requires* that cost increases can no longer be passed on easily. Consequently, businesspeople should assume that the current difficulty in raising prices will continue and should begin to develop permanent cost programs. This means that managers should not simply fire people but retain their positions on the organizational chart, because the temptation to fill the positions later will still exist. Instead, departments should be reorganized or combined to eliminate *positions*. Only then should people be chosen to fill the new, streamlined organization. Managers should ask themselves the very hard question, Which positions are absolutely essential and which can be dispensed with?

Eliminating minor and unprofitable lines of business is another way to cut costs permanently, as is reducing the number of suppliers. Being able to reward suppliers who meet quality standards with bigger orders helps control costs, and the larger orders to fewer suppliers will also tend to result in lower bids. Investment in labor-saving, productivity-enhancing capital equipment may not always have immediate payouts, but the long-term opportunities for cost saving can make such expenditures worthwhile.

Some of these investments may be unconventional. Corning Glass Works' new engineering building was designed with low partitions and other features to take advantage of the finding that engineers get a majority of their ideas from casual conversations with their colleagues, not in isolated offices. Corning says that with the new building design, 10% more projects are being handled by the same number of engineers.

Upgrading the purchasing function is another route to permanent cost control. In many firms, costs of purchased materials vastly exceed labor or other cost items, but purchasing agents tend to be low-level people, perhaps reporting to plant managers. Significant cost savings may be possible by upgrading these positions and perhaps having them report to the vice president of manufacturing. Furthermore, better cost results may be had if purchasing managers are engineers who have run plants and have a clear understanding of specifications and acceptable substitutes.

Permanent cost control can also result from a much more realistic attitude toward the value of executives' time. As consultants, we are basically selling our time and have a clear understanding of its value, but we observe many manufacturing executives at even the most senior level who are concerned with the cost of capital but who would be hard pressed to put an hourly value on their own time. Is it worthwhile to take a planeload of senior officers on an overnight trip to visit lawyers in their offices if the additional cost of having the attorneys visit the clients at home is only several thousand dollars?

Setting aside ego-building value, which is real and important, is the keynote address to a trade association really worth the time that the CEO and his or her staff spend in preparing and delivering it? These are tough questions, but developing the habit of asking them may help redirect executive time toward the most productive uses and perhaps even reduce the need for some high-priced talent.

Creating a competitive atmosphere among divisions or plants that produce similar products is another way of adding a permanent direction to cost control. Xerox has used this technique among its U.S., British, and Japanese units to encourage the production of parts and entire machines at the lowest costs. American employees of Xerox, threatened by internal, domestic external, and offshore competition, are joining quality-of-work-life circles and engaging in other productivity-enhancing activities. Other permanent cost-control opportunities are brought to mind by the possibility that Xerox's small copier may eventually be produced entirely in Japan, as may all of GM's small cars.

Of course, even in a noninflationary climate, some firms may continue to have a meaningful degree of control over the prices of their output. For most businesses, however, permanent cost controls probably will be the only route to success.

Pursue Volume Expansion

The second element in our winning strategy is volume expansion. With cost pass-through difficult and unit profitability under continuing pressure, as an end of inflation implies, volume expansion is the route to overall growth of profits. Therefore, the search for growth opportunities should occupy a considerable part of top management's time, particularly since volume expansion cannot be expected in every industry if inflation is brought under control and economic stability returns.

The process of controlling inflation is the process of eliminating people's convictions that they just can't miss by betting on continuing escalation in prices. After all the success many people and businesses have had in speculating in real estate and other tangible assets and in borrowing cheaply to do so, it probably will take even more pain and suffering than we've already had to dissuade them.

If inflation is killed, it will be because individuals and businesspeople have lost enough money to be much more cautious than has been the case for years. This doesn't preclude growth in spending, but it suggests that we need to look for specific and concrete reasons for growth. We have examined a number of growth-generating factors which appear to be firmly in place and not dependent on events yet to be decided.

Catch-ups resulting from earlier underspending bode well for autos and housing. The recessionary climate of the last several years has pushed auto scrappage well below normal levels just at the time that the models built in the early 1970s—the biggest production years ever, when all the gas hogs were turned out—are in sore need of replacement. Furthermore, low levels of new home construction in recent years have produced a huge backlog of unfulfilled demand and record low vacancy rates.

Demographic changes provide a second set of growth opportunities. Though these changes provide no help for autos—all the postwar babies are already drivers—the reverse is true for housing. Members of the postwar baby boom, who have been largely responsible for the growing backlog of housing demand, will still be forming families and looking for their first houses in the remainder of this decade. Obviously, housing and related industries such as appliances will benefit. However, with continuing high energy costs, smaller families, high real interest rates, and an end of the speculative urge to own a bigger and more expensive house than is really needed, the size of housing units may become smaller.

Housing strength will probably continue in the 1990s but shift then to second homes. In that next decade, the postwar babies will be in the 45- to 54-year-old age bracket, when earnings tend to be at career peaks and when offspring have left home and relieved parents of their financial responsibility. A significant part of the resulting jump in discretionary spending may be spent on vacation homes.

Heavily populated age groups can promote growth, but so too can lightly populated segments. As shown in Table 11-1, the number of people in the 14- to 25-year-old age group will decline 1.8% per year in the current decade. Since all of the people who will be in that bracket in the next 10 years are

Table 11-1 Average Annual Rate of Growth in
Population by Age
(1950–2000)

	1950–1960	1960–1970	1970–1980	1980–1990	1990–2000
	% Annually				
Total	1.7	1.3	1.0	0.7	0.7
Under 15 years	3.2	0.3	(1.5)	1.0	0.3
15–24	1.0	4.0	1.3	(1.8)	0.5
25–34	(0.5)	1.0	3.6	1.3	(1.7)
35–44	1.1	(0.5)	1.1	3.6	1.2
45–54	1.6	1.3	(0.3)	1.1	3.5
55–64	1.6	1.8	1.3	(0.2)	1.1
65+	3.0	1.9	2.2	1.8	0.7

SOURCE: U.S. Bureau of the Census.

alive today, this is one forecast about which we can be rea-
sonably sure. In this age range, people normally enter the
labor force, and so the dearth of new entrants is likely to
encourage purchases of labor-saving equipment.

Older women, the other major source of new workers, are
also likely to enter the job market less rapidly in the years
ahead because of an end of the inflation which earlier
reduced family purchasing power and pushed huge numbers
of them into the job market. Of course, purchases of labor-
saving, productivity-enhancing equipment will also be
encouraged by the recent tax liberalizations, by competitive
pressures for cost control, and by somewhat lower interest
rates.

Policy changes in Washington are also opening growth
opportunities, some of them in combination with demographic developments. A key change is the reversal of the
earlier policy of shifting income from upper-income people
to lower-income hands. We're all familiar with how that
mechanism worked: Given the progressive federal income
tax system, inflation pushed people into higher tax brackets,
and the government became a very efficient collector of revenue. Those funds as well as borrowed money were then
transferred to lower-income people in the form of welfare

outlays, unemployment insurance, Social Security payments, food stamps, and other transfer payments.

The current series of income tax cuts, however, are proportional to tax payments, and so they largely benefit those who pay the bulk of these taxes—higher-income households. At the same time, the offsetting planned cuts in nondefense spending almost have to be felt largely by the lower-income people who are the recipients of most of that spending. In effect, the earlier process of income transfer is being arrested.

As was noted in Chapter 5, higher-income people tend to be big savers, but they still spend the majority of their after-tax income. Consequently, the sorts of things they buy should benefit from this redirection of redistribution efforts. Higher-cost recreation and travel, especially by air, should benefit, and purchases of second homes should receive another boost. Financial services, better home furnishings, and specialty apparel should also benefit. This extra spending power may be what's needed to pay for those two-way home telecommunications systems that will let people do everything from ordering the groceries to taking a course in history to buying stocks and bonds.

The postwar babies will also help this phenomenon. As they move ahead in their careers in the next several decades, their incomes will advance sharply. This group will have a high percentage of its women members working and will have relatively few children. Consequently, its discretionary income will be substantial and its spending on quality purchases should grow significantly. The wave of older women who became job holders in the last decade should also gain income and purchasing power as they gain experience and skills.

As was discussed in Chapter 5, another new government approach is the deregulation of such industries as airlines, trucking, banking and financial services, rails, telecommunications, and investment banking. Deregulation and the resulting removal of cartellike pricing control tend to encourage consolidation, in which the financially strong are the winners.

Beyond that phase, though, industry growth is likely to exceed earlier rates because the lower prices induced by competition will enlarge the market. For example, freight-sensitive goods can be moved to more distant markets if trucking costs are lower. Deregulation of industries whose earlier cartellike behavior inhibited the introduction of new technologies can offer exceptional growth possibilities. The prospective application of computers to a deregulated tele-communications industry is a vivid example.

Finally, we note the policy change favoring strong defense. Barring a major accord with the Russians, spending in this area is likely to grow rapidly for some time.

Pent-up demand, demographic shifts, and changes in government policy will provide growth opportunities in the years ahead, but they will also create some weak areas which should be avoided. The other side of the after-tax income shift in favor of higher-income people is the lack of lower-income growth implied by the containment of federal transfer programs. In addition, the number of low-income people will be held down by the movement of many postwar babies and recently hired older women to higher income levels.

Obviously, these developments would reverse the patterns of the last several decades, with adverse implications for the things that lower-income people buy. When one thinks about it, many of the areas of consumer spending strength in the last 20 years have centered on the mass distribution of moderately priced items: fast food, door-to-door cosmetics, amusement parks, beverages, intercity food stores, and variety stores, for example. To the extent that these benefited earlier from government transfer payments and the influx of new wage earners, their outlook is now dimmed.

State and local government are likely to be buffeted by declining federal grants, less inflation-induced growth in revenues, pressure by liberals to pick up discontinued federal programs, and voters balking at any increases in tax or indebtedness.

The implications for state and local government spending are obvious: smaller outlays for construction, roads, pollution control, etc. Continuing low birthrates imply that educational expenditures will be weak as well. It goes without saying that a shrinking nondefense federal sector also will limit sales of many goods and services purchased directly by the federal government.

Other areas of likely weakness include commercial construction. As was discussed in Chapter 8, it may take some years to absorb the excess hotel, office, and shopping center space now under development. Industrial construction and capacity-enhancing equipment may also be weak. Tremendous excess capacity here and abroad, a continuing strong dollar, further pressure from imports, fierce competition abroad for U.S. exports, and sober and moderate growth worldwide following the transition to a less inflationary world all suggest a limited need for new industrial capacity in the years ahead.

Limited growth in export markets in the 1980s may make agriculture a fairly static industry. The earlier excesses in energy development and the ongoing conservation efforts suggest that it may be some time before domestic oil, gas, and coal activities resume strong growth trends.

It's interesting to compare this list of strong and weak areas with the supply siders' assumptions that future growth will favor capital spending while consumer-related activities will be weak. Our list suggests that it will be a mixed bag. In the area of capital outlays, there will be strength in labor-saving, productivity-enhancing equipment but not in commercial and industrial construction or in capacity-expanding equipment. On the consumer side, we see strength in autos, housing, and upper-income-related spending but not in goods and services purchased by lower-income people. Overall, and in contrast to the supply siders, we see more strength in consumer than in capital spending areas.

Before leaving this discussion of volume expansion we should note that it can be also achieved by simply holding down prices even in an industry that lacks strong growth characteristics. Tasty Baking Co., for example, has decided to forgo price increases on its products until unit volume picks up appreciably. Furthermore, the program may be succeeding. Management believes that high prices in earlier periods caused volume declines that sometimes exceeded 10% a year. With flat prices in the first half of 1982, however, unit volume increased about 5%.

Look for High Real Interest Rates, Especially Short-Term Rates

The third element in our winning strategy is the full recognition that real interest rates will remain high for some time, as was discussed in Chapter 5. Real bond yields, which averaged about 3% in the late 1960s and early 1970s, may be twice as high or more for some time, even after the 1980–1981 bulge of real interest rates subsides.

These additional interest costs can be a lot for a firm to absorb, especially if it is a heavy borrower. Consequently, borrowing should be reduced wherever possible and confined to areas where higher profits will offset higher borrowing costs. Cash flow should be emphasized, and business areas that no longer provide adequate returns on capital should become candidates for sale or liquidation.

Besides interest rates remaining high in relation to inflation, we also noted in Chapter 5 that the spread between short- and long-term interest rates may become considerably narrower than it was earlier. In effect, short-term rates would remain higher compared to earlier times for two reasons: first to come closer to long-term rates and second to join long-term rates in being higher in relation to inflation.

In these circumstances, the obvious objective is to hold down short-term borrowing. One way is to finance at least part of inventories, accounts receivable, and other items that normally are financed in the short term by borrowing long, but that strategy is risky. A more prudent approach is to find ways to reduce inventories, accounts receivable, etc., while still serving customers adequately. Perhaps production runs should be shortened, even with some loss of efficiency, in order to reduce inventories, or the number of models should be reduced, with more standardization of parts for those which remain.

In industries in which final assembly is a major aspect, perhaps suppliers should relocate closer to the assembly plants so that only minutes, not days, of inventories are tied up in transit. This, of course, is the Japanese *kanban* system in which inventories of purchased materials are controlled so precisely that suppliers deliver needed parts to the assembly line "just in time." In contrast, General Motors estimates that at any time, over half the firm's inventories are on trucks or trains.

Changes are in the wind, however. The Buick Motor division's Flint assembly plant found that they could reduce inventories of metal body stamping by over 80% by merely switching from rail deliverers every other day to truck deliveries three times a day. With changes of this sort, the use of fewer suppliers, and other techniques, a Booz, Allen & Hamilton, Inc., study estimates that GM could cut its inventory expenses more than two-thirds—a substantial amount. The study places the total cost of carrying GM's $9 billion of inventories—financial costs, handling, storage, defects, etc.—at $3 billion a year.

Unfortunately, many American firms still lack systems which adequately inform division managements of the high costs of carrying inventories or for that matter the costs of all capital invested in those divisions. We are amazed at how many large and well-managed companies have not yet begun to link their full cost of capital to division managements' incentive compensation in one way or another. Worse yet, some do charge their divisions for capital, but at rates well below the market, sometimes using the firm's historical average costs of capital, which can greatly undershoot the cost of new money. Capital at submarket rates can only mis-direct division-level efforts to control inventories and other capital-absorbing items. A good pep talk is probably better than a submarket interest charge, but the use of full market interest costs beats both.

A final interesting note: Domestically produced goods tend to spend much less time in transit than those imported from distant points, such as the far east. Consequently, higher inventory financing costs should make domestic pro-duction somewhat more competitive against imports. At least there's one plus for domestic producers.

Long-Term Performance, Not Short-Run Profits or Financial Manipulation

Fourth on our list of winning strategic elements is an orien-tation toward long-run business performance, not short-run profit maximization. This would reverse the inflation era approach of managing companies of any appreciable size like investment portfolios. With that approach there is little concern with what is actually produced by the various divi-sions but tremendous preoccupation with the return on assets employed. Divisions of the company are viewed essentially as portfolio components which compete for a lim-ited supply of investment funds, and any division that does not make the grade is replaced by something more attractive.

That orientation has also encouraged financial manipu-lation and the purchase of divisions or even whole compa-nies with the goal of cosmetically altering them in a financial sense and then selling either the whole operation or its broken-up pieces for a quick profit. The process was encour-aged by a depressed stock market, which, along with expec-tations of high inflation, convinced many that a takeover can-didate's assets were greatly undervalued and had nowhere to go but up.

An end of inflation and the opportunities it provides for

successful financial manipulation, along with higher stock prices and the newfound necessity for cost control and efficiency in production, means that this earlier orientation toward short-run results is no longer appropriate. Furthermore, the new environment suggests that those who thought they were making only a short-term investment in businesses even though they owned 100% may come to grief. The opportunities for quick and profitable resales to someone else infected by merger mania may disappear fast as the perception of grossly undervalued assets evaporates.

Robert H. Hayes and William J. Abernathy of the Harvard Business School, who have studied this situation extensively, point out that the old approach promotes caution instead of innovation because of what they call "managerial remote control." Executives are rewarded for short-term performance that often comes by milking assets at the expense of the investment and innovation which pay off big only in the long run. They urge that the focus be shifted away from financial techniques and toward technology and improved production.

Many managements have complained that it is really stockholders who have forced this orientation toward short-term results since the interruption of a steady climb in quarterly earnings could devastate their stocks' prices. Ironically, those same managers often put relentless pressure on the equity managers of their pension funds—which collectively account for the vast majority of equity trading—to turn in superior investment performance on a quarterly basis.

Leading companies are moving in the direction of this new philosophy, which is also akin to the Japanese idea of forgoing short-term profits in favor of investment and organization for long-term performance. Xerox has adopted this new approach. General Electric, which pioneered much of the profit-maximization philosophy and portfolio orientation of corporate management, is now worried that this orientation fosters caution and bureaucracy that are not up to meeting competitive threats, especially from abroad. The firm, under its new chief executive officer, John F. Welch, Jr., wants GE managers to behave as if they were entrepreneurs aggressively running a group of small businesses, but backed by the strength of a large company.

Avoid Tangible Asset Plays

The fifth element for a winning strategy is the avoidance of tangible asset speculation, which is echoed in our advice to investors as well. Most businesspeople would not admit to having engaged in this activity, but they certainly have in one way or another by buying land sites ahead of need, piling up unnecessary but rapidly appreciating inventories, taking over companies rich in natural resources, and borrowing heavily to finance these and other nonessential physical assets. But an end of inflation is tantamount to an end of the days when assets in or on the ground appreciate much faster than either overall inflation rates or borrowing costs. Instead, financial assets—stocks and bonds—are likely to be once again the more attractive investments.

Avoiding new speculation in tangibles is one thing, but dealing with past acquisitions is quite another. The best course of action may be simply to liquidate past mistakes, even at losses, particularly if those tangible assets are heavily leveraged by high-cost borrowing.

Accept Deregulation and an End of Government Bailouts

Sixth in our list of winning strategic elements, we believe that businesspeople should accept the reality of deregulation and the end of the cartellike pricing and industry consolidation that normally follow. For those in previously regulated industries, this suggests unrelenting efforts to slash costs, particularly those which are out of line with more competitive industries. Wages often fall into this category, and even though labor is often slow to understand the effects of an end of cartellike control, education efforts may be worthwhile. Moving toward the more competitive areas of an industry can also ease the shock of deregulation. Even before deregulation of their industry got into high gear, some unionized trucking companies started separate companies with lower-cost nonunion labor.

Perhaps most important, companies in industries in the process of deregulation should keep their powder dry. It's difficult to resist the urge to retaliate when a competitor moves into your territory, but the firm's resources can easily be dissipated in the process. Many trucking companies did exactly this when deregulation allowed them to expand easily coast to coast. The final results were a number of financially weakened, if not bankrupt, firms. This same misguided strategy of rapid expansion upon deregulation led to the failure of Braniff. It cannot be stressed enough that the winners in the consolidation that normally follows deregulation are the financially strong ones who move cautiously, husband their resources, and wait patiently to pick up the pieces when others fail.

This same cautious approach makes particularly good sense in an era when government bailouts are no longer the rule. The day when any firm or industry that was big enough could be assured of federal assistance in times of trouble regardless of how reckless or stupid it was is probably over. Now the attitude in Washington seems to be that the right to fail is an essential disciplinary element in the economic process and is needed to control inflation by keeping the system honest and reducing speculative excesses. The decision to let Penn Square Bank fail rather than bail it out with a merger may be the first concrete example of this new attitude. Obviously, more business caution is now in order.

Import and Export Competition Will Remain Fierce

Our seventh element is the full recognition of continuing competitive pressure from imports and fierce competition abroad for U.S. exports. The arrival of all-out protectionism on a global scale could change things dramatically, but barring that disaster, a continuing strong dollar, unemployed men and machines abroad, and almost irresistible political pressure there to put them to work all point to continuing problems for U.S. industries that compete with imports as well as for American exporters. In a growing number of cases, American firms are now competing not just with foreign companies but also with other countries. Foreign government-owned companies often compete aggressively for sales despite operating losses because policy decisions outweigh profit considerations.

Cost control, including foreign "sourcing" of parts, is always at least a partial answer to these problems. If you can't beat them, join them. In some cases, however, it may make sense simply to abandon certain markets and replant human and capital assets in more fertile ground.

Emphasize Financial Strength, Even at the Expense of Market Share Gains

The last recommendation in our list is to emphasize financial strength, even if that requires forgoing attractive opportunities to increase market share. We realize that market share is often the best indication of business success. The firm with the largest market share is normally the most profitable, perhaps because that firm has the most cumulative experience in turning out the item in question and hence is the lowest-cost producer. We are also aware of the findings of the Strategic Planning Institute that recessions are usually the best times to increase market share. Weaker competitors often drop out, and thus times of disruptive change can often be the times to seize the initiative.

The market share principle isn't always applicable, however. It works in industries with high labor content, complex assembly operations, or large volumes of standard products. But it seems less important where brand image, technological leadership, and marketing expertise instead of low manufacturing costs are the keys to success.

Much more important, however, today's conditions may

simply render earlier approaches inappropriate. We do not view the recent period of business weakness as a normal recession, nor do we see the period ahead as similar to the earlier postwar era. Today's financial risks are unprecedented in the business careers of almost everyone.

The need, in our view, is to conserve and build financial strength, not risk it on heavy advertising outlays or other attempts to grab market share. It may make more sense in this atmosphere to remain cautious and simply wait for less prudent competitors to fail. This, ironically, may be the quickest route to improvement in market share in the foreseeable future.

An end of inflation means an end of many of the problems that have made business so unpredictable and difficult in recent years. It does, however, present a fresh group of challenges and mandates a new business strategy, whose elements we've discussed in this chapter. Those firms whose managements understand the necessary changes and adopt them early should enjoy the benefits of the economic growth and stability we see ahead. Those which do not probably will not thrive and may even disappear or have their slow-moving managements replaced.

A noninflationary environment will also require changes in investment strategy, as we will explore in Chapter 12.

Investment Strategy: Rewarding but Different Opportunities

12

We looked at winners and losers in Chapter 10, but some further discussions of the investment implications of an end to inflation are clearly warranted. In a general sense, the end of inflation suggests seven major investment conclusions:

- Interest rates in nominal terms will drop significantly.
- Real interest rates, however, will remain high for some time to come.
- The distorting effects of inflation on consumer, business, and investor behavior will stop.
- Expectations of inflation will end.
- Volatility will diminish, and stability will return.
- The government's share of the economy will shrink.
- Tax rates will decline, and saving rates will rise.

Each of these developments should have a major, long-lasting effect on investments and investment strategy.

The Old Winners Are the New Losers

1. Tangible assets, the major winners in inflation, become the big losers in a noninflationary environment. Most forms of real estate, collectibles, diamonds, stamps, commodities, antiques, paintings, gems, strategic metals, farmland, siver coins, art, and raw land will suffer. The investment climate for them will move from the best of all possible worlds—rapidly rising real prices for tangibles and low or negative real financing costs—to the worst of all worlds—high real interest rates and declining real prices.

The future for gold is a bit harder to predict. High real interest rates make the cost of holding gold unattractive, and it should be remembered that gold not only offers no current return but also requires storage and insurance costs. Also, an elimination of expectations of inflation and diminished economic volatility would end much of the inflation-hedge motivation that made gold popular in the 1970s. Thus, if inflation ends, gold will have lost its luster and may be vulnerable to further price correction.

However, gold is also held as a hedge against political and banking risks. A major flare-up in the middle east or a major banking crisis either in the United States or abroad could make gold attractive again. Ironically, such crises may develop during the process of eliminating inflation.

2. Investments in natural resources, such as oil and gas, coal, aluminum, lead, zinc, forest products, silver, copper, and nickel, will be unattractive if inflation ends. These commodities benefited immensely from the inflationary era, and the companies producing them were frequent targets during the takeover craze. An end to expectations of inflation and shortages, however, should generally eliminate the attraction of natural resource investments and greatly reduce their appeal as takeover candidates.

3. Highly financially leveraged companies and those heavily in debt will be poor investments if inflation ends. Also, conglomerates or companies whose basic business is

acquiring others probably will be poor performers, particularly if leverage is used to make the acquisition, as is often the case. As noted, high real interest rates and an end of expectations of inflation would make debt and leveraged investment strategies of dubious merit.

Indeed, balance sheet analysis could become almost as important for stock investors as it is now for bond analysts. With continued concern over corporate liquidity, the classic liquidity ratios—the current ratio, the quick ratio (that is, cash and receivables divided by current liabilities), the ratio of short-term to long-term debt, the pretax interest coverage ratio (pretax income plus interest divided by interest), and the ratio of cash flow as a percentage of long-term debt—may become useful tools to the stock investor.

4. Tax shelters probably won't make as much sense as they did in the 1970s if inflation ends. First, most of the classic tax shelters, such as oil and gas, drilling rigs, and real estate, won't be good investment areas. Second, without inflation, bracket creep should no longer be an important issue, and this will further reduce the attractiveness of tax shelters. Also, one cannot dismiss the possibility that a flat-rate tax may win congressional support. In that case, the tax rate on additional income would be so low that there would be hardly any incentive for shelters.

Furthermore, some of the benefits for tax shelters of the 1981 tax law were rescinded by Congress in the 1982 tax act. Under the 1981 act, real estate and equipment leasing benefited from significantly shorter depreciation periods, and thus investors were able to get larger tax deductions in the early years of the shelter. As this book was being written, Congress was proposing to raise badly needed revenues by scaling back some of the increased depreciation allowances of the 1981 act.

Also, many people went into tax shelters in recent years to avoid taxation, and in most cases, little attention was paid to investment merits. That attitude is changing quickly. For one thing, many tax shelters have turned out to be financial

disasters. What's more, the financial and investment set-
backs that occur with the ending of inflation are creating a
preoccupation with capital preservation.

A final drawback for tax shelters is that many investors
in leveraged tax shelters are finding themselves on the hook
for additional money. Consider the case of a number of drilling funds financed by the Penn Square Bank. Now that the
bank is being liquidated, many investors are faced with the
prospect of standing behind the loans. If conditions deteriorate enough, most partnerships can require each limited
partner to put up an additional 10% to cover expenses, and
this could severely tarnish the image of tax shelters.

The New Winners Are the Old Losers

Quality stocks and bonds would be the clear winners with
the elimination of inflation. Both stocks and bonds were big
losers in inflation, particularly in the accelerating phase of
the 1970s. They were at the bottom of the list of performance
of the 16 investment categories discussed in Chapter 6.
Indeed, for the 10 years ended June 30, 1981, bonds ranked
last, with a 3.8% annual return, as against a rise in the CPI
during the same period of 8.3%. Stocks were third from the
bottom, with a 5.8% annual return.

Stocks would benefit from six out of seven of the investment characteristics accompanying the end of inflation. First,
they would be helped by declining interest rates, which have
provided stiff competition in recent years. The average yield
on the S&P 400 Index at this writing is 6.25%, a long shot
from the 12 to 14% available in the money markets and the
13 to 16% yield of the bond market in the summer of 1982.

An end to the distortions of inflation on consumer, business, and investor behavior as well as the demise of expectations of inflation and disappointments over losses in tangible assets could be a big plus for stocks. The flow of
investment funds would revert once again toward financial
assets and away from tangible assets as investors focused on

current return and genuine growth. Inflationary pressures would no longer squeeze corporate profits. In addition, the whole issue of underdepreciation of corporate assets and inventory profits, which is of great concern to investors in an inflationary era, would no longer be important. In a noninflationary environment, corporations would concentrate on rebuilding liquidity and reducing debt—a further attraction to investors.

A return to economic stability would also reduce the great interest in speculative financial vehicles such as options and commodity futures. In all probability, interest would shift toward long-term investments in the economy, and the best means of participating there may be through the stock of publicly held companies.

A smaller share of the economic pie claimed by government would mean growth opportunities in the private sector. Not only would private companies be able to gain market share from inefficient quasi-governmental suppliers of goods and services, but deregulation would lower costs and increase flexibility.

Finally, as was discussed in Chapter 5, declining tax rates and other factors would encourage people to save, particularly those with high incomes. A good portion of this money might find its way into the stock market.

Previously issued bonds would also benefit from a noninflationary environment. Bond yields would be expected to decline substantially—and bond prices to rise commensurately—even though real bond yields are expected to remain high by historical standards. Furthermore, the end of expectations of inflation would be a powerful stimulus to bond buyers. Pension funds, institutional investors, and individuals have been burned so many times in the past two decades that skepticism about the end of inflation is enormous. If inflationary expectations were truly broken, investors would rush to lock in historically high bond yields.

An end to volatility in the financial markets would also benefit bonds. As was discussed in Chapter 5, one of the reasons for the high real return on bonds in 1981–1982 was volatility, or the risk factor. Since bond prices can now fluctuate more in a week than they used to in a year, investors are demanding a risk premium. Obviously, if volatility lessened, so would that risk premium, although it might decline only slowly.

Make Market Timing All-Important

There are several important caveats to the investment case for stocks and bonds, however. Ending inflation is not a painless task; indeed, as was pointed out in Chapter 8, the risks are the greatest in 50 years. If the recession drags on, corporate profits will remain depressed and stocks may be uncertain investments. Alternatively, if the financial system does crack, stocks will be very unattractive. Also, as was pointed out in Chapter 7, bonds may be poor investments initially in a major financial crisis. In 1932, during the last crisis, even prices of quality bonds fell sharply during the rush for liquidity. Of course, in a financial crisis, when investors worry about who will visit the bankruptcy courts next, low-quality bonds make no sense at all.

When security markets recover it is probable that bonds will outperform stocks for a while, as usually occurs at market bottoms. Bonds are quick to respond to an easing in credit policy by the Federal Reserve, a reduction in private sector credit demands, and lowered expectations of inflation. Stocks, on the other hand, usually require an extended basing period because investor concern over corporate profits, dividend cuts, and bankruptcies weighs heavily. Nevertheless, a sharp decline in interest rates is bound to cause a significant rally in stock prices.

As far as stocks go, one group which should benefit from an end to inflation is the interest-sensitive stocks, such as insurance, finance companies, savings and loan associations, and utilities. Of course, the financial condition and the competitive environment of these companies will have to be evaluated closely. For instance, competition in casualty insurance and the pervasiveness of universal life have caused havoc in the insurance industry. Also, small loan companies may be affected by the amount of delinquent loans they have on their books.

At some point, cyclical stocks, such as rubber, chemicals, and machinery, should do better. For one thing, these companies have initiated massive cost-cutting programs, and so almost any amount of cyclical recovery could increase their earnings by multiples.

The telecommunications market may also offer investment opportunities. The deregulation of that industry is opening up an enormous market to efficient and low-cost producers and suppliers.

Deregulation is also opening up the transportation industry, and we are seeing a host of new small commuter airlines and mergers in the trucking industry. Obviously, there is further consolidation ahead, but in the long run the financially strong survivors should have good opportunities for growth by offering reduced rates.

Another group that should prosper if inflation ends are businesses that manufacture proprietary products and thus have control over pricing. They are not likely to be hurt as much by the price cutting in the economy as other businesses. Examples of such industries are drug companies and certain photographic companies.

Finally, investors should consider areas of long-term growth where the demographics, demand trends, and results of policy changes in Washington appear favorable, as was discussed in Chapter 11. Some examples of this are autos and housing, where there is a huge pent-up demand. Housing starts in recent years were not sufficient to handle the need for housing by the baby boom generation, and auto sales recently have been reduced so far that replacement demand alone could cause a substantial pickup in sales. Primary housing and vacation homes and related areas will also benefit from the demographic factors and policy shifts that are allowing more after-tax income to be retained by higher-income people. Other beneficiaries include specialty retailers, financial services, and air travel. Defense spending should do well unless America and Russia settle their differences. Finally, with the emphasis on cost control and a lack of new entrants to the labor force, labor-saving equipment should prosper, particularly equipment which can raise service-sector productivity and factory efficiency.

A final and most important criterion for evaluating stocks is corporate strategy, which we discussed in Chapter 11. It is very important that a corporation and its management be prepared for a noninflationary environment and understand its implications. Indeed, an investment in any company should first run the gauntlet of our eight-point checklist in Chapter 11. For example, is the company cutting costs permanently and with a vengeance? Are heavy debt burdens being reduced? Is the business being run as if inflation would soon return or as if inflation were dead? In other words, in a noninflationary climate, can revenues be translated into profits?

In sum, the end of inflation will usher in a totally new world, full of opportunities and difficulties. For those who are prepared, the possibilities are both exciting and enormous. For those who are not, the recession-ladened transition to this new era—the *trancession*—may be devastating.

References

Much of the research and thought contained in this book was originally laid out in the following publications.

A. GARY SHILLING & COMPANY, INC. REPORTS

*Inflation Outlook: *A Bet on Voter Attitudes,* 10/31/75.
*Worldwide Business Outlook: *The Aftermath of the Great Recession,* 11/14/75.
*Inflation by Fiat, 5/31/77.
*Inflation Forecast: *The Value of Farm Real Estate: An Inflationary Bubble about to Burst,* 10/28/77.
*Prospects for a Recession, 4/5/78.
Long-Term Business Outlook: *Will We Ever Get Out of This Mess?* First David Steine Lecture delivered at Vanderbilt University, Nashville, Tennessee, 3/30/79.
Special Report: *Is Real Estate Still a Sound Investment?* 11/15/78.
Special Report: *Will Housing Be Crunched?* 12/15/78.
Long-Term Business Outlook: *A Perspective on the 1980s,* 2/20/79.
Quarterly Financial Outlook: *Serious Storm Clouds Are Gathering,* 5/17/79.
Special Report: *Too Many Feet in the Trough,* 10/25/79.
To Our Clients and Friends, 11/6/79.
Economic Outlook: *The Consumer—Where Is He?* 11/20/79.
International Outlook: *International Banking: Just How Sick?* 1/7/80.
Economic Outlook: *Vulnerability in Housing: Prelude to a Vicious Circle?* 3/10/80.

*A. Gary Shilling, White Weld Economic Services.

257

Repercussions of Recession: The Murphy's Law Series: *It's Down Down on the Farm*, 5/7/80.

Economic Outlook: *Labor-Capital Substitution: A Time for Its Reversal*, 5/27/80.

Repercussions of Recession: The Murphy's Law Series: *Recession + Trade Aggression = Protectionism?* 6/9/80.

Dear Clients and Friends: *Economic Implications of the Conservative Sweep: Lower Inflation, But with a Bang or a Whimper?* 11/7/80.

Long-Term Business Outlook, 2/25/81.

Housing Outlook: Part I: *The Postwar Babies Run for Shelter*, 3/25/81.

Housing Outlook: Part II: *Don't Lose the Trees for the Forest*, 4/8/81.

Long-Term Agricultural Outlook: *Removing Some of the Bloom from the Export Rose*, 5/8/81.

Dear Clients and Friends: *The Economy beyond the Administration's Program*, 5/29/81.

Dear Clients and Friends: *What's Going On Here?* 9/22/81.

Reagan Economics—Will It Work? Delivered at Amherst College, Amherst, Massachusetts, 10/28/81.

Dear Clients and Friends: *1982—The Risks Are on the Downside*, 1/15/82.

Dear Clients and Friends: *The New Federalism—Aimed at Smaller Total Government*, 1/27/82.

Agricultural Outlook: *Looking for an Era of Surpluses*, 1/28/82.

Statement Before the Joint Economic Committee of the U.S. Congress: *The New Federal Tax Rate Cuts and Spending Restraints and Their Effects on Income Distribution and Saving: Desirable and Probably Necessary*, 2/10/82.

Economic Comment: *Patterns of Recovery*, 3/8/82.

Reducing the Federal Deficit: *It Makes a Difference How It's Done*, 4/2/82.

Productivity Growth in the 1980s, 4/6/82.

Dominoes? 5/17/82.

Inflation, Disinflation, and Corporate Profitability, 6/30/82.

Interest Rates in the 1980s: Part I: *Are Bond Yields Too High?* 7/1/82.

Interest Rates in the 1980s: Part II: *Are Treasury Bill Rates Too High?* 7/9/82.

PUBLISHED IN The Wall Street Journal:

The Conservative Mandate and Budget Realities, 2/3/81.
The Alternative Tax Bill Would Be a Mistake, 7/15/81.
American Labor—From Cartels to Competition, 1/21/82.

PUBLISHED IN Fortune:
Transitions: Disinflation—It's Not All Fun, 5/3/82.

Index